Early Christian Care for the Poor

MATRIX
The Bible in Mediterranean Context

EDITORIAL BOARD

John H. Elliott   John S. Kloppenborg
Anselm Hagedorn   Douglas E. Oakman
K. C. Hanson   Gary Stansell

PREVIOUSLY PUBLISHED VOLUMES

Richard L. Rohrbaugh
The New Testament and Social-Science Criticism

Markus Cromhout
Jesus and Identity

Pieter F. Craffert
The Life of a Galilean Shaman

Douglas E. Oakman
Jesus and the Peasants

Stuart L. Love
Jesus and the Marginal Women

Eric C. Stewart
Gathered around Jesus

Dennis C. Duling
A Marginal Scribe

Jason Lamoreaux
Ritual, Women, and Philippi

Ernest Van Eck
The Parables of Jesus the Galilean

Bruce J. Malina and John J. Pilch, edtiors
Biblical Social Values, 3rd ed.

Early Christian Care for the Poor

*An Alternative Subsistence Strategy
under Roman Imperial Rule*

K. C. RICHARDSON

CASCADE *Books* • Eugene, Oregon

EARLY CHRISTIAN CARE FOR THE POOR
An Alternative Subsistence Strategy under Roman Imperial Rule

Matrix: The Bible in Mediterranean Context 11

Copyright © 2018 K. C. Richardson. All rights reserved. Except for brief quotations in critical publications or reviews, no part of this book may be reproduced in any manner without prior written permission from the publisher. Write: Permissions, Wipf and Stock Publishers, 199 W. 8th Ave., Suite 3, Eugene, OR 97401.

Cascade Books
An Imprint of Wipf and Stock Publishers
199 W. 8th Ave., Suite 3
Eugene, OR 97401

www.wipfandstock.com

PAPERBACK ISBN: 978-1-4982-9652-6
HARDCOVER ISBN: 978-1-4982-9654-0
EBOOK ISBN: 978-1-4982-9653-3

Cataloging-in-Publication data:

Names: Richardson, Kristopher Carl, 1970–, author.
Title: Early Christian care for the poor : an alternative subsistence strategy under Roman imperial rule / K. C. Richardson.
Description: Eugene, OR: Cascade Books, 2018. | Matrix: The Bible in Mediterranean Context 11. | Includes bibliographical references and indexes.
Identifiers: ISBN: 978-1-4982-9652-6 (paperback). | ISBN: 978-1-4982-9654-0 (hardcover) .| ISBN: 978-1-4982-9653-3 (epub).
Subjects: LCSH: Charity—Biblical teaching. | Church work with the poor—Rome—History. | Church history—Primitive and early church, ca. 30–600.
Classification: BV4639 R53 2018 (print). | BV4639 (epub).

Unless otherwise noted, Scripture quotations are from New Revised Standard Version Bible, copyright © 1989 National Council of the Churches of Christ in the United States of America. Used by permission. All rights reserved worldwide.

Scripture quotations marked (NIV) are taken from the Holy Bible, NEW INTERNATIONAL VERSION®, NIV® Copyright © 1973, 1978, 1984, 2011 by Biblica, Inc.® Used by permission. All rights reserved worldwide.

For Angela, Stephen, and Sophia

Contents

Acknowledgments | ix
Abbreviations | xi

Introduction | xv

1. The Poor in the Roman World | 1
2. The Historical Jesus and Care for the Poor | 24
3. Care for the Poor in the Letters of Paul | 63
4. Care for the Poor in Luke–Acts | 101
5. Christian Care for the Poor in the Second and Third Centuries CE | 140

Conclusion | 187

Bibliography | 193
Index of Ancient Sources | 209
Index of Modern Authors | 214

Acknowledgments

THIS BOOK IS A revision of my doctoral dissertation completed in the Department of History at the University of California, Los Angeles, in 2008. I would first like to thank the members of my doctoral committee for their support and guidance, not only during the writing and completion of the dissertation, but also in the classes, seminars, and independent reading courses that I had the good fortune of taking with them during my doctoral studies at UCLA. Claudia Rapp introduced me to the exciting world of Roman Late Antiquity. Ronald J. Mellor enriched my understanding of the Roman Empire and its social history, particularly in his seminar on Roman religion. William M. Schniedewind, my outside reader from the Department of Near Eastern Languages and Cultures at UCLA, graciously welcomed me into his seminars on the Hebrew Bible. I would especially like to thank my mentor and doctoral adviser in the History of Religion program, S. Scott Bartchy, who was a constant source of encouragement, guidance, and friendship. Each of these individuals displayed a rare combination of scholarship, effective pedagogy, and collegiality that I can only hope to emulate in some small way in my own teaching. While each contributed significantly to this project, I alone assume full responsibility for the errors that remain.

Since 2007, I have had the privilege of being a member of the faculty at Hope International University in Fullerton, California. I would like to thank my colleagues for the very welcoming academic community they have created. I would particularly like to thank Curtis Holtzen and David Matson, who have been constant sources of rich conversation, encouragement, and friendship. I am grateful to the academic administration of Hope International University, especially Joseph C. Grana, Dean of the Pacific Christian College of Ministry and Biblical Studies; Steven D. Edgington, Dean of the College of Arts and Sciences; and Paul H. Alexander,

Vice President of Academic Affairs, for their tireless leadership and advocacy for both the faculty and students of our institution. I would also like to thank them for granting me a sabbatical leave in the spring semester of 2016, during which I was able to begin the revision process that now culminates in this book. Finally, I would like to thank Kent Anderson for his vision for theological scholarship and education in establishing the Kent Anderson Fellowship Program in the Pacific Christian College of Ministry and Biblical Studies at Hope International University. His generosity allowed me a reduced teaching load in the fall of 2017 that provided much-needed time for the final stages of this project.

Finally, I would like to thank my family. My parents, Steve and Elaine Richardson, provided my sister, Noël, and me with a wonderfully nurturing, supportive, and loving home. It is impossible to express adequately my gratitude for their continuing encouragement and boundless love. My children, Stephen and Sophia, have been part of this book from the very beginning, and I wish to thank them for their patience, their support, my enjoyment watching them play in countless baseball and softball games, and most of all for their affection, which reminds me of what is truly important in my life. And finally, to my wife, Angela, with whom I just celebrated twenty-five years of marriage: thank you from the bottom of my heart for your belief in me and constant love. I am truly grateful for our lives together.

Abbreviations

Ancient

Acts John	*Acts of John*
Acts Paul	*Acts of Paul*
Acts Pet.	*Acts of Peter*
1 Apol.	Justin, *First Apology*
Barn.	*Epistle of Barnabas*
Ben.	Seneca, *On Benefits*
Did.	*Didache*
Eleem.	Cyprian, *On Works and Alms*
Eth. nic.	Aristotle, *Nicomachean Ethics*
Ep.	Cyprian, *Epistles*
Gos. Thom.	*Gospel of Thomas*
Herm. Mand.	*Shepherd of Hermas, Mandates*
Herm. Sim.	*Shepherd of Hermas, Similitudes*
Herm. Vis.	*Shepherd of Hermas, Visions*
Hist. eccl.	Eusebius, *Church History*
Laps.	Cyprian, *On the Lapsed*
Off.	Cicero, *On Duties*
Peregr.	Lucian of Samosata, *The Passing of Peregrinus*
Quis div.	Clement of Alexandria, *Who Is the Rich Man that Shall Be Saved?*
Resp.	Plato, *The Republic*
Vit. beat.	Seneca, *On the Fortunate Life*

Vit. Cyp.   Pontius, *Vita Cypriani*

Modern

AB	Anchor Bible
ABD	Anchor Bible Dictionary
ACW	Ancient Christian Writers. 1946–
AJT	Asia Journal of Theology
ANF	Ante-Nicene FathersApol. Tertullian, *Apology*
BDAG	Frederick W. Danker, ed., *Greek-English Lexicon of the New Testament and Other Early Christian Literature*. 3rd ed. Chicago: University of Chicago Press, 2000
BECNT	Baker Exegetical Commentary on the New Testament
BJS	Brown Judaic Studies
BTB	Biblical Theology Bulletin
CAH	Cambridge Ancient History
CCSL	Corpus Christianorum: Series latina. Turnhout: Brepols, 1953–
ExpT	*Expository Times*
HTR	*Harvard Theological Review*
HTS	Harvard Theological Studies
HvTSt	*Hervormde teologiese studies*
JBL	*Journal of Biblical Literature*
JJS	*Journal of Jewish Studies*
JRS	*Journal of Roman Studies*
JSHJ	*Journal for the Study of the Historical Jesus*
JSNT	*Journal for the Study of the New Testament*
JSNTSup	Journal for the Study of the New Testament Supplement Series
JSOTSup	Journal for the Study of the Old Testament Supplement Series

JTS	*Journal of Theological Studies*
KJV	King James Version
LCL	Loeb Classical Library
LXX	Septuagint
NICNT	New Interntional Commentary on the New Testament
NovT	*Novum Testamentum*
NIV	New International Version
NRSV	New Revised Standard Version
NTS	*New Testament Studies*
PL	Patrologia latina [= Patrologiae cursus completus: Series latina]. Edited by J.-P. Migne. 217 vols. Paris: Migne, 1844–1864
RTR	*Reformed Theological Review*
SBL	Society of Biblical Literature
SBLDS	Society of Biblical Literature Dissertation Series
SBLECL	Society of Biblical Literature Early Christianity and Its Literature
SBLMS	Society of Biblical Literature Monograph Series
SBLSP	Society of Biblical Literature Seminar Papers
SBT	Studies in Biblical Theology
SC	Sources chrétiennes
SNTSMS	Society for New Testament Studies Monograph Series
SP	Sacra pagina
StPB	Studia Post-biblica
TDNT	*Theological Dictionary of the New Testament.* Edited by Gerhard Kittel and Gerhard Friedrich. Translated by Geoffrey W. Bromiley. 10 vols. Grand Rapids: Eerddmans, 1964–1976
TPINTC	TPI New Testament Commentaries
WBC	Word Biblical Commentary

WUNT	Wissenschaftliche Untersuchungen zum Neuen Testament
ZECNT	Zondervan Exegetical Commentary on the New Testament

Introduction

THE EARLY CHRISTIANS CARED for the poor. Beginning with the very earliest Christian sources, we find consistent expression, not only that the poor matter to God, but also that God's people should meet their needs. And this was more than empty rhetoric. Unsympathetic pagan observers also acknowledged Christian care for the poor. The fourth-century emperor Julian, heir of the Constantinian dynasty and pagan revivalist, grudgingly noted the popular advantage Christians enjoyed because of their concern for the needy. In a letter to a pagan priest, Julian insists that traditional Roman religion must meet the challenge of the "Galileans" or risk further decline: "We must pay especial attention to this point, and by this means effect a cure. For when it came about that the poor were neglected and overlooked by the priests, then I think the impious Galileans observed this fact and devoted themselves to philanthropy. And they have gained ascendancy in the worst of their deeds through the credit they win for such practices."[1] Two centuries earlier, Lucian had mocked Christian generosity in his *Death of Peregrinus*, a story of an unscrupulous itinerant missionary supported by gullible Christians who thought they were giving to a legitimate man of God.[2] To Lucian there was nothing admirable in the Christians' willingness to give; it was simply the indiscriminate generosity of a foolish and morally suspect religion. The early Christians cared for the poor and were widely recognized for doing so.

There is a lot of interest today in the topic of early Christianity and the poor. One reason for this is the importance of social and economic themes in recent historical research. Convinced that the stories of well-known historical figures have already been well told, historians now insist

---

1. Julian, "Fragment of a Letter to a Pagan Priest," 305C.
2. Lucian, *Peregr.* 11–13.

that the experience of common people is historically significant even though their names and individual stories have largely been forgotten. In the case of biblical scholars and religious historians, the experience of those who identified as followers of Christ is as important for understanding early Christianity as the ideas of the well-known shapers of doctrine. For others, interest in the topic arises out of their faithfulness to the New Testament and its concern for the poor. Commitment to social justice and compassion for the needy find expression not solely among so-called progressive Christians; such compassion reflects the aspirations of believers across the ecclesiastical and political spectrums.

Yet this recent interest in early Christian care for the poor is often accompanied by modern assumptions that potentially distort our understanding. In some cases, we erroneously assume a basic similarity between antiquity and the modern world in matters pertaining to the economy, society, religion, and politics. We tend to think, for example, that in the ancient world, as in ours, wealth was an accurate indicator of social status, or that a free market economy rewarded creative and hardworking individuals with limitless opportunities for upward mobility. Perhaps we assume that the Roman government provided a safety net to insure at least basic subsistence for those who fell on hard times, or we take for granted that religion promoted personal morality and made adherents more sensitive to the plight of the needy. As we will see, the ancient Roman world was very different from our own in these and many other respects, and it will be important to account for these differences as we examine the economic practices of the early Christians.

Biblical scholars and historians of early Christianity have also made assumptions about Christian care for the poor, but in this case the assumptions tend to emphasize the differences between the Christians and their larger society. In the view of some interpreters, Christian care for the poor appeared as something fresh and new in Roman society, a culture, they claim, that was largely devoid of human love and compassion. Jewish charitable giving preceded that of the Christians and provided an important foundation for them, but these scholars insist that the Christians were different in the universal and inclusive scope of their benevolence practices. In the estimation of some, the Christians practiced a love for neighbor that went beyond anything the world had seen previously. Gerhard Uhlhorn concluded the first chapter of his study of Christian charity with these words: "But amid all these remains the deep-lying difference between the ancient and the Christian life. Heathendom did not of itself produce a real, organized charity; that is, as it were, something quite new springing from Christianity. The ancient world stretched forth in this respect toward Christianity, but could not of itself produce what Christianity brings. It still is, and remains, a world without love."[3] Similarly for Adolf von Harnack, the practice of care for the poor grew out of the novel content of the Christian message: "The new language on the lips of the Christians," he writes, "was the language of love."[4] For other interpreters, compassion for the needy was an appealing practice that set the Christians apart and helped them attract new converts in the first three centuries CE.[5]

Other scholars emphasize a different kind of discontinuity, this time between the practices of the earliest Christians and those of later times. According to these interpreters, what began as an egalitarian movement of renunciation and communal sharing gradually turned into a socially and economically stratified church, whose leaders promoted care for the poor no longer as an expression of Christian sibling-love, but as a self-interested effort to sustain the church's institutional needs as well as their own positions of status and power.[6] Starting with the communities formed by Paul, the churches no longer required complete renunciation from their wealthier members, so long as they gave alms and practiced what Gerd Theissen refers to as "love patriarchalism."[7] This basic pattern continued in the churches reflected in Luke-Acts, a composition that alters the original intent of the Jesus movement in that it addresses an audience of urban, relatively wealthy householders and landlords.[8] By this time, care for the poor no longer reflected the Christians' egalitarian ethos but instead represented the means by which rich Christians could express their elevated social and economic status. It was now possible for wealthy Christians, in good conscience, to retain private ownership of their possessions, so long as they gave generously to those in need. These interpreters insist that early Christian care for the poor started out as a novel expression of economic mutualism, motivated by love and

3. Uhlhorn, *Christian Charity*, 43.
4. Harnack, *Mission and Expansion*, 149.
5. Dodds, *Age of Anxiety*, 136–38; Lane Fox, *Pagans and Christians*, 324; Stark, *Rise*, 161–62.
6. For variations on this theme see Countryman, *Rich Christian*; Garrison, *Redemptive Almsgiving*; and Brown, *Poverty and Leadership*.
7. Theissen, *Social Setting*, 107–10.
8. Oakman, "Countryside in Luke-Acts," 151–79.

directed toward the economically destitute, but changed over time into a system of patronage that reflected the values of Greco-Roman urban society and thereby opened the door to social and economic stratification in the Christian community itself. This process undermined the church's original egalitarian spirit and led ultimately to the corrupted church of late antiquity and the Middle Ages.

In this study I propose a different way for understanding early Christian care for the poor, which I hope more accurately reflects the social context of the ancient Mediterranean world under the Roman Empire. In one sense this means taking account of important differences between the ancient and modern worlds, and I will discuss many points of difference along the way. But perhaps more important, I wish to emphasize certain similarities between the Christians and their contemporaries as well as continuity over time within the Christian movement itself. The Christians did not live in a vacuum. They shared assumptions with and adopted some of the practices of the society around them. I hope to show that Christian care for the poor was not distinctly Christian in practice but was indeed supported by a uniquely Christian worldview. Christian economic behavior looked familiar to most onlookers, though the ideas Christians articulated to justify those behaviors may have sounded very strange.

The alternative model I propose here is based on two fundamental points. First, I argue that rather than being substantially different from the practice of their contemporaries, early Christian care for the needy was inspired by a very common and familiar economic model derived from the practices of the rural village. Second, I argue that Christian care for the poor remained remarkably consistent over the first three centuries, and that the observable changes do not fundamentally alter the basic model that was practiced in the earliest years of the movement. Rather than a story of decline from a radically egalitarian protest movement to a stratified and complacent institutional church, I propose that in terms of care for the poor at least, a fundamental continuity can be seen from Jesus to Cyprian, the two figures who represent the chronological limits of this study. Specifically, I argue that Christian care for the poor in the first three centuries CE is best understood as an alternative subsistence strategy that developed in response to social and economic conditions brought about by Roman imperial rule.

A crucial premise in this study is that the Christian *practice* of care for the poor looked quite familiar to most people in the Roman world.

In spite of the evidence for economic growth consisting of industry and trade under the Roman Empire, the Mediterranean economy remained fundamentally agrarian. This means that either the majority of the population worked as farmers and in affiliated occupations, or their livelihoods were closely linked to the uncertainties of agricultural production in one way or another. The rural village, therefore, shaped the economic assumptions of the majority of people. And one of these assumptions was that collectively the village had an obligation to meet the subsistence needs of its members in times of food shortage. This is what James C. Scott refers to as the "moral economy of the peasant."[9] In short, I will argue in this study that the early Christians implemented the "moral economy of the peasant" in their mostly urban house churches, and that their economic practice, which above all emphasized giving to the poor because of their *need*, was recognizable to the majority of the population of Rome's empire because it reflected their own traditional practices and assumptions.

I refer to Christian care for the poor as an "alternative subsistence strategy" because they practiced it in urban settings where a different set of economic assumptions, values, and behaviors typically prevailed. Perhaps contrary to popular opinion, wealthy Romans were generous and gave significant sums to their cities and personal clients. The wealthy had a moral obligation to give, and they were honored for doing so. The difference, however, between urban benefaction and the "moral economy of the peasant" lay in the importance of human need as a criterion for giving. The village community expected rural benefactors to meet the basic subsistence needs of their impoverished neighbors. Urban benefactors, in contrast, gave to those whom they deemed worthy, based on criteria such as social status, citizenship, or moral virtue, and not necessarily because of their poverty. The early Christians followed the model of the village and encouraged the wealthy to give to the poor, not because they were "worthy" according to some culturally constructed value system, but more fundamentally because they needed help to survive. The Christians brought these assumptions and practices to cities, a context in which their wealthier members would have been tempted to follow the urban model of giving rather than the rural one. As a result the Christians not only had to persuade their members to accept an alternative economic practice; they also had to support it with an alternative worldview in which giving

---

9. Scott, *Moral Economy*. I will explore Scott's model in more detail in chapter 2.

to the needy, on the basis of their need, seemed to make sense. It was this sustaining worldview expressed fundamentally as a narrative of God's activity in Christ that was distinctly Christian. In other words, the economic practice of the Christians was familiar; the ideological framework used to support it was not.

In the pages that follow, I examine Christian care for the poor from the time of the Jesus movement to Cyprian of Carthage. I try to show that the Christians' basic economic model for providing subsistence insurance to their needy members remained remarkably consistent as the movement expanded beyond rural Galilee into the urban centers of the Roman world, even as the church assumed an increasingly institutional form. Alongside my examination of the Christians' practice, I also follow the development of Christian ideological support for their commitment to caring for the poor and argue that we can see a basic continuity in this as well over the course of the first three centuries. From Jesus to Cyprian, Christian texts consistently insist that the relatively wealthy should care for their needy brothers and sisters in Christ, and these same texts provide Christian benefactors with an alternative worldview in which it makes sense for them to do so.

With the exception of pointing to archaeological research for economic conditions in the Roman Empire in general and in first-century Galilee in particular, I make my case in this study primarily on the basis of literary sources, beginning with the New Testament itself and continuing with selected Christian texts of the second and third centuries CE. I do this for two reasons. First, there is little in the way of material evidence from this period that directly contributes to our understanding of the economic attitudes and behaviors of the early Christians specifically. Second, my goal is to understand how the Christians themselves thought of their practice of care for the poor—the obligation to do so, whose responsibility it was, the logistics involved—as well as the ideological support they provided for their actual practice. Christian literature of this period refers to these topics extensively and provides a substantial database for Christian thought on care for the poor.

A brief overview is in order at this point. Chapter 1 provides historical context for this study. I begin with a description of the ancient Roman economy, paying particular attention to research on poverty and food shortage. I then summarize the work of James C. Scott on peasant responses to colonial rule and propose that his observations about the "moral economy of the peasant" help to illuminate the economic behavior of the early Christians under the Roman Empire.

In chapters 2 through 5, I turn to the Christian sources themselves. In chapter 2, I follow those who have described Jesus's ministry in early first-century Galilee as a movement of village renewal, and I argue that a major part of this effort involved promoting an alternative subsistence strategy for those who were negatively affected by Herod Antipas's efforts to integrate Galilee into the wider economy of the Roman Empire. Chapters 3 and 4 consider the influence of the economic morality of the Jesus tradition upon the Christian movement as it expanded into the cities of the Roman world, by first examining the letters of Paul and then turning to the two-volume Luke-Acts. Taken together these documents constitute the bulk of the New Testament and consequently provide its dominant theological perspectives. With regard to Paul, many scholars assume that he had little interest in the ministry and teachings of the historical Jesus, choosing instead to emphasize the eschatological and soteriological significance of the crucified and resurrected Christ. An analysis of Paul's economic morality and the theology he articulates to support it, however, reveals a close continuity between Jesus and Paul in their attempts to promote an alternative subsistence strategy. A similar continuity can be seen in Luke-Acts. Even though scholars have often thought of Luke as writing from a world far removed from the values and concerns of Jesus's Galilean village movement, a common goal in both cases was to promote care for the poor.

In a final chapter, I examine the theme of care for the poor in the Christian literature of the second and third centuries CE. Again I observe that when care for the poor is examined as an alternative subsistence strategy, the practice first promoted by Jesus appears to have remained rather durable through these centuries, despite the fact that the greatest change in Christian care for the poor is generally ascribed to this period.

CHAPTER 1

The Poor in the Roman World

Before turning to early Christian responses to poverty in the following chapters, I first consider here a number of preliminary issues. Who were the poor? Why were they poor? What survival strategies did they employ? I hope to answer these and related questions by briefly describing the social and economic context of poverty in the Roman world. A second goal of this chapter is to consider the economic effect of Roman imperial rule. Did the Roman Empire improve economic conditions for the poor or make them worse? This is a debated question. I hope to show that even though the economy grew during the Pax Romana, enabling some to enjoy a measure of upward mobility, Romanization disrupted traditional social relations upon which the poor had previously relied for certain kinds of subsistence strategies. For this discussion, I will draw upon the work of James C. Scott to show the way colonial rule adversely affected the poor by altering traditional economic behavior, even when the overall economy entered a period of expansion. At the conclusion of this chapter, I will then consider the Christians' efforts to care for the poor as an "alternative subsistence strategy" in response to the detrimental effects of Roman imperial rule.

Poverty and "the Poor" in the Roman World

Modern researchers encounter a number of challenges when attempting to identify the poor in the ancient Roman world. One is the problem of terminology. In ancient Greek literature a number of terms were used to designate the "poor," two of which, πένης and πτωχός, were most common. The word πένης stood for the working poor person, who had enough to live, but not enough for a life of leisure, a condition considered necessary for the practice of virtue. The term πτωχός, on the other hand, referred to the destitute beggar, who had little to no means of subsistence.¹ Similarly, in Latin the term *pauper* generally refers to one who owned a little, while the term *egens* corresponds to the Greek πτωχός, the one who is poor and on the brink of starvation.² To complicate matters, the New Testament uses πτωχός extensively and πένης relatively rarely. Why is this? Bolkestein concluded that the Christian use of the term must indicate that the number of πτωχοί increased in Roman society beginning in the first century CE.³ Alternatively, A. R. Hands pointed to the tendency toward hyperbole in the Hellenistic period.⁴ Another possible explanation is that the Christians had a greater awareness of the destitute than did their Greco-Roman contemporaries. Each of these explanations is plausible but impossible to verify. Perhaps the vocabulary for "the poor" was inexact and flexible, and it may be safest, therefore, to refrain from drawing hard conclusions about actual economic conditions based on the linguistic data.⁵

A second problem in identifying the poor in the ancient world is that many scholars envision a highly stratified society, starkly divided economically between the magnificently rich elite class and the impoverished majority. It is generally assumed that there was no "middle class" in Roman society, only a vast economic disparity between the tiny ruling class and the rest of the population which was poor and powerless.⁶ This view holds that the elite orders, made up of senators, equestrians, and decurions, and constituting no more than 1 to 2 percent of the population, controlled all of the surplus wealth, while everyone below the top social stratum lived in abject poverty, struggling to survive at the level of basic subsistence. While accurately representing the clear social and legal dichotomy between the elite and non-elite sectors of Roman society and correctly assessing the proportional relationship between the two groups, this view mistakenly assumes that a person's economic level

---

1. Bolkestein, *Wohltätigkeit und Armenpflege*, 181–85.
2. Ibid., 327–29.
3. Ibid., 184–85.
4. Hands, *Charities and Social Aid*, 63.
5. On these questions for the period of late antiquity see Brown, *Poverty and Leadership*, 1–44.
6. See for example, Finley, *Ancient Economy*, 35–61; MacMullen, *Roman Social Relations*, 88–97; Alföldy, *Social History of Rome*, 106–56.

equated directly to his or her social status. Certainly it is true that members of the elite classes were very wealthy compared with their non-elite contemporaries, but it is problematic to assume that all non-elites were therefore equally impoverished. To speak meaningfully of "the poor," it will be necessary to envision a smaller subset of the 98 percent who made up the non-elite segment of society.

An insufficient base of evidence is a third problem in trying to identify the poor. Not only do economic historians depend upon an incomplete archaeological record; they also have to contend with the fact that ancient people did not carefully record the sort of information needed for modern economic analysis. Archaeologists continue to expand the database of relevant material and documentary evidence, but the inherent limitations of this evidence hinder accurate analysis of the poor in the Roman world.

In spite of these challenges, Walter Scheidel and Steven J. Friesen have put forward a sophisticated attempt to assess the size of the economy and the distribution of income across every sector of Roman society.[7] Building on their earlier individual work on the subject,[8] the authors propose an alternative to viewing Roman society as composed of a "few super-wealthy surrounded by a mass of relatively undifferentiated poor."[9] Making use of available ancient data as well as comparative models from other premodern and early modern societies, Scheidel and Friesen have devised an income scale that differentiates various economic levels in the Roman world. Their argument is complex and detailed, but the results are easily summarized.[10] Scheidel and Friesen conclude that 15 to 25 percent of total income was controlled by 1.5 percent of the population, (i.e. the elite classes made up of the senatorial, equestrian, and decurial orders). The bottom 90 percent (approximately) of the population controlled around 50 percent of total income. This large majority, according to the authors, hovered right around the level of basic subsistence, some just above and others below, with most living right at subsistence level. A remaining 6 to 12 percent, whom Scheidel and Friesen refer to as a "middling" section of Roman society, also controlled approximately 15

---

7. Scheidel and Friesen, "Size of the Economy."

8. See, for instance, Scheidel, "Stratification, Deprivation"; and Friesen, "Poverty in Pauline Studies."

9. Scheidel and Friesen, "Size of the Economy," 62.

10. Ibid., 84–85.

to 25 percent of total income.[11] Thus, a small middle class, made up of freedmen, wealthy artisans, merchants, farmers, and soldiers, enjoyed as much spending power, collectively, as the elite classes. Put in terms of subsistence, this "middling" group had an annual income of 2.4 to 10 times the amount necessary for "bare-bone subsistence," or 1 to 4 times the amount necessary for "respectable" levels of consumption.[12]

Scheidel and Friesen's income distribution scale helpfully clarifies the identity of the "poor" in Roman society by drawing attention to subsistence as a key economic indicator. The vast majority of the population lived on the edge of subsistence, which means that they also faced chronic economic vulnerability. Any fluctuation in their economic situation—natural disaster, political instability, or personal misfortune—could immediately plunge them below the level necessary for survival. Being chronically *vulnerable*, however, did not necessarily mean that they were chronically *poor*, or that they would have considered themselves to be. In this study, I identify the "poor" as those who fell below subsistence level, either temporarily or permanently, as a result of some event that adversely affected their economic position. In other words, while close to 90 percent of the population lived under the cloud of potential poverty, a smaller segment of that number would actually be "poor" at any given time, and for many of these victims the situation would eventually be reversed.

This definition of the "poor" is consistent with the work of Roman historians who have begun to make a distinction between "structural" and "conjunctural" poverty.[13] This is a difference "between those who are born poor and remain poor until they die . . . and those who fall into that state as a result of misfortune."[14] The first is a form of poverty that results from the basic structure of society, while the other is situational, arising from specific individual circumstances.[15] The first tends to be chronic, while the second is circumstantial and, in most cases, temporary. A case

---

11. This range reflects Scheidel's and Friesen's "pessimistic" and "optimistic" estimates.

12. Scheidel and Friesen, "Size of the Economy," 84.

13. A number of the essays in Atkins and Osborne, *Poverty in the Roman World*, make this distinction. See, for example, Osborne, "Roman Poverty in Context"; Morley, "Poor in the City of Rome"; Parkin, "Pagan Almsgiving"; and Rathbone, "Poverty and Population."

14. Morley, "Poor in the City of Rome," 28.

15. Osborne, "Roman Poverty in Context," 1.

can be made that the ancient Roman world exhibited features of both types of poverty,[16] but in the estimation of some scholars, "conjunctural" poverty was much more common.[17] An advantage of identifying the poor as those who fall below subsistence level is that it makes the "poor" a real category by differentiating a subset from among the 98.5 percent non-elite population.

Scheidel and Friesen's income distribution scale also puts forward another helpful insight by drawing attention to a relatively affluent segment of the non-elite population. The authors emphasize the important economic role of the 6 to 12 percent of the population who though not belonging to the elite classes nonetheless collectively controlled as much wealth. These relatively wealthy non-elite households had substantial disposal income and, in the estimation of Scheidel and Friesen, accounted for a significant amount of economic activity, particularly with regard to local production and exchange.[18]

The Subsistence Strategies of the Poor in the Agrarian Economy of the Roman World

In contrast to the 7.5 to 13.5 percent of the population (the elite orders along with Scheidel and Friesen's non-elite "middling" class) who were sufficiently affluent and thereby free from subsistence concerns, up to 92.5 percent of the population faced ongoing economic insecurity. This does not necessarily mean (as suggested above) that they were chronically poor—this would be the case only when and if they fell below subsistence level—but it does mean that such households had to develop various subsistence strategies for protection against food shortage, a common occurrence in the predominantly agrarian economy of the Roman Empire. The ancient Mediterranean region was prone to regular and typically short-term food shortages, resulting, to a significant extent, from naturally occurring regional and annual climatic variation.[19] Even today, not only is rainfall erratic from year to year, but it also varies widely from

---

16. Morley, "Poor in the City of Rome," 36.
17. Rathbone, "Poverty and Population," 105–14.
18. Scheidel and Friesen, "Size of the Economy," 88–91.
19. Garnsey, *Famine and Food Supply*, 6–9. This observation is also a key component in the work of Horden and Purcell, *Corrupting Sea*, particularly 53–88.

region to region in any given season.[20] For those who lived at the edge of subsistence, not only peasant farmers but also those employed in affiliated occupations, planning for the inevitable shortage was a necessary fact of life.

Peter Garnsey has described a number of subsistence strategies employed by ancient Greco-Roman farmers to insure survival in times of shortage.[21] Garnsey classifies some of these as production strategies, which could include the dispersal of landholdings, diversification of crops, and the storage of surplus.[22] Dispersion and diversification helped to alleviate overall shortfall when one region faced drought conditions or when one type of crop failed. Regarding storage, Garnsey notes that present-day Mediterranean peasants typically aim for a surplus of about two years' worth of grain and guesses that ancient farmers set similar goals.[23] Other historians add that the cultivation of cash crops for the marketplace should also be included as a production-based subsistence strategy.[24] That Roman peasant farmers voluntarily grew cash crops might seem to contradict the conventional wisdom that the Roman economy was by nature primitive and risk-averse, and that small farmers avoided innovation and long-range planning for the sake of profit.[25] But when evaluated on the basis of subsistence, taking on the risk of growing cash crops was a matter of survival in difficult times and not an indicator of a profit motive in the modern sense.

Production strategies often proved insufficient, however, forcing needy peasant farmers to adopt other measures to insure their survival. Sometimes this meant turning to one's social network for assistance.[26] Typically this network included horizontal relations with their extended kinship group and neighbors in the village as well as vertical ties with a rural patron. When these measure failed, needy farmers might finally adopt what Garnsey refers to as "demographic behaviors," some of which were particularly distasteful and embraced only reluctantly.[27] The expo-

20. Garnsey, *Famine and Food Supply*, 9.
21. Ibid., 48. See also Wilson, *For I Was Hungry*, 81–132.
22. Garnsey, *Famine and Food Supply*, 48–55.
23. Ibid., 54.
24. Horden and Purcell, *Corrupting Sea*, 175–97; See also De Ligt, *Fairs and Markets*, 106–54.
25. Finley, *Ancient Economy*, 95–122.
26. Garnsey, *Famine and Food Supply*, 55–63.
27. Ibid., 63–68.

sure of infants was one such demographic behavior, though its frequency is impossible to determine.[28] Another option was for surplus rural laborers to migrate to distant regions, either to establish a colony or to seek employment in a town or city.[29] As a last resort, peasants might even consume various types of substandard "famine" foods.[30] These foods were not generally considered part of the human diet but were "nevertheless eaten in emergencies" and might include the flesh of dogs and cats, twigs, shoots of trees and bushes, bulbs, and the roots of indigestible plants.[31]

Urban residents generally enjoyed a somewhat higher degree of food security than rural peasants during periods of food shortage.[32] For one thing, the basic political, social, and economic relationship between the city and the countryside tended to favor the urban dweller. The surplus of the countryside was in large measure controlled by the city, so it would be the peasant who felt the greatest stress in times of smaller harvests, especially when rents and taxes remained at prefamine levels. Urban dwellers also sometimes benefited from state intervention. In Rome and later in Constantinople, the grain dole sponsored by the imperial government was of some benefit, though citizenship, rather than need, was the criterion for eligibility. In other urban areas, city councils sometimes intervened by placing controls on prices when speculators released their hoards into the market in times of shortage.[33] In spite of these examples, however, the cities of the ancient Mediterranean world generally "did not develop an extensive framework of institutions and laws capable of protecting the ordinary citizen consumer from hunger and starvation."[34] There was, in other words, no official, government-sponsored safety net to insure basic subsistence for the poor. Far more important were the private, individual efforts of patrons and benefactors who assisted their clients and the population of their cities in times of need.

Patronage was a fundamental and enduring institution which helped counteract the inherent inequality of Rome's highly stratified social

28. Ibid., 64.
29. Ibid., 31–32, 64–65.
30. Garnsey, *Food and Society*, 36–41.
31. Ibid., 37. See also Horden and Purcell, *Corrupting Sea*, 178–97.
32. Garnsey, *Food and Society*, 41.
33. Garnsey, *Famine and Food Supply*, 74–79.
34. Ibid., 85.

structure.³⁵ As defined by Richard Saller, three features characterized a patron-client relationship: "First it involves the reciprocal exchange of goods and services. Second, to distinguish it from a commercial transaction in the marketplace, the relationship must be a personal one of some duration. Thirdly, it must be asymmetrical, in the sense that the two parties are of unequal status and offer different kinds of goods and services in the exchange—a quality which sets patronage off from friendship between equals."³⁶ In exchange for various types of services, not least of which was the honor and prestige his clients bestowed on him, the patron provided his dependents with a number of important benefits, including legal and economic protection, meals and entertainment, and in some cases assistance in attaining social or political advancement.³⁷ Patronage defined connections up and down the social hierarchy, with the result that the clients of some could also be the patrons of others.

Civic benefactors were patrons on a large scale, funding public services for entire cities or for a particular segment of the urban population. The Roman system of government depended upon these local elites to carry out the administration of the empire and to promote Romanization at the local level.³⁸ Not only did they oversee the collection of taxes for Rome and establish local law and order, but they also erected public buildings, administered civic services, and funded religious festivals and public entertainments. In the case of food shortage, the civic benefactor might make donations of money or food, but more commonly his generosity simply involved making his hoarded surpluses available to the market, below the going rate perhaps, but still for a profit.³⁹ Benefactors performed these services voluntarily but did so under a sense of moral obligation.⁴⁰ According to Paul Veyne, one seeks in futility for the material motives of euergetism.⁴¹ The notable class gave to demonstrate their social superiority and, accordingly, their right to rule: "Euergetism . . . always had two sides. It was civic, in that it benefited the city or the citizens as a whole, and it was the act of a class, the notables, who gave because

---

35. Wallace-Hadrill, "Patronage in Roman Society," 63–87.
36. Saller, *Personal Patronage*, 1.
37. Hands, *Charities and Social Aid*, 26–61.
38. Lintott, *Imperium Romanum*, 129–53.
39. Garnsey, *Famine and Food Supply*, 83.
40. Veyne, *Bread and Circuses*, 101–31.
41. Ibid., 153.

they felt they were superior to the mass of the people. That second aspect was essential: euergetism was the expression of a political ascendancy— the city was split in two, between those who received and those who gave."[42] Benefactors gave generously in order to be recognized for their civic virtue, rather than from a sense of moral obligation to the poor as such. This will be discussed at greater length in subsequent chapters, but at this point, suffice it to say that for urban patrons and benefactors, the worthiness of one's beneficiaries (defined in terms of Greco-Roman concepts of virtue) was a more important criterion for bestowing generosity than the recipient's economic need. Thus, while the urban poor could sometimes count on assistance from social elites in times of food shortage, they received these benefits for reasons other than their poverty: either because they were citizens of the city to which a benefactor gave a general distribution, or because they had been deemed virtuous and had therefore been taken on as clients by a wealthy patron.[43] Even though a manual laborer may generally have had better prospects for employment in the city, he was also more vulnerable in times of shortage than his rural counterpart if he had no citizenship rights or the support of a wealthy patron. The main point in all of this, however, is that for the majority of people, whether living in a rural village, town, or city, subsistence was a perennial concern, and their survival depended upon cultivating successful subsistence strategies to see them through periods of shortage.

The Economic Impact of Roman Imperial Rule

If most people in the ancient Mediterranean world were constantly concerned about food shortage and spent significant time and effort taking precautions against it, how did Roman imperial rule affect these basic economic conditions? Did the economy improve during the period from the late Republic through the early Empire (approximately 200 BCE to 200 CE)? Were the "poor" better off, or did the Romans make matters worse?

The answer to these questions is the subject of substantial debate among economic historians. An emerging consensus, however, is that in spite of the greater burden of taxes and rents faced by households under the Roman Empire, such losses were offset, overall, by gains in

---

42. Ibid., 104.
43. Hands, *Charities and Social Aid*, 62–115.

productivity, growing wealth, and a higher standard of living, even among the humble classes.[44] This growing body of research also supports Scheidel and Friesen's conclusions about the significant spending power of the "middling" class and suggests that this moderately wealthy, non-elite segment of society found new social and economic opportunities under Roman rule. Beginning with Augustus, the Pax Romana brought relative peace after decades of socially and economically devastating civil wars, created an integrated economy across the empire, encouraged industry and trade, and provided new opportunities of upward mobility for some. Nevertheless, even a growing economy did not significantly ease the strain of poverty. Evidence suggests that a larger number of people consumed a more nutritious diet, including meat,[45] but even if they ate better most of the time, they still faced the problem of recurring food shortage. To put it in modern terms, most people remained just "one paycheck away" from financial ruin, even though they were generally somewhat better off than their predecessors. In short, the vast majority of the population under the Roman Empire remained very concerned about subsistence, and significant numbers were "poor" at any given time.

More important, Roman imperial rule disrupted traditional social relations that the poor had normally relied upon in difficult economic times. As we have seen, Roman rule enabled a growing number to enter a sort of economic "middle class" and thereby enjoy earnings that provided both personal security against food shortage as well as significant amounts of discretionary income. But this positive economic development had serious social repercussions. Which social sphere would provide the basic frame of reference for this class of non-elite but economically upwardly mobile individuals? Would the prosperous farmer look to the village, his traditional home alongside his neighbors of humble means, or to the nearby city with its alluring amenities, opportunities for social advancement, and symbols of Roman power? The same questions would also apply to successful artisans, prosperous merchants, soldiers, centurions, military veterans, and wealthy freedmen—groups whose relative affluence provided opportunities to rise socially. Would these fortunate few be influenced by the cultural tastes and expectations of the elite class

---

44. For the current state of the debate on economic conditions under the Roman Empire, see the chapters by Kehoe ("Production"), Morley ("Distribution"), Jongman ("Consumption"), and Lo Cascio ("The State and the Economy") in Scheidel, Morris, and Saller, *Cambridge Economic History*, 543–647.

45. Jongman, "Consumption," 613–14.

and aspire to be linked with them, or would they remain connected to their non-elite peers?

The behavior of this segment of society, Scheidel and Friesen's "middling" class, may hold the key for understanding developments in the Roman economy and may provide insights into the condition of the poor under the Pax Romana. As a group, compared with the elite orders and the majority who lived at subsistence level, the relatively wealthy non-elites experienced the greatest social and economic change. It is true, of course, that beginning with Augustus the senatorial and equestrian orders expanded, enrolling increasingly larger numbers from the provinces. Likewise new local elites joined the ranks of the decurial order in towns and cities throughout the empire. But in terms of the overall percentage of the population, the size and economic impact of these elite orders changed relatively little. Similarly, the majority of people remained subsistence level farmers, laborers, and artisans whose struggle to survive determined their economic behavior as much as ever. But it was the prosperous middle class, though relatively small as an overall percentage of the population, who enjoyed more disposable income along with new opportunities for the social and cultural advancement that came with it. As I will argue in the following chapters, Christian sources also indicate the prominent role in early Christian communities of this middle-income segment of the population.

James C. Scott and the Peasant Moral Economy

Comparative analysis of modern peasant societies can add another layer of support to this picture of the ancient Roman world by illuminating economic and social dynamics in an agrarian economy under colonial rule. The work of James C. Scott holds special promise in this regard. In his first major work, *The Moral Economy of the Peasant*, Scott analyzed the peasant rebellions in Southeast Asia during the Great Depression of the 1930s.[46] Doing so, Scott developed an important general description of peasant economic behavior, which intersects at a number of points with features of ancient Roman society. Scott explained the ideological assumptions that support peasant behavior and showed how colonial rule, with its new ideological system, could disrupt these traditional

---

46. Scott, *Moral Economy*, 3.

practices.⁴⁷ Scott also showed that these peasant communities typically engaged in indirect forms of resistance to colonial rule, inspired by an alternative ideological system, which not only helped to alleviate their struggles but also provided a sense of cohesiveness that sustained their efforts toward mutual assistance. As we will see, Scott's model provides important insights for this present study, demonstrating not only that Christian care for the poor should be understood as one of many subsistence options available in the Greco-Roman world but also why the Christian subsistence strategy emerged when it did, and why certain themes continually reappear in Christian theology that support this practice.

According to Scott, peasant communities typically observe two fundamental ethical principles that encourage village unity and mutual assistance when food shortage occurs. The first principle is the norm of reciprocity, the notion that by giving to one in need, the giver creates an obligation on the part of the receiver to make a comparable return at some future time when called upon to do so.⁴⁸ Research has shown this to be a widely known, perhaps even universal, phenomenon.⁴⁹ Marshall Sahlins has developed this basic concept further by observing that the form of reciprocal exchange varies depending upon the degree of intimacy in the relationship between the two parties.⁵⁰ Interaction between enemies tends to feature "negative reciprocity," a form of competitive exchange in which each party seeks to gain an advantage while also inflicting harm upon the other. Exchange between neutral partners—neither friends nor enemies—tends to be of the "balanced" variety. In this form of exchange, participants pay close attention to fairness and equality in what is given and received. Interaction between close kin or village neighbors, by contrast, tends to feature "generalized reciprocity," a type of exchange in which a return may possibly be delayed or even different in kind from the original gift. For example, parents providing food and shelter for a dependent child may expect only respect and gratitude in the short term but more tangible assistance during their old age in the distant future. Similarly, in times of food shortage a neighbor may help a neigh-

47. Ibid., 3–4.
48. Ibid., 167–76.
49. A few examples of important research in this field include the following: Mauss, *The Gift*; Gouldner, "Norm of Reciprocity," 161–78; and the collection of essays in Komter, *The Gift*.
50. Sahlins, "Sociology of Primitive Exchange," 185–275.

bor, knowing that repayment will be made not immediately but at some undetermined time when the roles are reversed and he himself experiences need. It is important to note, however, that even in relationships characterized by "generalized reciprocity," a gift obligates the receiver to reciprocate in some manner even though the nature and timing of the return may remain undefined.

A second assumption guiding peasant economic morality is that subsistence is a fundamental right for each member of the community.[51] That all members have the right to subsistence does not necessarily result in egalitarian social relations in the village community; differences in wealth and status are generally taken to be natural features of rural social life.[52] But it is also assumed that in times of food shortage, the village has a collective obligation to assist its struggling members. As Scott observes, "the operative assumption of the 'right to subsistence' is that all members of a community have a presumptive right to a living so far as local resources will allow. This subsistence claim is morally based on the common notion of a hierarchy of human needs in which physical survival takes priority over all other claims to village wealth."[53] It seems that poorer members of the village community are willing to tolerate economic inequality so long as the relatively affluent share their excess wealth in times of need.

According to Scott, these two moral principles allow us to "grasp the peasant's sense of social justice."[54] Scott writes:

> There is good reason for viewing both the norm of reciprocity and the right to subsistence as genuine moral components of the "little tradition." Reciprocity serves as a central moral formula for interpersonal conduct. The right to subsistence, in effect, defines the minimal needs that must be met for members of the community in the context of reciprocity. Both principles correspond to vital human needs within the peasant economy; both are embodied in many concrete social patterns that owe their strength and longevity to the force of moral approval or disapproval that villagers can bring to bear.[55]

---

51. Scott, *Moral Economy*, 176–92.
52. Ibid., 40–44; 167–79.
53. Ibid., 176.
54. Ibid., 167.
55. Ibid.

These two ethical assumptions provide an important guide to understanding relations in the village, not only among kin and close neighbors but also between the poor and the relatively affluent. Membership in the peasant community implies a basic commitment to these fundamental norms. Village residents not only claim a set of rights that they can draw upon in times of need but also accept the obligation to do their part to insure the welfare of their neighbors.

Scott points out that the first line of defense for peasants is generally to turn to close kin and village neighbors for assistance.[56] This tends to be a reliable strategy in that the closer the relationship, the more likely it is that assistance will be given. But the problem is that one's kin or close neighbors may not be in a significantly better financial position to help. Though reliable from a social standpoint, this strategy often proves insufficient.[57] Wealthier villagers represent a more promising source of assistance because of the larger reserves at their disposal, but their willingness to give depends upon the strength of the peasant economic morality in that village and the extent to which the relatively affluent identify themselves with the community. Observing the phenomenon in Southeast Asia, Scott writes:

> The social strength of this ethic, its protective power for the village poor, varied from village to village and from region to region. It was, on balance, strongest in areas where traditional village forms were well developed and not shattered by colonialism ... It is in precisely those areas where the village is most autonomous and cohesive that subsistence guarantees are strongest. Given control over their local affairs, then, peasants choose to create an institution that normally insures the weakest against ruin by making certain demands on better-off villagers.[58]

In Scott's analysis needy peasants were more likely to receive assistance from the relatively affluent in villages where the traditional communal ethic remained strong and relatively undisturbed by colonial rule.

In these communities, better-off villagers accepted the expectation that they would contribute to the well-being of their poorer neighbors. But why? What persuaded them to do so? Scott observed that the village

---

56. Ibid., 26–28.
57. Ibid., 27–28.
58. Ibid., 40–41.

community pressed its demands upon the affluent through a combination of rewards and sanctions:

> The prosaic, even banal, character of these social controls belies their importance. Well-to-do villagers avoid malicious gossip only at the price of an exaggerated generosity. They are expected to sponsor more conspicuously lavish celebrations at weddings, to show greater charity to kin and neighbors, to sponsor local religious activity, and to take on more dependents and employees than the average household. The generosity enjoined on the rich is not without its compensations. It redounds to their growing prestige and serves to surround them with a grateful clientele which helps validate their position in the community. In addition, it represents a set of social debts which can be converted into goods and services if need be.[59]

In closely knit communities, positive and negative social incentives—particularly those related to the community's capacity to ascribe honor and shame—had the power to compel the rural wealthy to act in an economically ethical way. Sanctions against the wealthy did not necessarily arise out of a general sense of resentment about economic inequality; rather, community reproach occurred only when the wealthy failed to meet their expected obligations to the village poor.[60]

What happened under colonial rule to the economic condition of the rural village? For one thing, Scott found that colonial governments imposed economic policies that adversely affected the rural poor, despite the fact that overall per capita income actually increased.[61] For example, Scott noted that even though peasants had been accustomed to taxation under previous authorities, colonial governments, administered by a far-reaching bureaucracy and backed by a strong military, had the ability to exact taxes more thoroughly and systematically year in and year out.[62] Colonial regimes also disrupted traditional peasant production practices, forcing small farmers to cultivate cash crops for the market, whereas before they had been able to grow their own food.[63] Depending upon price fluctuations, yields which had formerly met a family's subsistence needs

---

59. Ibid., 41–42.
60. Ibid., 40.
61. Ibid., 56–57.
62. Ibid., 65–68.
63. Ibid., 58–60.

might no longer be sufficient.⁶⁴ Additionally, peasants often lost "secondary subsistence resources," foraging and hunting for instance, when colonial governments took over formerly common lands and assigned them to farmers for cultivation.⁶⁵

Perhaps even more destructive to the peasant economy than the government's economic policies was the fact that colonialism disrupted the communal ethic of the village and the implicit sense of mutual obligation between rich and poor that had formerly guided their economic behavior. On the one hand, as mentioned above, taxes and the insecurity of producing for the market further reduced the already small surplus that subsistence-level villagers had at their disposal to assist needy family members and neighbors. Even more consequential, colonialism eroded affluent villagers' paternalistic concern for their needy neighbors when these wealthy rural patrons began to discover new bases of social, economic, and legal validation outside the village: "The objects of envy and pressure within the village, though hardly impervious, became less vulnerable to the demands of the local poor. The moderately well-to-do who did not actually leave the village were no longer so dependent on local validation and support for their position. Now the courts and the constabulary could, if need be, enforce their title to land and their claim to contractual debt. This new outside backing allowed them to incur local disapproval at less risk."⁶⁶ Those who had previously identified themselves closely with their home village, who had sought legitimacy primarily in the eyes of their neighbors, and who had acted in accordance with the consensual morality of their community, discovered under colonial rule new outlets by which to define themselves and new opportunities for social and political advancement. In short, their primary frame of reference changed. No longer were they most concerned about being acceptable to the rural village but rather to the colonial government and its agents. With this change of reference came also a fundamental shift in values. The market orientation of the colonial government came into direct conflict with the communitarian ethic of the village,⁶⁷ and the rural wealthy were forced to choose between the two. For many, the rewards to be gained through cooperation with the colonial regime proved too

64. Ibid.
65. Ibid., 61–65.
66. Ibid., 61.
67. Ibid., 56–90.

enticing, and the relatively wealthy turned from the village in order to pursue these opportunities. Consequently, a fundamental component of the peasant subsistence strategy was undermined, and the strategy as a whole became less and less reliable.

Peasant responses varied when colonial rule led to the breakdown of traditional economic practices. In some cases, peasants revolted, but Scott insists that this is only a small part of the story because "to speak of rebellion is to focus on those extraordinary moments when peasants seek to restore or remake their world by force. It is to forget how rare these moments are and how historically exceptional it is for them to lead to successful revolution."[68] Rebellion was rare in part because peasants had a difficult time unifying against their overlords and also because they faced substantial risks of reprisal if they did so.[69] Nevertheless, Scott observed that peasants did not remain passive in accepting the economically destructive effects of colonialism. For example, some communities continued, perhaps even more vigorously than before, to press their traditional demands upon their relatively affluent village neighbors. Scott writes, "where such social controls survived with some vigor in the colonial period they tended to block the growth of sharp class cleavage within the village."[70] Active resistance to the detrimental economic effects of colonial rule is also represented by the willingness of normally conservative peasant communities to embrace innovative measures for the sake of survival. Sometimes these might involve distasteful practices such as "putting all of the family to work, eliminating valued ceremonial obligations, emigrating, sharing poverty, seeking charity, or serving in a landlord's gang against one's fellow villagers."[71] Innovation may also include forms of "self-help" among the village poor, as in "burial societies, social welfare groups, rotating credit associations, and local efforts to spread the work and food resources as far as possible."[72] As Scott observed, however, these forms of "lower class communitarianism" typically proved not to be viable in the long term due to the lack of sufficient resources.[73]

68. Ibid., 203.
69. Ibid., 195–201.
70. Ibid., 42.
71. Ibid., 204.
72. Ibid., 206.
73. Ibid., 207.

Up to this point I have been discussing Scott's analysis of peasant economic morality and the adverse effects of colonialism, but I want to take up briefly one more element in Scott's work that has a bearing on this present study, namely, the ideological support necessary for peasant communities to resist the changes brought on by colonial governments. Traditional peasant subsistence strategies rest upon a deeply engrained set of values, a consensual economic morality that sustains the cohesiveness of the peasant community in its efforts to care for the needs of its members. When these traditional strategies begin to fail as the result of colonial rule, and alternative subsistence strategies become necessary, an alternative ideology is also needed to sustain the peasant community as they attempt to implement these new practices. In other words, peasant communities need an alternative ideology to counteract the colonial ideology that has begun to undermine the traditional practices. In a later work, *Domination and the Arts of Resistance*, Scott examines the ways subordinate classes resist the worldview and social order of the dominant class. Scott characterizes this as a confrontation between the "public transcript" and the "hidden transcript."[74] The public transcript refers to the worldview of the ruling class and the way subordinate classes appear to "play by the rules" of this worldview. The hidden transcript, on the other hand, refers to the "backstage" discourse of subordinate groups. In the hidden transcript these groups give voice to their resentment and animosity toward those who oppress them.

Since the hidden transcript appears publicly only on occasions of overt rebellion, and since, as mentioned above, such occasions are exceedingly rare, does this mean that subordinate groups historically have been cowed into quiet compliance? One of Scott's chief arguments is that Marxist interpretations, which emphasize the "false consciousness" of the proletariat as the key inhibitor to concerted acts of resistance, are insufficient for analyzing the political activity of oppressed groups.[75] Scott's point is that outward compliance with the public transcript should not be equated with political passivity. Rather, he argues that a close examination of various forms of non-elite cultural expression reveals moments when the hidden transcript begins to make its way into the public discourse. Here, Scott argues, one can see evidence of both an ideology and concrete acts of resistance to the dominant social order: "[This is a] third

---

74. Scott introduces these concepts in *Domination*, 1–16.
75. Ibid., 70–107.

realm of subordinate group politics that lies strategically between the first two. This is a politics of disguise and anonymity that takes place in public view but is designed to have a double meaning or to shield the identity of the actors. Rumors, gossip, folktales, jokes, song, rituals, codes, and euphemisms—a good part of the folk culture of subordinate groups—fits this description."[76] This is what Scott refers to in another place as the "Little Tradition," which is in constant dialogue with the "Great Tradition," the culture, values, and master narrative of the ruling elite.[77]

Though the Little Tradition may appear either to support or, alternatively, to be of no real threat to the Great Tradition, a close examination reveals a clear aim to distort or subvert it. The Little Tradition offers an alternative worldview to those who embrace it. It is frequently based on a narrative of reversal, which imagines the present world order coming to an end and a new one, which is more just and responsive to the needs of the oppressed classes, emerging to take its place. Scott writes: "At the level of systematic social doctrine, subordinate groups confront elaborate ideologies that justify inequality, bondage, monarchy, caste, and so on. Resistance at this level requires a more elaborate riposte, one that goes beyond fragmentary practices of resistance. Better put, perhaps, resistance to ideological domination requires a counterideology—a negation—that will effectively provide a general normative form to the host of resistant practices invented in self-defense by any subordinate group."[78] In short, subordinate groups require an alternative ideology for supporting acts of resistance, including their own alternative subsistence strategies. There needs to be a contrasting worldview that resists the worldview advanced by the colonial power, one in which it makes sense not only for the poor of the village to practice "lower-class communitarianism" but more important for the wealthy to continue meeting their traditional obligations to the needy in their village.

---

76. Ibid., 18–19.

77. Scott, "Protest and Profanation," 1–38, 211–46. "Little Tradition" and "Great Tradition" are terms that originated with Robert Redfield; see, e.g., Redfield, *Little Community*; and Redfield, *Peasant Society and Culture*.

78. Scott, *Domination and the Arts of Resistance*, 118.

The "Moral Economy of the Peasant," the Roman Empire, and Early Christian Care for the Poor

Scott's model includes several salient ideas that are particularly helpful in understanding not only economic conditions in the Roman Empire, but also early Christian responses to the problem of poverty. Let me summarize the key points. Peasant villages function according to a communal economic ethic in which it is understood that the village, collectively, will provide for the subsistence needs of those who become poor, whether from personal misfortune, an inadequate harvest, or some other cause. Every household in the village plays a role in this collective sharing, but the greater burden falls upon the relatively well-off rural patrons, who in exchange for honor, prestige, and leadership in the village, contribute to the basic needs of those who have fallen below the level necessary for survival. The fact that there is an economic disparity between the relatively wealthy and the subsistence-level farmer tends not to be a point of contention or resentment in the village. Inequality is taken as a fact of life and only becomes divisive when the affluent are perceived as ignoring their traditional role as caretakers of the poor.

Scott observed that when peasant villages come under the control of a colonial government, the new regime disrupts the economic equilibrium created by the communal ethic. Not only do subsistence-level farmers have even less surplus to share with poor family members and neighbors in times of need, but even more devastating, the village patron no longer feels obligated, as he once did, to offer assistance. The colonial regime provides a new frame of reference, new social connections, new legal privileges, and a new set of values, which conflict with those of the village. In response to these changed circumstances and the grave implications for economic well-being that result, peasant communities redouble their efforts. They continue to exert collective pressure on wealthy villagers, seeking to preserve the traditional moral economy of the peasant in the face of modernization and change.

Similar patterns seem to have been at work in the ancient Roman world as well. The Roman economy was predominantly agrarian, and since most people were farmers, the communal economic ethic of the village would have been familiar to them. Wealthy patrons, in exchange for honor and preeminence in the village, reciprocated with a paternalistic and protective concern for the poor. But these traditional relationships within the village suffered under the expansion of Rome. The Roman

Empire had been spreading for many centuries and had come to dominate both the western and eastern regions of the Mediterranean by the latter years of the first century BCE. However, beginning with Augustus and his efforts to integrate and Romanize the provinces,[79] Roman imperial rule, along with its supporting ideology of the arrival of a "golden age" and the Pax Romana, exerted a more powerful and unified force throughout the empire than it had previously under the Republic, characterized as that period was by the diffused and competing interests of its conquering generals. In other words, under Augustus and his heirs, local communities throughout the Mediterranean world experienced the presence of Rome and its claims to universal authority in a more direct and powerful way.

For some residents of the empire, the Roman presence was a welcomed liberation from their former constraints and restricted ways of life, providing these fortunate few with a path of upward mobility. New men from the provinces began to fill the senate and join the equestrian order. City councilors cultivated new relationships with Roman nobles, governors, and even sometimes the emperor himself. Roman outreach to the elite classes of provincial society and the efforts to win them over to the Roman way is a well-known feature of this period.[80] But there were some, outside the elite orders, who also found new opportunities for social and economic advancement under the Roman Empire. Wealthy freedman enjoyed the honor of overseeing the cult of the emperor as *Augustales* in cities throughout the empire.[81] An enormous market, both urban and rural, for consumable goods, along with the relative safety of travel under the Pax Romana, provided new business opportunities for suppliers, manufactures, merchants, and traders.[82] Upon discharge, soldiers received Roman citizenship, if they did not already possess it, as

---

79. For a study of the architectural, artistic, and ceremonial aspects of the propagation of Augustan ideology, see Zanker, *Power of Images*. More recently, see MacMullen, *Romanization in the Time of Augustus*.

80. See for example, Garnsey and Saller, *Roman Empire*, 214–16.

81. Alföldy, *Social History*, 147–48.

82. For manufacturing, see Kehoe, "Production," 559–66. Kehoe notes that large landowners benefited primarily from supplying the raw materials used in manufacturing consumable items such as olive oil, wine, ceramics, and textiles, while those of more humble social status dominated manufacturing itself, typically conducted in small-scale workshops in both rural and urban areas. For the impact of the Roman Empire on trade (and distribution more generally) see Morley, "Distribution," 571–91. See also, Horden and Purcell, *Corrupting Sea*, 342–400.

well as a cash payment that might enable them to become landowners.[83] Centurions were often able to meet the property requirements for joining the decurial order, and in some exceptional cases even to be recruited into the equestrian class.[84] Wealthy farmers sometimes found new opportunities for advancement as they were drawn into the social and economic circles of the nearby city.[85]

It was these sorts of people who constituted Scheidel and Friesen's "middling" class, a group that, as we have seen, played a much more significant role in Roman society than their relatively small numbers (6 to 12 percent of the population by Scheidel and Friesen's estimates) would suggest. As a group, they controlled a significant amount of disposal income, a surplus which provided not only food security for themselves but also the means to assist the needy if they chose to do so. Yet, what would they do? With the allure of Roman values and the opportunity for social promotion, would they use their surplus resources in an "honorable" way, as defined by Roman cultural assumptions about what it meant to be virtuous? Or would they remain sensitive to the needs of the poor whom they had previously assisted in accordance with the moral economy of the peasant? Far more destructive to the economic condition of the poor than taxation or imperial manipulation of the economy would have been that many relatively wealthy non-elites chose to forsake their traditional responsibility to the needy in hopes of personal social advancement.

It is my contention that the early Christians focused on recruiting this "middling" segment of society for their efforts in creating an alternative subsistence strategy for their members. There is no clear evidence for elite participation in the Christian movement in the foundational period, and it is not until the end of the fourth century CE that the church could claim substantial numbers of upper-class members and count on them to contribute to the economic needs of poor Christians.[86] Prior to this, Christian groups appealed primarily to those among their members who, though of non-elite social status, possessed sufficient surplus wealth to meet not only their own needs during periods of food shortage but also the needs of their fellow members in the Christian assemblies who on those occasions fell below the level of subsistence. As indicated in the in-

---

83. Garnsey and Saller, *Roman Empire*, 146.
84. Ibid.
85. MacMullen, *Roman Social Relations*, 15.
86. Peter L. Brown tackles this subject in a number of publications. See particularly his *Poverty and Leadership* and *Through the Eye of a Needle*.

troduction, I have called the Christians' effort an "alternative" subsistence strategy, primarily because they typically introduced the economic ethos of the rural community into urban-based, house-churches. Under such a scenario, these relatively wealthy, non-elite members played the role of village patrons who in the rural farming community felt the expectations of their neighbors to meet the subsistence needs of the poor among them. In other words, the Christians imported a time-tested and traditional subsistence strategy into a new social context in the Greco-Roman city. Therefore it was an alternative subsistence strategy.

To recruit these new patrons, the Christians needed to promote a new worldview, an alternative ideology to counteract the temptations of the Roman "golden age." Roman ideology was proclaimed through a variety of media—artistic images, sculpture, architectural forms, religious ceremonies, coins, inscriptions, and literary compositions—all of which sought to convey the blessings of the universal peace and prosperity made possible by Roman rule. To be fair, publicity about the accomplishments of the Roman Empire was not empty propaganda. The Romans accomplished many remarkable things: relative peace, sophisticated infrastructure like roads and aqueducts, law and order, and a growing economy to name a few. Even the Christians, with the exception of some noteworthy periods of persecution, benefited from the Pax Romana, seeing their religious movement expand both numerically and geographically over the course of the first three centuries CE in large measure because of the stability offered by the Roman Empire. Yet, the Christians also recognized that the claims the Romans made about the eternal and divine nature of their empire were idolatrous and in conflict with their own proclamation of the kingdom of God and the Lord Jesus Christ. These competing worldviews likewise promoted competing ways of life, including ideas about the proper way to be generous. Embracing the values of the Pax Romana led to benefaction which made the recipient's virtue the main criterion, but when the Christians sought to recruit members of the "middling" class, they had to convince this group of the validity of their own ideology in which the act of caring for the poor, on the basis of need rather than virtue, makes sense. This Christian message and their economic practices, I argue, remained consistent from Jesus to Cyprian and will be my focus in the following chapters.

CHAPTER 2

The Historical Jesus and Care for the Poor

CITING THE BOOK OF Deuteronomy, Jesus famously stated, "you always have the poor with you . . ."[1] Modern interpreters have puzzled over the meaning of this statement, but one thing seems clear: in Jesus's day, as in ours, no matter how affluent a society might be, there are many who cannot enjoy the benefits of that prosperity. Whatever its causes, poverty persists, and the presence of the poor among us stands as a constant reminder that all is not right in our world. In this chapter, I examine Jesus's response to poverty and the ways he promoted care for the poor among his followers. Even a cursory look at the gospel materials reveals the prominent place of economic matters in the Jesus tradition and suggests that addressing poverty was one of the salient features of his movement. In parables, aphorisms, and lengthier units of discourse, Jesus is remembered to have spoken frequently about matters pertaining to wealth, poverty, and giving to the poor. Regardless of the historicity of any given unit of material, the overall picture is consistent and indicates clearly that economic issues were a major concern for Jesus and formed a crucial aspect of his public program.

During the early decades of the first century CE, Galilee was under the authority of Herod Antipas, a client ruler whom the Romans designated with the title of "tetrarch" after he inherited Galilee and the region of Perea upon the death of his father, Herod the Great, in 4 BCE. The lengthy reign of Antipas, lasting until 39 CE when he was deposed and exiled under suspicion of treason by the emperor Caligula, suggests that Antipas ruled with competence and cordial relations with Rome. Scholars remain divided, however, regarding the extent and quality of Antipas's

---

1. Mark 14:7; cf. Deut 15:11. (Unless otherwise indicated, references to the biblical text are taken from the NRSV.)

impact upon social and economic conditions in Galilee. A number of recent interpreters have adopted a "conflict model" to describe the political, social, and economic situation of first-century Galilee and propose a "political Jesus" whose top priority was to address these problems. In the estimation of these scholars, Antipas introduced a period of intense Romanization, which aroused resentment and sowed the seeds of anti-Roman sentiment that eventually resulted in the Jewish War of 66–70 CE. The activities of Jesus, they claim, should be understood in the context of this growing anti-imperial mood as a program of protest and nonviolent resistance, conducted approximately three decades prior to the outbreak of the revolt. Meanwhile, other recent interpreters challenge the "conflict" view of first-century Galilee. In their assessment, Antipas presided over a period of relative peace, prosperity, and sound government when Jewish religion and culture were respected, and economic growth led to a rising standard of living for significant numbers of people. On the basis of this picture of a peaceful and prosperous Galilee, these scholars either reject altogether the "political Jesus" model or, at the very least, propose a reconsideration of how central political aims were in Jesus's ministry.

One's choice of which of these two paradigms more accurately describes first-century Galilee and the ministry of Jesus plays a crucial role in one's interpretation of the gospel material and especially Jesus's teaching on social and economic matters. Interpreters who presuppose a context of conflict tend to read the entire body of Jesus's discourse as veiled anti-imperial rhetoric, while those who reject the conflict view assume that the bulk of Jesus's teaching had to do with spiritual and "otherworldly" matters. Thus, depending upon our presuppositions, we may arrive at very different, even contradictory, conclusions about Jesus's sense of identity and purpose, all the while drawing from the same textual evidence.

I begin this chapter, then, by examining these competing assessments of the social and economic conditions of first-century Galilee and the paradigms for understanding the nature of Jesus's ministry that result in order to draw some conclusions about the state of Galilean society under Herod Antipas. After establishing a picture of social and economic conditions that draws from both the "conflict" and "nonconflict" models, I then consider how the historical Jesus responded to social and economic conditions in Galilee by examining elements of the Jesus tradition that illustrate his program for creating an alternative subsistence strategy among the villages and towns of Galilee.

Jesus of Nazareth and the Economics of First-Century Galilee

The Galilean Conflict Model

For some historians and biblical interpreters, the relationship between the ruling elite and the peasant population of Galilee under Herod Antipas was one of exploitation and conflict.[2] Following John Kautsky, these scholars identify Rome as an "aristocratic empire," a state with a fundamentally agrarian economy in which a very small elite class of rulers and large landowners controls the surplus produced by the peasant class, thus leaving the vast majority of the population at the very edge of subsistence.[3] Through a combination of taxes, rents, government control of industry, forced labor, and peasant debt, the elites enjoyed enormous wealth, which they spent primarily for conspicuous consumption rather than for investment and economic growth.[4] In the estimation of some, rural Galilee was even more hard-pressed than other Roman provinces in that its population suffered under three levels of tribute-taking authorities: the Romans themselves, the Herodian rulers set up as client kings, and the priestly aristocracy that ruled the temple in Jerusalem.[5] Because elite wealth in an aristocratic empire is derived primarily from the surplus produced by the agrarian class, and not from investment and entrepreneurship as in a modern free-market economy, exploitation of the powerless is an inexorable feature of this economic system. Thus, whether or not there is clear evidence (in the works of Josephus, for example) to indicate a period of oppressive government, it must be assumed that the economy of Galilee, by virtue of its very structure, served to enrich the ruling class while depressing living conditions for the rest of the population. In other words, in an aristocratic empire, there is no other way for the elites to amass great wealth other than by

---

2. Recent contributions by notable scholars representing this position include the following: Horsley, *Galilee*; Oakman, *Political Aims*; Crossan and Reed, *Excavating Jesus*; Borg, *Jesus: Uncovering*; and Herzog, *Prophet*.

3. Kautsky, *Politics of Aristocratic Empires*; see Hanson and Oakman, *Palestine in the Time of Jesus*, 57–91, for an application of this model to first-century Palestine.

4. Oakman, *Political Aims*, 62–65.

5. Horsley, *Jesus and Empire*, 15–34. See Hamel for a detailed assessment of the taxes, rents, debts, and land tenure arrangements that oppressed the peasant class in Roman Palestine during this period (*Poverty and Charity*, 142–63).

extracting it from peasant labor.

In Rome's aristocratic agrarian empire, the rulers carried out their extraction of peasant surpluses by quasi-legal means, backed by brutal violence and a reign of terror. According to Richard A. Horsley, "[The] new world order established by Rome . . . meant disruption and disorder for subjected peoples of the Middle East such as the Judeans and Galileans. In conquering and reconquering them the Roman military forces repeatedly slaughtered and enslaved the inhabitants and destroyed their houses and villages, particularly in the area of Jesus' activity around villages such as Nazareth and Capernaum."[6] One of the characteristics of an aristocratic empire is a "monopolization of the means of violence and control of the law courts."[7] Peasant populations, therefore, typically have no viable means to resist the brutality they face and likewise no hope of legal recourse against their oppressors. This explains why peasant resistance movements typically employ what James C. Scott has called the "weapons of the weak," which include subtle and less overt forms of resistance (such as tax evasion) thereby reducing the risk of violent reprisals by those in power.[8]

Scholars who adopt this view insist that an accurate assessment of Jesus's ministry in Galilee must take into account a sociopolitical context of violence and economic exploitation. This means that concepts that modern interpreters typically think of as "religious" take on a clearly "political" significance. For example, when Jesus proclaimed the kingdom of God, he was not primarily concerned with a future, otherworldly, utopian realm, but rather with God's imminent rule in *this* world.[9] Jesus's proclamation was both an announcement of God's coming judgment of sinful oppressors as well as a call to covenantal renewal for God's own people.[10] Moreover, proponents of the "political" Jesus insist that the separation of religion and politics is a modern anachronism and inappropriate for understanding the reality of the ancient world.[11] What we call "religion" was thoroughly intertwined with political and economic concerns. The

---

6. Horsley, *Jesus and Empire*, 34.
7. Oakman, *Political Aims*, 49.
8. Ibid., 42; citing Scott, *Weapons of the Weak*.
9. Ibid., 70–78.
10. Horsley, *Jesus and Empire*, 79–128.
11. Horsley, *Galilee*, 2–4.

kingdom of God for Jesus was therefore a political reality with tangible social and economic consequences.

Douglas E. Oakman argues that Jesus targeted especially the problems of debt and taxation as the preeminent threats to peasant subsistence.[12] Debt was one of the "major mechanisms" for the elites to increase their wealth at the expense of the poor by providing the legal means for seizing "ownership of the patrimonial land of the Judean and Galilean peasantry."[13] Oakman envisions what may have been a common scenario: "A bad harvest or excessive taxation, coupled with the need of the Palestinian peasant to feed his family and set aside grain for animals or the next crop, led to arrears. When this was compounded with low productivity or successive bad years, default ensued. The tax collector or a wealthy man advancing credit, might insist on securing a fiscal debt through property. The peasant, obviously, would try to secure it with the labor power of his offspring or something less valuable."[14] The result of "escalating debt" was the "growth of tenancy and the landless class."[15] In Oakman's estimation, "more and more land came under the control of fewer and fewer landowners" as a result of this process.[16] Jesus addressed this concern through parables, such as the parable of the unforgiving servant (Matt 18:23–35) and the parable of the dishonest manager (Luke 16:1–9) and particularly in the prayer he taught his disciples, who are to ask the Father to forgive their debts as they forgive the debts of others (Luke 11:2–4 // Matt 5:9–13).[17] Likewise, by eating with tax collectors and "sinners," Jesus sought to broker tax relief for indebted peasants (i.e., the "sinners") by bringing them to the table with those in a position to reduce their tax burden.[18]

Roman authorities ultimately put a stop to Jesus's subversive activities by executing him by crucifixion in Jerusalem. Proponents of the political Jesus point out that crucifixion was a political penalty, designed to suppress popular uprisings by means of fear and intimidation. The Romans were not concerned about Jewish religion or theological disputes,

---

12. Oakman, *Jesus, Debt*, 17–118
13. Ibid., 18.
14. Ibid., 32.
15. Ibid., 33.
16. Ibid.
17. Ibid., 42–91.
18. Oakman, *Political Aims*, 97–99.

sometimes assumed to be the reason for Jesus's crucifixion; rather, they were concerned about the political threat that Jesus posed to the Roman order.[19] Though Jesus had no intentions of leading a violent revolt,[20] the ruling authorities nevertheless recognized his patterns of "everyday resistance" as the politically disruptive behavior that it was. As Oakman states, "The cross was the Roman punishment reserved for seditious provincials."[21]

In short, proponents of a political Jesus argue that his public activities must be understood in the context of a region under the rule of an aristocratic agrarian empire. Most residents of Galilee were poor peasants who struggled for mere survival because of the oppressive burden of paying financial tribute, in a variety of forms, to a small class of social superiors. The aristocracy extracted surpluses from these peasant farmers by ostensibly legal but typically violent means, producing a downward cycle of debt and desperation, which exploded ultimately in armed revolt in 66 CE. The Jesus movement appeared approximately three decades prior to the Jewish War, and, in the view of these scholars, offered active resistance to Roman imperial rule, even though Jesus eschewed the path of violent revolt. Jesus's frequent treatment of economic matters found throughout the gospel materials indicates his genuine concern, along with constructive strategies, for meeting the subsistence needs of the village population of first-century Galilee. His economic program had political implications.

The Galilean Prosperity Model

Other recent scholarship has challenged this picture of a political Jesus by questioning the assumption that *conflict* best describes conditions in first-century Galilee. A number of scholars particularly in the field of archaeology, have argued that a profusion of archaeological activity over the last three decades is building a very different picture of Antipas's Galilee: one of relative peace and increasing prosperity.

Based on an analysis of literary, archaeological, and numismatic evidence, Morten Hørning Jensen argues that the effect of Herod Antipas's reign on Galilean society was far more modest than proponents of

---

19. Horsley, *Jesus and Empire*, 129.
20. Oakman, *Jesus, Debt*, 94–95.
21. Ibid., 116.

the political Jesus generally assume.[22] Rather than a powerful monarch who successfully transformed Galilee into a highly urbanized region that was fully integrated into the Roman economy, Jensen concludes instead that "Herod Antipas was a minor ruler with a moderate impact."[23] He bases this conclusion on several lines of argumentation. Regarding the literary evidence for the reign of Herod Antipas, Jensen observes that even though Josephus depicts Antipas in a manner that is consistent with his generally negative assessment of Herodian rulers, he is nevertheless unable "to come up with any real examples of cruelty or tyranny."[24] Similarly, the New Testament documents "correspond with the portrayal of Josephus, namely the ambivalence and indecisiveness of Antipas in a stressful situation."[25] Surveying the evidence of archaeological reports, Jensen comes to two important conclusions. First, the excavations of Sepphoris and Tiberias have uncovered very little in the way of public and monumental architecture that can be securely dated to the early first century; thus in Jensen's view Galilee experienced only "modest urbanization" under Herod Antipas.[26] Second, Jensen concludes that there is little in the material remains of rural Galilee to indicate that the policies of Antipas had any significant negative impact on the overall quality of life in Galilean villages. In fact, the evidence suggests instead that Antipas's "government provided the stable conditions needed for expansion and growth."[27] With respect to the coinage minted under Antipas, Jensen also makes two important claims. First, Antipas avoided pagan images on the coins that he minted, utilizing instead traditional Jewish imagery, a practice that suggests that Antipas tried to be sensitive to Jewish religious concerns, especially when compared with his brother Philip, who made heavy use of pagan images in his coinage.[28] Second, the relatively small output of coins under Antipas suggests that his goal was not necessarily to monetize the Galilean economy for more efficient extraction of peasant surplus.[29] In contrast to those who propose a political Jesus and a

22. Jensen, *Herod Antipas*; Jensen, "Friend or Foe."
23. Jensen, *Herod Antipas*, 254.
24. Ibid., 100.
25. Ibid., 125.
26. Ibid., 185.
27. Ibid., 186.
28. Ibid., 204–11.
29. Ibid., 212–14.

conflict model for assessing first-century Galilee, Jensen concludes that "Antipas was a minor Roman client ruler, mediocre in both his successes and failures," that a "picture of conflict cannot be substantiated to any notable degree by referring to the reign of Antipas," and that "the picture of the historical Jesus as provoked by and opposed to the reign of Antipas cannot be substantiated."[30]

A key assumption of the conflict model is that an excessive tax burden in first-century Galilee led to widespread poverty and growing resentment toward their rulers on the part of peasants, but this assumption has also been challenged in recent studies.[31] Fabian E. Udoh argues that Jewish Palestine was not subject to annual Roman tribute payments during the rule of Herod the Great and his successors,[32] thereby challenging the widespread view that Galileans suffered under three levels of taxation during the period of Herod Antipas.[33] In Udoh's view the Herodian tax system depended primarily on a land tax, a sales tax, and tolls and duties on trade goods passing through Herod's domain.[34] The majority of Herod's subjects, therefore, paid their taxes primarily in kind, and the level of taxation seems to have depended on the productivity of any given year; for example, Josephus reports occasions when Herod reduced taxes in response to drought conditions.[35] Most interpreters assume that Herod depended upon the land tax to fund his extensive building program, but Udoh points out the modesty of Herod's building program in the early years of his reign, between 37 and 30 BCE, a period in which he focused primarily on internal security and constructed just a few fortifications throughout the land.[36] The high point of Herod's building program in the 20s and 10s BCE, however, took place only after Octavian had greatly expanded Herod's kingdom, giving him lands beyond Judea as well as control of cities and trade routes upon which he could impose tolls and duties.[37] Thus, Udoh rejects the contention that Herod's lavish building program and beneficence to foreign cities was funded on the backs of

30. Ibid., 257–58.
31. Richardson, *Herod*, 28; Udoh, *To Caesar*; Udoh, "Taxation."
32. Udoh, *To Caesar*, 113–59.
33. Ibid., 285. For discussion of the three levels of taxation, see Horsley, *Jesus and Empire*, 15–34.
34. Ibid., 159–80.
35. Ibid., 204–5.
36. Ibid., 195–97.
37. Ibid., 197.

the peasantry and argues instead that these projects should be attributed to "the prosperity of his realm and to his personal wealth."[38] While not treating the period of Antipas in detail, Udoh nevertheless maintains that Galilee experienced only a moderate level of taxation under his reign as well.[39]

As I mentioned above, recent archaeological research also supports a picture of political stability in Galilee and growing prosperity in its villages in the early decades of the first century. Numerous studies over the last thirty years seem to reveal a picture of relative peace and economic growth in this period, but in consideration of space constraints, I briefly discuss here only a few recent syntheses that summarize the current state of the research.

Mordechai Aviam argues that after years of neglect during the reign of Herod the Great, a "great change" took place when Herod Antipas became tetrarch and established Sepphoris as his capital city.[40] Far from draining the Galilean peasantry of its limited surplus, Aviam argues, Antipas invested in Sepphoris and so "provided employment, stimulated trade, and in general raised the level of prosperity."[41] Aviam supports this claim with reference to two representative towns, Yodefat and Gamla, the remains of which show evidence of economic expansion.[42] Since both communities were destroyed in 67 CE and were never resettled, the material remains can be dated precisely to the first half of the first century; thus these towns serve as important test cases for assessing conditions under the reign of Antipas.[43] Excavation in Yodefat suggests that the town's approximately two thousand residents were not uniformly poor. The majority of houses were simple structures built with local materials, but "a small, elite community probably occupied the higher eastern slope of the town's hill where they lived in large, beautifully decorated mansions."[44] Yodefat also appears to have been the home to various industries—olive oil production, a clothing industry, and pottery manufacture—which suggest that the town's economic base went beyond mere subsistence ag-

38. Ibid., 190.
39. Ibid., 189.
40. Aviam, "People, Land," 16.
41. Ibid., 20.
42. Ibid., 21–29.
43. Ibid., 21.
44. Ibid., 23.

riculture, and that trade with other villages provided additional income.[45] Only about half the arable land is suitable for agriculture (the other half is hilly and rocky); this leads Aviam to suppose that animal herding was another important element in the diverse economy of Yodefat.[46] Likewise, excavations in Gamla have revealed evidence of luxury items, olive oil production, a mill, and hoards of silver coins and jewels.[47] Aviam's survey leads him to conclude: "The results of the excavations at Yodefat and Gamla prove that villages in the Galilee were not poor. Galilean villagers were not peasants. Both poor people and rich people lived in cities, towns, and villages."[48]

C. Thomas McCollough provides a similar synthesis of research for the city of Sepphoris and the village of Khirbet Qana during the period of Herod Antipas.[49] Though Antipas aspired to the example of his father by building cities on a Roman urban model, McCollough claims that there is little evidence to indicate "monumental construction" in the early decades of the first century, and that significant urban development only occurred in the second century CE, long after the period of Antipas.[50] Yet, modest as it was, Antipas's urbanization efforts did impact village life in Galilee in a generally positive, nonoppressive manner. McCollough states: "The evidence for Khirbet Qana (and Yodefat) argues for a positive correlation between urban foundations and the village economy. At the same time, the modest dimensions of the urban development limited the extent of the intrusion on village life and culture . . . Antipas's building efforts did more to invigorate rather than spoil the villages of Lower Galilee in the first decades of the first century."[51] Khirbet Qana exemplifies the positive effect of Antipas's urbanization efforts. Village dwellings suggest "social and economic differentiation" as well as a clear sense of Jewish "ethnic/religious" identity.[52] Two public buildings, one of which appears to have been a synagogue, McCollough dates to the early decades of the first century and states that these structures also "point to a village that is

45. Ibid., 26–28.
46. Ibid., 28.
47. Ibid., 28–29.
48. Ibid., 43.
49. McCollough, "City and Village in Lower Galilee."
50. Ibid., 55.
51. Ibid., 56.
52. Ibid., 60.

at once economically stable, if not thriving, as well as sustaining a robust Judaism."[53] Evidence for industrial activities, which include *columbaria* (dovecotes for domesticated birds) and a possible glass-making installation, suggest that like Yodefat and Gamla, Khirbet Qana "diversified its activities beyond agriculture."[54] The lack of a road between Qana and Sepphoris in the early first century CE, however, suggests that trade took place mainly between villages, along foot and donkey paths that followed the contours of the hills and valleys of Galilee.[55] Based on these observations, McCollough states the following conclusion: "The evidence that surrounding villages were growing and thriving in the pre-70 period suggests that the initial phase of the construction of Sepphoris (and Tiberias) had a positive economic impact on Lower Galilee," which "seemed to strengthen and benefit interconnectivity between villages rather than fostering strong ties between village and city."[56] It was only after 70 CE, and not during the lifetime of the historical Jesus, that Galilee experienced intense Romanization that "brought increases in militarization, monetization, and mobility to the region," along with the social and political strife that such changes would entail.[57]

Sharon Lea Mattila argues that it is now necessary to reassess the social and economic conditions in Capernaum in light of evidence that indicates the presence of a wider range of economic diversity and greater wealth in the village than proponents of the political Jesus (who claim that the population of Capernaum consisted of subsistence-level fishermen and farmers) are willing to acknowledge.[58] Mattila begins by refuting the claim that "there were no luxury items or other indications of wealth"[59] in first-century Capernaum by pointing to discoveries of fine imported pottery and elegant glassware.[60] Mattila admits that the quality of this tableware does not match the level found in a city like

---

53. Ibid., 62.
54. Ibid.
55. Ibid., 67.
56. Ibid., 71.
57. Ibid.
58. Mattila, "Revisiting Jesus' Capernaum." Throughout the essay, Mattila engages chiefly with Reed, *Archaeology and the Galilean Jesus*, and Crossan and Reed, *Excavating Jesus*.
59. Mattila, "Revisiting Jesus' Capernaum," 90, citing Crossan and Reed, *Excavating Jesus*, 85.
60. Ibid., 90–95.

Jerusalem but argues that these discoveries nevertheless indicate the presence in Capernaum of at least some residents who "lived at a level significantly above subsistence."[61] Mattila also points to the evidence of three large houses that have been excavated in Capernaum as indicative of wealth above subsistence.[62] Finally, Mattila challenges the view that the undressed basalt stone walls of the houses in Capernaum necessarily indicate subsistence-level poverty. Drawing upon the analogy of the mud brick houses of the Egyptian village of Karanis, Mattila suggests that attention to decorative features, both on the exterior and in the interior of the homes in that village which would not have survived the passage of time and thus not in evidence from modern excavations, indicates that even in non-elite houses in Capernaum some residents may have had the economic wherewithal to add beautifying touches to their surroundings.[63] In all, Mattila establishes her modest argument that "at least some of the villagers in the Capernaum of Jesus' time—fishers and farmers though many of them probably were—enjoyed wealth beyond subsistence."[64]

Assessment and Summary

The evidence for rural Galilean prosperity, in my estimation, is not sufficient for overturning the fundamentals of the Galilean Conflict Model. The limited number of revenue-streams in an ancient agrarian economy left few options, other than extraction of peasant surplus, for the economic support of ancient empires.[65] The sociopolitical-economic system was designed to benefit the elite class; thus, material evidence for prosperity, by itself, tells us very little about how widely Galilean prosperity reached and what percentage of the population experienced improved living conditions as a result. Oakman is certainly correct to observe that "both prosperity and oppression can be true for first-century Galilee. The more appropriate question is *cui bono*? Who in fact benefitted from an obviously prosperous economic development in Herodian Galilee?

---

61. Ibid., 95.
62. Ibid., 114–24.
63. Ibid., 124–29.
64. Ibid., 130.
65. Douglas E. Oakman refers to the "regularity of premodern patterns of elite organization of political economy" ("Execrating? Or Execrable Peasants," 151).

Prosperity, if shared or controlled inequitably, could reasonably be perceived by some like Jesus of Nazareth as the other side of oppressive and exploitative social relations."[66] Even if it were possible to establish that Herod Antipas was milder than other ancient rulers, as proponents of the prosperity model suggest, this would not change the fact that the vast majority of the Galilean population lived at the very edge of subsistence. Food shortage was common and remained a perennial concern for the people of the Mediterranean world, regardless of political circumstances.[67] Relatively peaceful conditions might ease the burden somewhat, but at no time would an entire population be immune to subsistence concerns. Moreover, Antipas's urbanization and economic program in Galilee, even if relatively modest, would have had at least an indirectly negative effect on the Galilean poor by undermining traditional peasant subsistence strategies. As discussed in chapter 1, James C. Scott observed that one of the effects of the introduction of colonial rule in peasant societies is that the local village elite find new social and cultural opportunities in connection with the colonial rulers, which allow them to be less responsive to the traditional demands made upon them by the village poor. I argue in this chapter that first-century Galilee was experiencing a similar social transformation and that Jesus called upon the village patrons to fulfill their traditional responsibilities while also recruiting new patrons to fill this role.

The evidence for rural prosperity does support Scheidel and Friesen's view that 6 to 12 percent of the non-elite population had a level of wealth that provided them with personal food security as well as enough for substantial discretionary spending. In light of the possibilities suggested by Scheidel and Friesen's income scale, we need not assume that evidence of rural wealth—large homes and luxury items discovered in Galilean villages, for instance—necessarily indicates the presence of the social elite class in these villages.[68] Rather, it is more likely that these material remains point to relatively wealthy non-elites who lived in Galilean villages, side by side with those of humbler means. These individuals were, perhaps, relatively large landowners or owners of village industries, who

---

66. Oakman, "Socio-Archaeology and Dimensions of Exploitation," 347.

67. Hamel has detailed the difficult agricultural conditions in Roman Palestine and shows that basic subsistence was a challenge even apart from the added burden of taxation and rents (*Poverty and Charity*, 91–141).

68. As suggested by Oakman, "Oppressive or Prosperous," 349–51.

as rural patrons were expected to meet the needs of their poor neighbors according to the demands of the "moral economy" of the peasant.

At this point, let me now propose the following scenario for understanding the context of Jesus's economic teaching and his program of care for the poor. When Herod Antipas became tetrarch of Galilee in 4 BCE following the death of his father, he embarked on an intentional effort to urbanize and integrate Galilee into the larger Roman political, cultural, and economic system. Due to his limited resources, mediocre personal capabilities, and what appears to have been a reluctance to antagonize his piously religious Jewish subjects, Antipas's achievements were relatively modest. The cities of Sepphoris and Tiberias, though built by Antipas, experienced significant development and intense Romanization only long after the time of Antipas, in the second century CE. Under Antipas's much more modest urbanization and Romanization efforts, however, Galilee did experience a period of relative peace and a prosperity that appears to have brought increased wealth to Galilean villages by encouraging the growth of industries and intervillage trade. Presumably this led to an overall improvement in the rural standard of living and perhaps to a higher degree of food security for a greater number of people. But that this growing economy and increased prosperity did not solve the problem of poverty is evidenced by the recurrence of this theme in the Jesus tradition. Most residents of Galilee were still vulnerable to naturally occurring food shortages and required alternative subsistence strategies for survival during those times. Though many of these families lived, perhaps, a bit more comfortably over the level of basic subsistence during the time of Antipas, they were still not immune to the possibility of falling into poverty as a result of crop failure or personal misfortune. And we can only assume that Galilean villages were quite familiar with such scenarios; many of their families experienced poverty in any given year.

To counteract this type of conjunctural poverty, village residents cultivated traditional social subsistence strategies, by appealing to their neighbors—those of modest means and, more important, relatively wealthy villagers—for assistance during difficult times. It was upon these social strategies that the urbanization and Romanization efforts of Antipas had the most detrimental effect. Even if we grant that Antipas's urbanization and Romanization efforts led to overall relative improvement in the economic condition of Galilean peasants, I would argue that these policies were nevertheless detrimental to the Galilean poor in that rural patrons now had new social, legal, and economic opportunities that drew them away from their traditional obligations in the village. James C. Scott observed this phenomenon in the villages of Southeast Asia when they came under colonial rule, and I argue that the same thing was happening in the villages of Galilee in the early decades of the first century CE.

This scenario helps us make sense of the economic material that we see in the Jesus tradition. Jesus promoted an alternative subsistence strategy to deal with changing social conditions created by urbanization and a growing economy under Antipas. In spite of increased general prosperity the poor were perhaps worse off because they could no longer confidently rely on the social subsistence strategies that had sustained them in the past. In the remainder of this chapter, I examine key examples in the Gospels to argue that Jesus engaged in three different strategies to promote peasant subsistence: (1) Jesus engaged in a conservative effort to encourage rural patrons to continue to fulfill their traditional economic obligations to the poor in their communities; (2) Jesus promoted self-help strategies among those at subsistence level, what Scott has referred to as "lower-class communitarianism"; (3) finally, Jesus promoted the innovative measure of recruiting new patrons to fulfill the economic responsibility being abandoned by those who had traditionally played this role.

Before examining evidence from the Jesus tradition in the Gospels, let me briefly say a word about methodology. In this chapter, I limit my investigation, with only a couple of exceptions, to the Gospel of Mark and "Q" (the Gospel sayings source reconstructed on the basis of material common to Matthew and Luke but absent from Mark). Scholars generally consider these to be the earliest and most valuable sources for our knowledge of the historical Jesus.[69] The question of which of the two, Mark or Q, represents an earlier expression of the Jesus tradition is a matter of substantial debate.[70] Nevertheless, most scholars assign a date prior to 70 CE for each,[71] and many argue further that both were com-

---

69. Cf. Crossan, who assigns a number of non-canonical Gospels (including the Gospel of Thomas) to the earliest "first stratum" of evidence for the historical Jesus (*Historical Jesus*, 427–29).

70. The work of John S. Kloppenborg has been particularly controversial and, in some quarters, influential, in Gospel studies due to the priority it gives to the Q material over the Markan material. See particularly, Kloppenborg, *Formation of Q* and Kloppenborg-Verbin, *Excavating Q*, along with a number of other books, essays, and articles. See Dunn, *Jesus Remembered*, 149–58, for a critique.

71. In the case of Mark, most scholars would say "around 70"—either immediately before or after.

posed in Palestine.⁷² Thus, while it cannot be assumed that Q and Mark preserve unfiltered Jesus tradition, they are nevertheless basically reliable guides. This is especially true if one is interested more with the general themes that emerge from these sources than with the precise wording of any given saying or the historicity of any particular event.

Since even these earliest sources appear in written form no sooner than a full generation after Jesus's execution, James D. G. Dunn has observed that historical Jesus research is more appropriately construed as the study of Jesus as he was "remembered" by his followers.⁷³ Yet, one should not assume by this that the portrait of Jesus preserved in the Gospels is pure fiction, created by early Christians as a myth of origins to distance themselves from their Jewish brethren following the Great Revolt⁷⁴ or for any other reason conducive to their purposes. In fact, by way of analogy with other nonliterate societies, one may assume that the oral transmission of the early Christian memories of Jesus achieved a remarkable level of stability. Variations in the tradition occurred along the way not as a result of editorial redaction but from the flexibility allowed in the context of oral performance.⁷⁵ In Dunn's view, "performance includes both elements of stability and elements of variability—stability of subject and theme, of key details or core exchanges, variability in the supporting details and the particular emphases to be drawn out."⁷⁶ Indeed, the idea of "performance" suggests that in each retelling of the traditions about Jesus, the early Christians saw themselves as passing along a living and present reality. This approach to the historicity of the Gospels is useful for my purposes in this chapter. An examination of Mark and Q reveals a number of thematic similarities, which, taken together, lend support

---

72. This is less certain for Mark than for Q. Ched Meyers accepts a compositional setting in "agrarian Palestine" (*Binding the Strong Man*, 41). Other scholars seem to be more comfortable positing a more general Semitic setting. Gerd Theissen and Annette Merz observe that Mark's use of "Palestinian Jesus traditions with rich local coloring alongside pre-Pauline Hellenistic traditions" suggests a locale such as Antioch of Syria (*Historical Jesus*, 26).

73. Dunn, *Jesus Remembered*, 130-32.

74. As argued by Mack, *Myth of Innocence*, 353-57.

75. Dunn, *Jesus Remembered*, 192-254. Dunn relies in this section on a number of publications of Kenneth Bailey: "Middle Eastern Oral Tradition," 563-67; Bailey, "Informal Controlled Oral Tradition," 34-54; Bailey, *Peasant Eyes*; and Bailey, *Poet and Peasant*.

76. Dunn, *Jesus Remembered*, 249.

to the contention that part of the mission of the historical Jesus was to establish a new basis for peasant subsistence in rural Galilee.

Care for the Poor in the Jesus Tradition

Conservative Measures

A number of texts indicate that Jesus sought to preserve traditional social subsistence strategies in Galilean villages as an active response to the social and economic changes that were undermining those strategies. As we have seen, James C. Scott observed that increased access to elite institutions outside of the village caused wealthy rural patrons in Southeast Asia to become less concerned with the social norms that had formerly compelled them to assist the village poor. A similar situation seems to have been at work in Jesus's Galilee. The urban lifestyle and the perceived opportunities for social and economic advancement undoubtedly enticed many wealthy rural patrons away from their home villages to a new social context in the city. To put it simply, they were caught between two worlds and therefore had to decide which of the two, the village or the city, they would allow to shape their worldview, define their identity, and dictate their social obligations. Many of the activities and teachings of Jesus appear to be aimed at persuading this class of people to remain connected to the village and to provide for the poor among them.

The story of the wealthy man who approached Jesus inquiring about "eternal life" (Mark 10:17–22) is a prime example of this aspect of Jesus's alternative subsistence strategy. Considering that Mark's narrative never places Jesus in the cities of Galilee, Mark presumably intended his audience to identify this man as a wealthy rural landowner.[77] In response to his question about attaining eternal life, Jesus begins by reciting a number of commandments from the Decalogue. This is significant because it establishes the covenantal framework within which Jesus's subsequent instructions should be understood. The man claims that he has observed the commandments since his youth, but Jesus points out that this alone is insufficient for what he seeks. Jesus says, "You lack one thing; go, sell what you own, and give the money to the poor, and you will have treasure in heaven; then come, follow me."[78] The phrase, "whatever you have" (ὅσα

---

77. He is simply "one" in Mark, not a "ruler" (ἄρχων) as in Luke's version (18:18).
78 "Ἕν σε ὑστερεῖ. ὕπαγε, ὅσα ἔχεις πώλησον καὶ δὸς [τοῖς] πτωχοῖς, καὶ ἕξεις

ἔχεις) is ambiguous. Luke adds the word "all" (πάντα) in his version of the story, presumably to clarify the ambiguity of Mark's statement. But the ambiguity of Mark's version may actually capture the original intent of Jesus's words. In light of the moral economy of the peasant it is more likely that Jesus was instructing the man to share his *surplus* wealth with the poor, rather than sell everything he owned. By giving out of his surplus, the wealthy man would fulfill his customary obligation to provide for the village needy.

Richard A. Horsley has argued that Mark's readers would have understood the man's claim of faithfulness to the Decalogue as patently false.[79] If the only way to amass wealth in a traditional society was at the expense of one's neighbors, as Horsley assumes, then the man was clearly guilty of violating the commandments against covetousness and stealing. Two considerations suggest this was not the case, however. First, Scott's analysis indicates that relative inequality between rich and poor in the village was not, in and of itself, necessarily a cause for resentment.[80] Rather, it was the extent to which the wealthy man gave generously that determined the legitimacy of his social status in the eyes of his neighbors. Jesus did not call him to a life of poverty or ascetic itinerancy but rather into a community of sharing.[81] Second, Jesus does not challenge the man's claim of faithful observance of the Ten Commandments but instead points out that this alone is insufficient for inheriting eternal life. More would be required, namely caring for the poor. It is likely that Mark intends his readers to hear in this exchange an allusion to the Covenant Code, which follows directly after the Ten Commandments in the book of Exodus (Exod 21:1—23:19). Much of the Covenant Code deals with care for the poor and represents the subsistence strategy of the ancient Israelite people. Even in the midst of various historical changes affecting Israel—the rise of the monarchy, exile, and restoration in the land—these laws continued to guide rural relations in the subsequent centuries. It is possible, however, in first-century Galilee, as it was undergoing urbanization and economic integration into the larger Roman world, that the rural-oriented laws of the Covenant Code were falling out of favor because they seemed too archaic and inapplicable to the urbanization underway

θησαυρὸν ἐν οὐρανῷ, καὶ δεῦρο ἀκολούθει μοι (Mark 10:21).

79. Horsley, *Hearing*, 191.

80. Scott, *Moral Economy*, 40–44, 167–79.

81. A point made by S. Scott Bartchy on a number of occasions in personal conversations.

in Galilee. Whatever the case may be, Jesus here challenges this rural patron to fulfill his traditional role as caretaker of the village poor rather than to embrace the values and new social opportunities of the city.

Certain aphorisms and parables also illustrate Jesus's attempt to bolster traditional social subsistence strategies. The saying, "Do not store up for yourselves treasures on earth, where moth and rust consume and where thieves break in and steal; but store up for yourselves treasures in heaven, where neither moth nor rust consume and where thieves do not break in and steal,"[82] reflects the practice of the rural wealthy of storing their grain surplus. Saving a portion of one's harvest in an especially good year was an acceptable facet of an effective subsistence strategy, but this saying suggests a level of grain reserves that goes far beyond what is needed for personal subsistence insurance. So much grain is saved that the excess goes to waste instead of being used to feed the poor; the surplus is so great that it benefits no one. This saying may also reflect the practice of the wealthy who hoarded their surplus grain in order to release it into the market at a substantial profit when shortages occurred, a practice that is well documented in the ancient sources.[83]

The parable of the hoarding farmer in Luke 12:16-21 also fits this context and expresses the futility, from a peasant standpoint, of amassing more wealth than one could actually use.[84] From the peasant perspective, long-term planning for a life of ease and luxury would have been utterly pointless, considering the constraints of basic subsistence. It would have come as no surprise to Jesus's peasant audience, therefore, that the farmer's grandiose plans fail due to his sudden death. From an urban perspective, however, the behavior of the hoarding farmer would have been perfectly intelligible. The farmer's initial indecision about what he should do with his great harvest (v. 17) suggests that the wealthy farmers in Jesus's audience may have also been experiencing the tension between urban and rural economic values and practices.

---

82. Μὴ θησαυρίζετε ὑμῖν θησαυροὺς ἐπὶ τῆς γῆς, ὅπου σὴς καὶ βρῶσις ἀφανίζει καὶ ὅπου κλέπται διορύσσουσιν καὶ κλέπτουσιν; θησαυρίζετε δὲ ὑμῖν θησαυροὺς ἐν οὐρανῷ, ὅπου οὔτε σὴς οὔτε βρῶσις ἀφανίζει καὶ ὅπου κλέπται οὐ διορύσσουσιν οὐδὲ κλέπτουσιν (Q = Matt 6:19-20 // Luke 12:33. The editors of the *Critical Edition of Q* follow Matthew for this Q saying).

83. Garnsey, *Famine and Food Supply*, 74-79.

84. For the most part, I am focusing on Q and Mark in this chapter. However, on a few occasions I consider parables and sayings which are singly attested in Matthew or Luke.

The parable of the great feast expresses a similar tension between rural and urban values, perhaps a hint that the primary audience for this story was again this class of wealthy rural farmers who were influenced by the new cities of Galilee.[85] Scholars have recognized the significance of table fellowship for Jesus's announcement of the kingdom of God. S. Scott Bartchy writes: "One distinctive feature of the historical Jesus' public life was his practice of a radically inclusive, status-leveling, and honor-sharing fellowship at table as a central strategy in his announcement and redefinition of the in-breaking ruling of Israel's God. In so doing, Jesus of Nazareth presented a living parable and model of his vision of a renewed Israel. His actions profoundly challenged the inherent exclusivism and status consciousness sustained by the prevailing cultural values and social codes."[86] Bartchy goes on to state, "traditional meal practices provided easy opportunities for males in his [Jesus's] culture to seek honor and display their ascribed or acquired status."[87] Thus by engaging in "radically inclusive" table fellowship, Jesus sought to challenge these cultural values in an "especially prominent venue."[88] These principles are poignantly dramatized in the parable of the great feast.

While the substantial differences between Matthew's and Luke's versions of the parable make an assessment of its original form especially difficult, the similarities between the Gospel of Thomas and the Lukan version provide some grounds for giving priority to the latter.[89] The parable opens with a scene that would have been familiar in the context of the urban elite: a wealthy man hosts a meal and invites his social and economic peers. Yet, very quickly everything goes wrong and the scene fails to develop as one would expect when the invited guests refuse the host's invitation. In doing so, they not only dishonor the hopeful host but also signal that they have no intention of nurturing a reciprocal relationship with him. It is clear that he should expect neither to receive future invitations from them, nor to enjoy the broader benefits and prestige of being part of their social circle.[90] In response to this great insult, the host com-

---

85. The parable is attested in Luke 14:16–24; Matt 22:1–10; and *Gos. Thom.* 64.
86. Bartchy, "Reversal of Honor at the Table," 175.
87. Ibid., 182.
88. Ibid.
89. Horsley, *Spiral of Violence*, 180; *Gos. Thom.* 64.
90. Marcel Mauss has observed: "To refuse to give, to fail to invite, *just as to refuse to accept*, is tantamount to declaring war; it is to reject the bond of alliance and commonality" (*Gift*, 13; emphasis added).

mands his slave, "Go out at once into the streets and lanes of the town and bring in the poor, the crippled, the blind, and the lame."[91] When this is accomplished, the slave declares that there remains room for more. To this the host responds, "Go out into the roads and lanes and compel people to come in, so that my house may be filled" (v. 23).[92]

For whom did Jesus intend this parable? Since one must rely primarily on Luke's version, it is impossible to determine which details may be Lukan glosses and therefore reflective of the presumed concerns of Luke's audience.[93] If it can be assumed, however, that Luke's version is basically consistent with the original, then Jesus appears again to be addressing particularly the rural wealthy of Galilee. Like the host in the parable, they also experienced the tension of competing values. To prepare a feast for other wealthy men meant having to ignore their poor fellow villagers. On the other hand, fulfilling their customary obligations to the needy meant having to forgo the opportunities available to them in Herod's new cities. What should they choose? The prospect of associating with the urban elite was undoubtedly very appealing to many wealthy rural farmers, but Jesus issues here a cautionary tale for those contemplating such a move: by making advances toward the elite, the wealthy farmer risked being rebuffed and effectively put "back in his place." He risked the humiliation of a failed attempt to join an elite class whose practices and values were foreign to him. To turn to the city meant having to become an obsequious client rather than an honored patron in his home village. It was a decision with grave consequences.

In the end, the wealthy farmer in the parable comes full circle and acts in a manner appropriate to his position (according to peasant values, at least): inviting and welcoming the poor, crippled, blind, and lame of the village into his home for a feast. In this story Jesus reaffirms traditional Israelite peasant values. He hopes to persuade those wealthy farmers, who may have begun to see these old values as obsolete and passé, to reconsider this evaluation and return to their traditional place in the village community.

---

91. "Ἔξελθε ταχέως εἰς τὰς πλατείας καὶ ῥύμας τῆς πόλεως καὶ τοὺς πτωχοὺς καὶ ἀναπείρους καὶ τυφλοὺς καὶ χωλοὺς εἰσάγαγε ὧδε (Luke 14:21).

92. "Ἔξελθε εἰς τὰς ὁδοὺς καὶ φραγμοὺς καὶ ἀνάγκασον εἰσελθεῖν, ἵνα γεμισθῇ μου ὁ οἶκος.

93. Luke's tendency to use the term πόλις ("city") for all types of settlements, regardless of size or legal status, is one such gloss and can be seen in 14:21.

Jesus's recommendation to resolve conflicts locally may also have been intended particularly for wealthy rural landowners. Disputes concerning debt and land seizure were undoubtedly a common source of conflict in rural society.[94] In the context of the village, the elders of the community presumably adjudicated such disputes in accordance with the peasant subsistence ethic, which favored the poor, and under normal conditions the wealthy farmer's need to preserve and increase his honor among his fellow villagers would typically have provided sufficient motivation to act generously. But in the case of Southeast Asia, Scott observed that the rise of colonial rule allowed the rural wealthy to disregard local opinion because they could now take their cases to urban law courts.[95] A similar situation, in which the rural wealthy sought legal judgments in the city rather than in the village, may have begun to develop in first-century Galilee.

The model prayer that Jesus taught his disciples may be relevant in this context. The second petition of the prayer states, "and forgive us our debts, as we have also forgiven our debtors."[96] By teaching his followers to seek forgiveness from God as they themselves forgive the debts of others, Jesus implies that his hearers have some control over judicial proceedings, and that debt forgiveness should be decided at the local level in the context of the village. The burden of the obligation to forgive debts lay primarily with the wealthy, who frequently assisted needy farmers with much-needed loans, which in the Israelite legal tradition were supposed to be interest-free.[97] This is not completely unusual, however. Liberal food loans are also known in other rural societies and constitute a typical feature of peasant subsistence systems.[98] In other words, peasants knew that such loans were sometimes necessary for survival and were grateful to the wealthy persons who were willing to lend. The problem was that a farmer was often unable to repay the loan, in which case he would lose his land to the creditor. The cycle of debt had already had devastating

---

94. See Horsley, *Spiral of Violence*, 251–55, for discussion of this issue.

95. Scott, *Moral Economy*, 61.

96. καὶ ἄφες ἡμῖν τὰ ὀφειλήματα ἡμῶν, ὡς καὶ ἡμεῖς ἀφήκαμεν τοῖς ὀφειλέταις ἡμῶν (Luke 11:4). Horsley notes that Luke replaces debts (ὀφειλήματα) with sins (ἁμαρτίας), so the Matthean version is given priority in that it is more true to Jesus rural Galilean context (*Spiral of Violence*, 253).

97. Exod 22:25; Lev 25:36–37; Deut 23:19–20.

98. Scott, *Moral Economy*, 50–51.

social and economic consequences in Judea.⁹⁹ Galilee may have faced a similar problem, even if, as discussed above, the policies of Herod Antipas did not have quite the negative impact that many assume. Jesus's call for the forgiveness of debts, therefore, was an attempt to stem the tide of this destructive cycle.¹⁰⁰

Again we might ask, for whom was this teaching intended? Jesus's call for the forgiveness of debts probably had little effect upon the urban-based absentee landlords who heard Jesus rarely, if ever. Thus, we should assume that Jesus spoke these words primarily to the rural wealthy, many of whom he hoped would still be influenced by his advocacy for the peasant moral economy. Jesus's saying concerning the avoidance of law-courts seems to indicate the same point.¹⁰¹ The Lukan version reads: "When you go with your accuser before a magistrate, on the way make an effort to settle the case, or you may be dragged before the judge, and the judge hand you over to the officer, and the officer throw you into prison. I tell you, you will never get out until you pay the very last penny."¹⁰² This advice is specifically for poor debtors who were being called into court, but the implication is that their wealthy creditors could possibly be persuaded to accept some form of extrajudicial resolution, perhaps the traditional justice of the village.

As we can see from these examples, one component of Jesus's alternative subsistence strategy involved calling rural patrons back to their traditional role as caretakers for the needy. As Galilee became more urbanized and economically prosperous during this period, the rural wealthy had new opportunities for social and economic advancement. Jesus tried to help them resist the allure of the city and remain oriented toward the village. He did so by reminding them of their traditional obligations, rooted in the Israelite covenant, and also by warning them of the inherent risk of rejection and humiliation in seeking social advancement.

---

99. Goodman, "Jewish Revolt," 417–27.

100. On the question of whether Jesus was calling for a Jubilee in Israel as a whole, see Wright, *Jesus and the Victory of God*, 294–95. Wright thinks it more likely that Jesus "intended his cells of followers to live 'as if' the Jubilee were being enacted" (295).

101. Q (Luke 12:57–59; Matt 5:25–26).

102. ὡς γὰρ ὑπάγεις μετὰ τοῦ ἀντιδίκου σου ἐπ' ἄρχοντα, ἐν τῇ ὁδῷ δὸς ἐργασίαν ἀπηλλάχθαι ἀπ' αὐτοῦ, μήποτε κατασύρῃ σε πρὸς τὸν κριτήν, καὶ ὁ κριτής σε παραδώσει τῷ πράκτορι, καὶ ὁ πράκτωρ σε βαλεῖ εἰς φυλακήν. λέγω σοι, οὐ μὴ ἐξέλθῃς ἐκεῖθεν, ἕως καὶ τὸ ἔσχατον λεπτὸν ἀποδῷς (Luke 12:58–59).

Part of Jesus's alternative subsistence strategy, then, was simply a reaffirmation of traditional rural values.

Innovation: Self-Help Measures

Other elements in the Jesus tradition reflect more innovative measures. This is consistent with Scott's observation that when customary subsistence strategies begin to break down, peasants are forced to seek new means of meeting their food needs.[103] Jesus focused his appeal on the rural wealthy who could still be influenced by traditional peasant values, yet this alone may not have been enough. Jesus also promoted sharing among the poor themselves, what Scott has referred to as "lower class communitarianism."[104] Such measures demand tremendous sacrifices. Entire villages may have to reduce caloric intake or eat sub-standard food items in order to insure that every member has at least the bare minimum required for survival in the short term.[105] Moreover this sort of self-sacrificing behavior demands significant levels of trust among the poor who would naturally resist cooperation when they have no real surplus to share. Indeed, Scott points out that in periods of severe competition for scarce food resources, "self-help" sometimes pits neighbor against neighbor, which might involve, for instance, "serving in a landlord's gang against one's fellow-villagers."[106] Not surprisingly, these activities "entail great human costs."[107]

In the Gospels one finds abundant indirect evidence that Jesus attempted to mitigate these socially destructive behaviors by encouraging the poor to practice forms of "lower class communitarianism." To be sure, these were only stopgap measures. Considering Jesus's other strategies which targeted the rural wealthy, and as we will see below, the "retainers" of the urban wealthy, it is clear that Jesus did not think of shared poverty as the ultimate goal of his efforts. However, it is likely that such practices

---

103. Scott, *Moral Economy*, 203–25.

104. Ibid., 205–7.

105. Ibid., 206–7. Such practices are known also from Greco-Roman antiquity and resulted in serious nutritional deficiencies over the long term. See Garnsey, *Food and Society*, 34–61.

106. Scott, *Moral Economy*, 204.

107. Ibid.

were sometimes necessary as temporary measures in order to guarantee at least basic subsistence in the short term.

One means by which Jesus encouraged sacrificial sharing among the poor was to speak frequently about trusting in God's provision. Living at the edge of subsistence, a peasant by necessity took a defensive stance toward those around him (aside from close kin) and would have hesitated to make sacrifices that might put him and his family in further jeopardy. Thus, when Jesus attempted to persuade the poor to trust in God for their well-being he was providing a theological rationale for sacrificial behavior. The basic message was, share today and do not worry about tomorrow because God will provide.

This point is stated eloquently in two well-known sayings found in the Q material. In Luke 12:22–31 Jesus says this to his disciples:

> Therefore I tell you, do not worry about your life, what you will eat, or about your body, what you will wear. For life is more than food, and the body more than clothing. Consider the ravens: they neither sow nor reap, they have neither storehouses nor barn, and yet God feeds them. Of how much more value are you than the birds! And can any of you by worrying add a single hour to your span of life? If then you are not able to do so small a thing as that, why do you worry about the rest? Consider the lilies, how they grow: they neither toil nor spin; yet I tell you, even Solomon in all his glory was not clothed like one of these. But if God so clothes the grass of the field which is alive today and tomorrow is thrown into the oven, how much more will he clothe you—you of little faith! And do not keep striving for what you are to eat and what you are to drink, and do not keep worrying. For it is the nations of the world that strive after these things, and your Father knows that you need them. Instead, strive for his kingdom, and these things will be given to you as well.[108]

---

108. Διὰ τοῦτο λέγω ὑμῖν· μὴ μεριμνᾶτε τῇ ψυχῇ τί φάγητε, μηδὲ τῷ σώματι τί ἐνδύσησθε. ἡ γὰρ ψυχὴ πλεῖόν ἐστιν τῆς τροφῆς καὶ τὸ σῶμα τοῦ ἐνδύματος. κατανοήσατε τοὺς κόρακας ὅτι οὐ σπείρουσιν οὐδὲ θερίζουσιν, οἷς οὐκ ἔστιν ταμεῖον οὐδὲ ἀποθήκη, καὶ ὁ θεὸς τρέφει αὐτούς· πόσῳ μᾶλλον ὑμεῖς διαφέρετε τῶν πετεινῶν. τίς δὲ ἐξ ὑμῶν μεριμνῶν δύναται ἐπὶ τὴν ἡλικίαν αὐτοῦ προσθεῖναι πῆχυν; εἰ οὖν οὐδὲ ἐλάχιστον δύνασθε, τί περὶ τῶν λοιπῶν μεριμνᾶτε; κατανοήσατε τὰ κρίνα πῶς αὐξάνει· οὐ κοπιᾷ οὐδὲ νήθει· λέγω δὲ ὑμῖν, οὐδὲ Σολομὼν ἐν πάσῃ τῇ δόξῃ αὐτοῦ περιεβάλετο ὡς ἓν τούτων. εἰ δὲ ἐν ἀγρῷ τὸν χόρτον ὄντα σήμερον καὶ αὔριον εἰς κλίβανον βαλλόμενον ὁ θεὸς οὕτως ἀμφιέζει, πόσῳ μᾶλλον ὑμᾶς, ὀλιγόπιστοι. καὶ ὑμεῖς μὴ ζητεῖτε τί τὰ ἔθνη τοῦ κόσμου ἐπιζητοῦσιν, ὑμῶν δὲ ὁ πατὴρ οἶδεν ὅτι χρῄζετε τούτων. πλὴν ζητεῖτε τὴν βασιλείαν αὐτοῦ, καὶ ταῦτα προστεθήσεται ὑμῖν.

Similarly Matt 7:7–11 says:

> Ask, and it will be given to you; search, and you will find; knock, and the door will be opened for you. For everyone who asks receives, and everyone who searches finds, and for everyone who knocks, the door will be opened. Is there anyone among you who, if your child asks for bread, will give a stone? Of if the child asks for a fish, will give a snake? If you then, who are evil, know how to give good gifts to your children, how much more will your Father in heaven give good things to those who ask him![109]

In the first saying Jesus encourages the poor to trust God as Creator who through the natural order sustains all the world's creatures, however insignificant they might seem.[110] The natural environment, as God created it, is fully capable of providing a good life for all people, even though this is hindered by the fact that the "nations of the world strive after these things" (Luke 12:30). Nevertheless, according to Jesus, the poor could be confident that through the created order, God would provide. Additionally, in both passages, God is depicted as a father, who lovingly provides for his children. It is noteworthy that Jesus seems intentionally to have de-emphasized the image of the dominating ancient father, replacing it with an image of fatherly care and provision.[111]

Jesus also conveyed the notion of God as provider when he announced the imminence of the kingdom because he believed its arrival would be of particular benefit to the poor.[112] For example, Luke's version of the Beatitudes state: "Blessed are you who are poor, for yours is the kingdom of God. Blessed are you who are hungry now, for you will be

---

109. Αἰτεῖτε καὶ δοθήσεται ὑμῖν, ζητεῖτε καὶ εὑρήσετε, κρούετε καὶ ἀνοιγήσεται ὑμῖν· πᾶς γὰρ ὁ αἰτῶν λαμβάνει καὶ ὁ ζητῶν εὑρίσκει καὶ τῷ κρούοντι ἀνοιγήσεται. ἢ τίς ἐστιν ἐξ ὑμῶν ἄνθρωπος, ὃν αἰτήσει ὁ υἱὸς αὐτοῦ ἄρτον, μὴ λίθον ἐπιδώσει αὐτῷ; ἢ καὶ ἰχθὺν αἰτήσει, μὴ ὄφιν ἐπιδώσει αὐτῷ; εἰ οὖν ὑμεῖς πονηροὶ ὄντες οἴδατε δόματα ἀγαθὰ διδόναι τοῖς τέκνοις ὑμῶν, πόσῳ μᾶλλον ὁ πατὴρ ὑμῶν ὁ ἐν τοῖς οὐρανοῖς δώσει ἀγαθὰ τοῖς αἰτοῦσιν αὐτόν. (The editors of the *Critical Edition of Q*, 214–220, follow Matthew's version, based partly on the fact that Luke has "Holy Spirit" for Matthew's "good things" in the concluding verse).

110. Freyne, *Jesus, A Jewish Galilean*, 45–48.

111. Moxnes, *Putting Jesus in His Place*, 115–24.

112. That Jesus proclaimed the kingdom of God is nearly a consensus among scholars. James D. G. Dunn states, "the centrality of the kingdom of God (*basileia tou theou*) in Jesus' preaching is one of the least disputable, or disputed, facts about Jesus" (*Jesus Remembered*, 383).

filled. Blessed are you who weep now for you will laugh."[113] When Jesus proclaimed that the kingdom of God was at hand, part of what he meant was that the poor no longer had to rely upon their social superiors but rather could look directly to God, the good king, to supply their needs.

The image of God as provider is also found in Mark's Gospel, with the narrative of Jesus feeding the multitude as the paradigmatic expression of this theme. This story is especially well attested in the gospel sources. Not only does Mark include two feeding episodes (6:30–44 and 8:1–10), the Gospel of John, believed by most scholars to be independent of the Synoptics, also contains a version (6:1–15).[114] It is likely that Mark intended this story to recall YHWH's provision for the people of Israel by evoking the memory of both Elisha's feeding of the crowd (2 Kgs 4:42–44) as well as YHWH's care during Israel's desert wanderings following the exodus from Egypt.[115] Horsley observes that even though the miraculous nature of this story lies beyond the historian's capacity to comment, these narratives are "nevertheless to be understood as portrayals of how God was finally feeding the people with miraculous abundance despite appearances of paucity."[116] By feeding the crowds with only five loaves and two fish, Jesus enacts God's miraculous ability to provide for the subsistence needs of his people in spite of the meager resources with which to accomplish this task.

The agrarian parables in Mark 4 likewise allude to God's providential care for humanity.[117] In the parable of the sower, the seed produces an abundant harvest in spite of the many natural factors that thwart productivity.[118] In the second parable, the farmer plants the seed, and it grows on its own without the farmer even being aware of it. In the parable of the mustard seed, the smallest seed grows into a mighty shrub, which provides shelter for the birds of the air. This is probably an allusion to the tree planted by YHWH on Zion (Ezek 17:23; 31:6), also an image of the kingdom of God and its protection of the weak.[119] In each of these

---

113. Μακάριοι οἱ πτωχοί, ὅτι ὑμετέρα ἐστὶν βασιλεία τοῦ θεοῦ. μακάριοι οἱ πεινῶντες νῦν, ὅτι χορτασθήσεσθε. μακάριοι οἱ κλαίοντες νῦν, ὅτι γελάσετε (Luke 6:20–21).

114. For discussion, see Bammel, "Feeding of the Multitude," 211–40.

115. Horsley, *Hearing the Whole Story*, 89.

116. Horsley, *Spiral of Violence*, 179.

117. Oakman, *Jesus an the Economic Questions*, 95–139.

118. Ibid., 103–9.

119. Scott, *Hear then the Parable*, 373–87, refers to the "burlesque" quality of the parable in that Jesus makes the great cedar of Ezekiel into an unclean shrub. It suggests

parables, the growth is surprising or miraculous and can be attributed to God's benevolent care for creation. This points to another, related theme, which emerges particularly in the parable of the mustard seed—that the kingdom of God begins inconspicuously and humbly but miraculously grows into something quite significant.[120] Thus, another possible layer of meaning presents itself: not only does God provide for the humble and weak; they are the ones who, in fact, constitute his kingdom. This is in direct contrast with the kingdoms of the world, which are characterized by power and magnificence. Yet, while appearing insignificant, the kingdom of God possesses great power of a different sort, power that is related to the benevolent features of kingly rule. In light of Jesus' attempt to create an alternative subsistence strategy, one point of these parables may be that while God is the one who miraculously provides, it is incumbent upon those who make up his kingdom, namely the poor, to live out the values of God's rule among themselves. Jesus encouraged the poor in rural Galilee to trust God for their basic needs so that in spite of their own lack of resources they would have the confidence to act more generously toward their neighbors. Jesus's conception of the kingdom of God was that it required the active participation of the people. In short, God's ability to provide demanded the people's willingness to share.

Jesus hoped to stimulate generosity and "lower class communitarianism" among the poor by encouraging trust in God, but another strategy he employed for this purpose was to redefine the family.[121] In light of the changes facing first-century Galilee, Jesus believed that family could no longer be narrowly defined by blood kinship but should extend to all those who join together in a covenant relationship with God. This is the clear intent of the well-known passage in Mark 3:31–35:

> Then his mother and his brothers came; and standing outside, they sent to him and called him. A crowd was sitting around him; and they said to him, "Your mother and your brothers and sisters are outside, asking for you." And he replied, "Who are my mother and my brothers?" And looking at those who sat around

---

Jesus' proclamation of a "kingdom of insignificance" in which "God's mighty works are among the unclean and insignificant" (387).

120. Wright, *Jesus and the Victory of God*, 241.

121. This issue has been developed by a number of scholars. See, among others, Lohfink, *Jesus and Community*, 39–50; Horsley, *Spiral of Violence*, 231–45; Hellerman, *Ancient Church as Family*, 59–91; Moxnes, *Putting Jesus in His Place*, 46–71.

him, he said, "Here are my mother and my brothers! Whoever does the will of God is my brother and sister and mother."[122]

Similarly in Mark 10:28–30, Jesus has just stated how difficult it is for the rich to enter the kingdom. Then, Peter asserts that those following Jesus "have left everything" (ἀφήκαμεν πάντα). In response, Jesus says, "there is no one who has left houses or brothers or sisters or mother or father or children or fields, for my sake and for the sake of the goods news, who will not receive a hundredfold now in this age—houses, brothers and sisters, mothers and children and fields."[123] Though some of his followers had to leave behind the security and sense of place that blood kinship provided, the Jesus movement compensated for this with the promise of new familial relations and the abundant material benefits that would come as a result.[124] In the words of Gerhard Lohfink, Jesus did not call his disciples "into solitude and isolation . . . He called them into a new family."[125]

Sayings in Q also indicate that followers of Jesus sometimes experienced separation from their natural families. The urgency of the Jesus movement was such that its claims upon participants superseded those of their natural families:

> As they were going along the road, someone said to him, "I will follow wherever you go." And Jesus said to him, "Foxes have holes, and birds of the air have nests; but the Son of Man has nowhere to lay his head." To another he said, "Follow me." But he said, "Lord, first let me go and bury my father." But Jesus said to him, "Let the dead bury their own dead; but as for you, go and proclaim the kingdom of God." Another said, "I will follow you, Lord; but let me say farewell to those at my home." Jesus said to

---

122. Καὶ ἔρχεται ἡ μήτηρ αὐτοῦ καὶ οἱ ἀδελφοὶ αὐτοῦ καὶ ἔξω στήκοντες ἀπέστειλαν πρὸς αὐτὸν καλοῦντες αὐτόν. καὶ ἐκάθητο περὶ αὐτὸν ὄχλος, καὶ λέγουσιν αὐτῷ, Ἰδοὺ ἡ μήτηρ σου καὶ οἱ ἀδελφοί σου ἔξω ζητοῦσίν σε. καὶ ἀποκριθεὶς αὐτοῖς λέγει, Τίς ἐστιν ἡ μήτηρ μου καὶ οἱ ἀδελφοί [μου]; καὶ περιβλεψάμενος τοὺς περὶ αὐτὸν κύκλῳ καθημένους λέγει, "Ἴδε ἡ μήτηρ μου καὶ οἱ ἀδελφοί μου. ὃς ἂν ποιήσῃ τὸ θέλημα τοῦ θεοῦ, οὗτος ἀδελφός μου καὶ ἀδελφὴ καὶ μήτηρ ἐστίν.

123. οὐδείς ἐστιν ὃς ἀφῆκεν οἰκίαν ἢ ἀδελφοὺς ἢ ἀδελφὰς ἢ μητέρα ἢ τέκνα ἢ ἀγροὺς ἕνεκεν ἐμοῦ καὶ ἕνεκεν τοῦ εὐαγγελίου, ἐὰν μὴ λάβῃ ἑκατονταπλασίονα νῦν ἐν τῷ καιρῷ τούτῳ οἰκίας καὶ ἀδελφοὺς καὶ ἀδελφὰς καὶ μητέρας καὶ τέκνα καὶ ἀγροὺς (Mark 10:29–30).

124. Moxnes, *Putting Jesus in His Place*, 46–71.

125. Lohfink, *Jesus and Community*, 42.

him, "No one who puts a hand to the plow and looks back is fit for the kingdom of God."¹²⁶

Other sayings in Q discuss the separation from unsupportive families that some of Jesus's followers had to face. For instance, Jesus says that he came not to bring "peace" (εἰρήνην) but "division" (ἢ διαμερισμόν), which would manifest itself particularly with conflict in the household, between father and son, mother and daughter, and between mother-in-law and daughter-in-law (Luke 12:49-53). Similarly, Jesus says in Luke 14:26: "Whoever comes to me and does not hate father and mother, wife and children, brothers and sisters, yes, and even life itself, cannot be my disciple."¹²⁷

On the basis of these sayings, a number of scholars have argued that the Jesus movement consisted of a group of rootless wanderers who had renounced possessions, household, and family, and that, in fact, renunciation was a precondition for joining the movement.¹²⁸ Halvor Moxnes writes:

> The sayings of Jesus were primarily addressed to young men, calling them to leave their position in the household. Most of these young men do not seem to have been in a marginal position in society (e.g., poor or "sinners," sick, etc.), but well integrated into their place in the house and village structure. Therefore, by leaving to follow Jesus they experienced the effects of separation: they became displaced; they were stripped of that which defined their position and status. They entered into a liminal stage, outside the known and accepted structure of their household and village society.¹²⁹

126. Καὶ πορευομένων αὐτῶν ἐν τῇ ὁδῷ εἶπέν τις πρὸς αὐτόν, Ἀκολουθήσω σοι ὅπου ἐὰν ἀπέρχῃ. καὶ εἶπεν αὐτῷ ὁ Ἰησοῦς, Αἱ ἀλώπεκες φωλεοὺς ἔχουσιν καὶ τὰ πετεινὰ τοῦ οὐρανοῦ κατασκηνώσεις, ὁ δὲ υἱὸς ἀνθρώπου οὐκ ἔχει ποῦ τὴν κεφαλὴν κλίνῃ. Εἶπεν δὲ πρὸς ἕτερον, Ἀκολούθει μοι. ὁ δὲ εἶπεν, [Κύριε,] ἐπίτρεψόν μοι ἀπελθόντι πρῶτον θάψαι τὸν πατέρα μου. εἶπεν δὲ αὐτῷ, Ἄφες τοὺς νεκροὺς θάψαι τοὺς ἑαυτῶν νεκρούς, σὺ δὲ ἀπελθὼν διάγγελλε τὴν βασιλείαν τοῦ θεοῦ. Εἶπεν δὲ καὶ ἕτερος, Ἀκολουθήσω σοι, κύριε: πρῶτον δὲ ἐπίτρεψόν μοι ἀποτάξασθαι τοῖς εἰς τὸν οἶκόν μου. εἶπεν δὲ [πρὸς αὐτὸν] ὁ Ἰησοῦς, Οὐδεὶς ἐπιβαλὼν τὴν χεῖρα ἐπ' ἄροτρον καὶ βλέπων εἰς τὰ ὀπίσω εὔθετός ἐστιν τῇ βασιλείᾳ τοῦ θεοῦ (Luke 9:57-62).

127. Εἴ τις ἔρχεται πρός με καὶ οὐ μισεῖ τὸν πατέρα ἑαυτοῦ καὶ τὴν μητέρα καὶ τὴν γυναῖκα καὶ τὰ τέκνα καὶ τοὺς ἀδελφοὺς καὶ τὰς ἀδελφὰς ἔτι τε καὶ τὴν ψυχὴν ἑαυτοῦ, οὐ δύναται εἶναί μου μαθητής.

128. See Theissen, *Sociology of Early Palestinian Christianity*, 11-12.

129. Moxnes, *Putting Jesus in His Place*, 71. Moxnes understands Jesus's call to leave family against the background of the social fragmentation resulting from the

Others argue, however, that these sayings do not necessarily require a break with one's family but rather indicate only that separation may be necessary if the family is not supportive.[130] According to William Arnal, the severity of the Q sayings is for rhetorical effect, to emphasize that "following Jesus requires unconditional commitment, even at the cost of responsibilities otherwise deemed unquestionably inescapable."[131] This seems correct. In many cases commitment to the Jesus movement must have caused a breach with one's family, but such a complete separation was not a condition for becoming a follower. Thus, the significance of Jesus's teaching on the family lies in its constructive force. Leaving family was not valued for its own sake. Rather, as a new kind of kinship group, the Jesus movement served a positive social function for those who were without the benefits customarily received from one's natural family.

As I described above, the urbanization efforts of Antipas undermined the cohesion of kinship groups in rural Galilee. The inability of small farmers to repay their indebtedness frequently resulted in the loss of family land. Migration to the cities, either forced or by choice, separated families by some geographical distance. In first-century Galilee, therefore, it is very likely that for some, natural kinship no longer provided a reliable means of subsistence insurance. In response, Jesus proposed a form of fictive kinship, a new family constituted by those who do the will of God (Mark 3:35) and who belong to the covenant community. This redefinition of the family provided a new and greatly enlarged set of potential helpers for those whose natural families could no longer give them the assistance they needed. As the parable of the good Samaritan (Luke 10:25–37) illustrates, one's neighbor was no longer narrowly defined in conventional terms as a kinsman or fellow-villager but instead was defined in a broadened sense to include anyone in need.

In one sense this was an innovative strategy that may not have been well received by many Galilean peasants. This may help explain the lack

---

new economic order that Antipas established in Galilee. In this context, fathers were losing their authority over their households because of their inability to provide. As a result, many sons left home. Moxnes writes, "In a situation in which the values and social viability of the traditional household were threatened by the new economy of Herod Antipas, Jesus must have appeared to join forces with those who put the household at risk" (*Putting Jesus in His Place*, 151).

130. For example, see Horsley, *Spiral of Violence*, 229; Arnal, *Village Scribes*, 174-77; Dunn, *Jesus Remembered*, 592-99.

131. Arnal, *Village Scribes*, 175.

of evidence for Christianity in Galilee prior to the fourth century CE.[132] Milton Moreland writes, "Any movement that promoted a transformation of the traditional kin-based, social, and economic structures of a peasant village would find it difficult to maintain a long-term involvement in that context."[133] Moreland holds a relatively optimistic view of economic conditions in Antipas's Galilee and argues on this basis that most peasants would have been unwilling to embrace Jesus's innovative strategies when Galilee was enjoying such a period of widespread peace and prosperity. While there is evidence for prosperity in first-century Galilee (as discussed above), I have argued in this chapter that Antipas's urbanization efforts had an indirectly adverse effect upon economic well-being by disrupting social subsistence strategies upon which the poor had customarily relied in times of food shortage. Nevertheless, Moreland's assessment that the Jesus movement was largely rejected by the peasantry may still be correct. Even in poor economic conditions peasant resistance to Jesus's subsistence program is still quite plausible due to a natural defensive stance in times of shortage. Jesus's attempt to establish new families may simply have appeared too radical for those Galilean peasants who were getting by, albeit just barely. Solidarity with those on the other side of that fine line was undoubtedly not consistent with the typical peasant's "safety-first" approach.

Innovation: Recruiting New Patrons

I have argued in this chapter that even though the residents of Galilee, overall, experienced an extended period of relative prosperity under Herod Antipas, poverty nevertheless persisted, and the poor found it even more difficult than before to survive when they faced food shortage resulting from personal misfortune or crop failure. The reason for this is that as Galilee experienced modest urbanization and economic growth, traditional rural patrons (wealthy non-elites who made their homes in Galilean villages) discovered new social and economic opportunities that drew them away from their villages and the customary obligation to provide for the poor. As we have seen, part of Jesus's program was to appeal to these traditional patrons to stay in the village and to fulfill their responsibilities there. Jesus also promoted innovative self-help strategies

132. Moreland, "Galilean Response to Earliest Christianity," 37–48.
133. Ibid., 44.

by encouraging the poor to support one another, at least at the level of minimal subsistence, during times of severe food shortage by reminding them that God provides. In this last section, I examine one more innovative strategy that Jesus employed as an alternative subsistence strategy, namely, the recruitment of new patrons from among a class of people whom the rest of the population normally viewed with suspicion and distrust.

It is clear from the gospel accounts that Jesus frequently engaged with members of the retainer class, a social stratum typically found in complex agrarian societies.[134] Members of this segment of society served as lower-level administrators, such as scribes, property managers, and tax collectors. Owing their social position, wealth, and power to the rulers they served, retainers typically had little room for independent decision-making or action. We see on a number of occasions, however, that Jesus reached out to these people, calling them to participate in the coming kingdom of God. I argue that part of Jesus's purpose in doing so was to recruit them as new patrons who would provide generously for the rural poor. These retainers, in other words, were an important component of Jesus's alternative subsistence strategy. In the paragraphs that follow, I examine the role of two categories of retainers, tax collectors and property managers, as new recruits for Jesus's economic program.

That Jesus associated with and had sympathy for "tax collectors and sinners" is a secure element in the historical Jesus tradition. Not only is the tradition multiply attested,[135] but it also fulfills the criterion of embarrassment. Jesus's practice is usually interpreted in a primarily religious sense, as an indication of his openness to those who did not meet the standards of Jewish piety and were therefore considered moral outcasts. Tax collectors were "hated as collaborators with Rome" and were "widely regarded as dishonest and rapacious."[136] On the basis of later rabbinic evidence, scholars typically understand "sinners" to have been the *'am-ha'aretz*, the "people of the land," who were unable to observe the law with the rigor required by the Pharisees, along with those who, such as

---

134. Lenski, *Power and Privilege*, 243–48; Horsley and Tiller, "Sociology of the Second Temple"; and Wright, "Discourse of Riches and Poverty," 559–78.

135. Triple Tradition: Mark 2:13–17 // Luke 5:27–32 // Matt 9:9–13; Double Tradition: Luke 7:33–34 // Matt 11:18–19; M: Matt 21:31–2; L: Luke 15:1–2, 18:9–14, and 19:1–10.

136. Wright, *Jesus and the Victory of God*, 266.

prostitutes, "deliberately flouted the Torah."[137] Thus, Jesus substituted a politics of "mercy," with its corresponding strategy of inclusion, for the Pharisaic politics of "holiness" and separation.[138]

Jesus's practice of eating with tax collectors and sinners, however, most likely included a socioeconomic dimension in addition to this "religious" element. William R. Herzog writes:

> Not only were they [tax collectors and sinners] a limiting case of God's forgiveness, but they were functionaries in an oppressive system, whether low-level functionaries (toll collectors) or wealthier exploiters (chief toll collectors). If they could experience God's forgiveness with its demand for the justice of the reign of God, then they could become allies, not enemies, of the peasant villagers, artisans, and merchants, agents of redistribution rather than agents of exploitation. This means that Jesus' table companionship with toll collectors and sinners was an integral part of Jesus' economic concern for the people of the land and expressed his interest in redirecting the redistributive economies that dominated Herod's client kingdom, the temple's collaborationist hegemony and Rome's imperial control.[139]

As Herzog suggests here, though tax collectors did not establish the rate of taxation, they did have plenty of discretion regarding how tax policy would be implemented: for example, whether they would be forgiving and flexible or demanding and violent when collecting tax payments. Similarly, Douglas E. Oakman identifies the "sinners" as tax debtors; thus when Jesus eats with "tax collectors and sinners," he does so "to broker tax relief."[140] The story of Zacchaeus, though unique to the Gospel of Luke and clearly tailored to Luke's literary intentions,[141] may nevertheless reflect, in an idealized manner, the sort of response Jesus aimed to achieve by engaging with tax collectors, hoping that they would use both their official position as well as their own personal wealth to assist the poor.[142]

The property manager (οἰκονόμος) who oversaw the dispersed landholdings of an "absentee landowner" was a familiar figure in the ancient world and also appears occasionally in Jesus's parables. In Luke 12:41–48,

137. Ibid. See also Borg, *Conflict, Holiness, and Politics*.
138. Borg, *Conflict, Holiness, and Politics*, esp. 123–43.
139. Herzog, *Jesus, Justice, and the Reign of God*, 224.
140. Oakman, *Political Aims*, 98. See also Oakman, *Jesus, Debt*, 92–118.
141. Discussed more fully in chapter 4 below.
142. Oakman, *Political Aims*, 98.

for example, Jesus contrasts the faithful manager, who carries out the will of the householder (κύριος) and is then rewarded with even greater responsibility in the oversight of all the master's possessions, with the harsh and exploitative manager who beats his fellow slaves and is, himself, then severely punished[143] when the householder returns.[144] In the parable of the talents, the householder entrusts his property to his δούλους rather than to an οἰκονόμος, but the scenario is the same: an absentee landowner entrusts his property to the management of his slaves who are then answerable, upon his return, for the stewardship of his property.[145] In the context of the early church the image of the οἰκόνομος provided a fitting metaphor for leaders who oversaw the Christian community during the interim between Christ's ascension and his anticipated future return at which time they would be held accountable for the fruit of their leadership. In the context of the historical Jesus, however, references to the household manager may have had a more literal sense, suggesting the possibility that Jesus also sought to recruit these retainers to participate in his economic program.

In what way could the οἰκόνομος have been useful to Jesus's program of alternative peasant subsistence in Galilee? Like the tax collector, the property manager did not own and therefore did not have full control over the landholdings of his master; however, he was in a position to determine how he would implement the owner's policies, perhaps for example, deciding how much force he would use in collecting the rents and debts from his master's dependents. The parable of the dishonest steward (Luke 16:1–8) may be instructive here.[146] From the second century on, this parable has caused problems for interpreters.[147] According to the story, an absentee landowner hears that the agent in charge of his property has been "squandering" (v. 1) his resources. The verb here is διασκορπίζω, which has the basic meaning of "scatter," or "disperse," ei-

---

143. διχοτομήσει αὐτὸν καὶ τὸ μέρος αὐτοῦ μετὰ τῶν ἀπίστων θήσει ("He will cut him in pieces and put him with the unfaithful," Luke 12:46).

144. In Matthew's version of the parable, the manager is referred to as a δοῦλος; the οἰκόνομος in the Greco-Roman world was often of servile status.

145. Luke 19:11–27 // Matt 25:14–30.

146. This parable is unique to Luke, but the difficulty surrounding its meaning, evidenced already in Luke's (or his source's) attempt to find an appropriate application, suggests authenticity.

147. See Bailey, *Poet and Peasant*, 86–110, for a survey of interpretive views and commentary from a cross-cultural perspective.

ther of seed in planting or of a flock of sheep in the face of danger.[148] The idea of "squander" is rare among ancient authors. Its use for this concept in later Christian sources may be dependent upon Luke's use of the word here in 16:1 and in 15:3 with reference to the behavior of the prodigal son who "squanders" his inheritance. "Squander," however, may not do justice to the larger significance of Luke's depiction of "prodigal" behavior throughout Luke-Acts. This will be developed in more detail in chapter 4. Suffice it to say at this point that one plausible interpretation of the misdeeds of the manager is not that he was stealing for himself or that he was simply a poor manager who let the master's resources slip through his fingers; rather, he was intentionally "dispersing" these revenues to others, perhaps to the poor. Consequently, the master dismisses the manager and demands the accounting records (v. 2). At this point the manager panics: he is too weak to dig and too proud to beg (v. 3), so he begins to formulate a plan that he hopes will bring him honor in the eyes of the community, thereby guaranteeing his well-being following his dismissal (v. 4). One by one he calls his master's debtors, presumably renters on the owner's properties who are in a fixed-rent agreement which is to be paid in kind.[149] The steward tells each one to change his written contract to reflect a reduced rental agreement (vv. 5–7).

The main difficulty for interpreters of this parable centers on the question of how Jesus could have presented the dishonest manager as a positive exemplar to his followers. Attempts have been made to allegorize the story whereby the manager, like the prodigal son, is the prototypical sinner who is treated graciously by a forgiving God.[150] I would propose, however, that this parable be interpreted in a more literal sense, and that the intended audience was a clearly defined subgroup among Jesus's followers or potential followers. It is very possible that Jesus told this story in order to recommend this very behavior to members of the "retainer" class who were open and amenable to his program. These agents of the ruling class were in a powerful position. They could manipulate taxes, rents, and legal judgments in favor of the peasantry burdened by the demands of their overlords. Moreover, rather than seeing this as "dishonest," Jesus judged the steward's behavior as just in light of his proclamation of the kingdom of God and the concept of righteousness implied by that reality.

---

148. BDAG, 236.
149. Bailey, *Poet and Peasant*, 91–94.
150. See Bailey for discussion, ibid., 105–10.

Additionally, Scott's point that fixed rents, more frequent under colonial rule and absentee landlordism, are more oppressive than those that allow for flexibility depending on the yield may also be a factor here.[151] Thus, the landowner in this story is typical of the new style absentee landlords in the increasingly urbanized Galilee under Herod Antipas.[152] To deceive this sort of landlord, from the perspective of the "moral economy of the peasant," would not be dishonest or unjust but would rather constitute one component of a larger subsistence strategy, which was presently under stress as a result of changing social and economic circumstances in first-century Galilee.

One question remains, however: why would the master have been pleased in the end by his manager's deeds? In my view, Bailey offers the most satisfying explanation. The master has two alternatives for dealing with the deeds of his manager: "He can go back to the debtors and explain that it was all a mistake, that the steward had been dismissed, and thus his actions were null and void. But if the master does this now, the villagers' joy will turn to anger, and he will be cursed for his stinginess. Second, he can keep silent, accept the praise that is even now being showered on him, and allow the clever steward to ride high on the wave of popular enthusiasm."[153] In Jesus's parable the owner is influenced by public opinion. Perhaps, this was merely wishful thinking in reality, but from Jesus's perspective it was worth a try. The deceitful actions of retainers could potentially force the landowning elites into positions they might not otherwise adopt. Such deeds might compel them to be generous, whether their hearts were in it or not. But this was ultimately beside the point. Jesus's aim was to ease the burden on peasant farmers, and presenting the dishonest manager as praiseworthy was part of the alternative subsistence strategy he was attempting to promote.

Conclusion

Jesus proclaimed the kingdom of God at a time when Galilee was experiencing modest urbanization and economic growth under Herod Antipas. Though living conditions generally seem to have improved during this period, poverty remained a persistent concern in Galilee's fundamentally

---

151. Scott, *Moral Economy*, 67.
152. Schwartz, "Josephus in Galilee," 302–4.
153. Bailey, *Poet and Peasant*, 102.

agarian economy. Though farming families could meet their subsistence needs and perhaps even save a little in most years, the many variables affecting farm production, not to mention the ever-present possibility of individual personal misfortune, meant that those who generally lived just above subsistence, could easily fall below that level at any time. This was really nothing new. Peasant farmers had always needed a repetoire of subsistence strategies, including both production and relational strategies, to guard against these inevitable times of shortfall. What I have argued in this chapter is that the government of Herod Antipas did not directly make matters worse; in fact, overall conditions improved. The impact of Antipas's policies was instead indirect. Urbanization and growing prosperity, as modest as they may have been, disrupted relational subsistence strategies in which the poor had traditionally turned to their wealthy village neighbors for assistance when they experienced times of shortfall and need. Jesus, I argue, addressed this situation, first by appealing to village patrons to continue to play the role of caretaker of the poor. Jesus encouraged these individuals not to be enticed by new opportunities for social advancement in the cities and larger villages but to stay in their home villages and to continue enjoying the honor of their neighbors by being reliable sources of help in times of need. When these efforts failed, Jesus tried other approaches. He encouraged the poor to look after each other, to be willing even in the short term to share sacrificially in order to meet the basic food needs of all villagers. He promoted this sort of behavior with the message that God is faithful to provide for created beings, and therefore worry is unnecessary. But perhaps the most innovative, and controversial, strategy was to recruit new patrons from the so-called retainer class, most notably household managers and tax collectors, to take the places of the former patrons and caretakers of the poor. Individuals who functioned in this capacity in Galilean society, while not necessarily possessors of great wealth themselves, had positions and responsibilities over substantial financial resources that they could potentially manipulate in order to help the poor. Jesus encouraged these individuals, at times, to act in ways that might seem "dishonest," but in light of the "moral economy of the peasant" were actually righteous and pleasing to God.

An important part of the ministry of Jesus, then, was to support traditional subsistence strategies, as well as to encourage new and innovative ones, in a time of political, social, and economic change. In the next chapter, we turn to the writings of Paul of Tarsus to see the extent to which he shared the economic concerns of Jesus, and whether or not he tried to shape an "alternative subsistence strategy" for his urban house churches.

CHAPTER 3

Care for the Poor in the Letters of Paul

AT THE CONCLUSION OF his farewell address to the Ephesian elders in the book of Acts, Paul of Tarsus is remembered as saying, "We must support the weak, remembering the words of the Lord Jesus, for he himself said, 'It is more blessed to give than to receive'" (Acts 20:35).[1] The historicity of Paul's speech on that occasion as well as the authenticity of this otherwise unattested saying of Jesus may be open to question. Nevertheless, this passage in Acts establishes an important point: it was vital for at least some in the early church to acknowledge continuity between Jesus of Nazareth and Paul of Tarsus, not simply in the fact that Jesus's crucifixion and resurrection were the key themes of Paul's proclamation, but also to show that the teachings of Jesus influenced and shaped the conduct of Paul's own ministry.

Some modern interpreters reject this conclusion, however. Instead of continuity between Jesus and Paul, they claim that there were fundamental differences between the two figures. Jesus announced the coming kingdom of God, but Paul preached Christ's cross and resurrection. Paul made Jesus into a divine being, something that was completely foreign to the self-concept of the Jewish Jesus. In short, Paul invented "Christianity," by fundamentally changing the Galilean Jesus movement into a very different new religion as he proclaimed his gospel and established small Christ-groups in a number of key cities of the Roman Empire. Supporting this conclusion is the fact that while Paul repeatedly reflects on the significance of Jesus's death and resurrection, only rarely does he appeal to Jesus's teaching, and never does he mentions episodes from Jesus's ministry such as those later recorded in the Gospels.

1. δεῖ ἀντιλαμβάνεσθαι τῶν ἀσθενούντων, μνημονεύειν τε τῶν λόγων τοῦ κυρίου Ἰησοῦ ὅτι αὐτὸς εἶπεν, Μακάριόν ἐστιν μᾶλλον διδόναι ἢ λαμβάνειν.

Yet, Luke's depiction of Paul referring to the words of Jesus—"It is more blessed to give than to receive"—points to a different interpretation that will be borne out in the course of this chapter, namely, that there was indeed continuity between Jesus and Paul regarding behavioral norms for their followers, notably with regard to caring for the poor. In the previous chapter, I examined parts of the Jesus tradition that indicate that creating communities for alternative subsistence insurance in rural Galilee was an important component of the ministry of the historical Jesus. Here I argue that an analysis of the other earliest block of Christian writings, the letters of Paul, reveals a similar concern. Like Jesus, Paul also gathered into new communities people who were adversely affected economically by Roman rule. In fact, this effort to create communities whose purpose was, in part at least, to alleviate the struggles of the poor is a key, but often overlooked, point of continuity between the rural Galilean Jesus movement and Paul's urban Christian assemblies and suggests that addressing human need was a defining feature of the Christian movement in the foundational period.

Like Jesus, Paul founded small communities of faith steeped in the covenantal morality of Israelite religion, a key principle of which is the importance of caring for the poor. Paul's covenantal communities were open to Jews and Gentiles alike because of the Christ-event, which in his view was the decisive intervention of God in human history and, as such, the fulfillment of Jewish apocalyptic expectations. The majority of participants in the Pauline groups lived at the level of basic human subsistence and as a result were particularly vulnerable to food shortage. Though it is doubtful that the Pauline assemblies counted any members from among the social elite, there were some who were relatively well-off and comfortably secure from personal subsistence concerns. As we will see, Paul appealed particularly to these individuals to provide for their poor Christian brothers and sisters. As Jesus focused on the role of the village patron in his effort to bolster the traditional subsistence strategies of Galilean villages, so also did Paul focus on relatively wealthy non-elites to play a similar role in his urban gatherings of Christ followers. Though Paul's letters give no explicit indication of anti-imperial sentiments, he did articulate an ideological alternative to the Roman Empire by which he hoped to encourage the relatively wealthy in his churches to take a leading role in caring for the poor.

I begin this chapter by addressing the general effect of Roman rule upon the economic well-being of the population of cities within the empire; this is followed by a discussion of the composition of the Pauline churches. I then turn to the issue of whether or not care for the poor was even a serious concern for Paul and his churches, relying especially on the work of Bruce Longenecker. Following these preliminary discussions, I then examine the Pauline material itself and describe both the model of care for the poor that Paul advocated as well as the ideas that he used to support these practices in his house churches.

The Economic Effect of Roman Imperial Rule on the Population of Greco-Roman Cities

The Romans relied upon cities for ruling their Mediterranean empire, in a manner that has been described as "government without bureaucracy."[2] Instead of large bureaucratic governments in the provinces, the Romans generally relied upon local city councils to work in conjunction with the Roman governor and his limited staff for the protection of Roman interests as well as for the administration of local and regional matters affecting the daily lives of their urban residents. The cities of the empire were classified under a variety of statuses indicating their legal and economic relationship with the city of Rome, ranging from the Roman colony (*colonia*), which was populated typically by military veterans and established as an outpost of Roman authority, law, and culture, to the "free and immune cities" (*civitates liberae et immunes*), which enjoyed not only legal autonomy but also exemption from taxation.[3] This system illustrates Rome's political flexibility and the desire to find an appropriate balance between freedom and control as a means of preserving larger interests throughout the empire: primarily peace and consistent revenue. In the eastern provinces, Rome was able to co-opt well-established cities, so that only light touches of "Romanization" are evidenced in the archaeological record from the first century.[4] By contrast in the west, material remains show a significant number of urban foundations in the first century that were clearly modeled after the Roman style.[5] Under the empire, Walter Scheidel estimates that between one-eighth and one-ninth of the imperial

---

2. Garnsey and Saller, *Roman Empire*, 35–54.
3. Ibid., 41–42.
4. MacMullen, *Romanization in the Time of Augustus*, 1–29.
5. Ibid., 30–123.

population resided in cities,[6] a total of seven to nine million people living in urban areas ranging in size from Rome's one million residents to small settlements no larger than the size of some villages. Most urban dwellers, though not all, were employed in nonagrarian occupations.[7]

While Roman urbanization efforts undoubtedly resulted in political, social, and economic upheaval, particularly during the phase of initial conquest and urban re-organization under the late Republic, by the time of the Principate, the economic benefits of Roman rule most likely outweighed the disadvantages in most cities. According to Neville Morley, "The rule of the emperors brought the benefits of peace, the unification of the Mediterranean and the development of the legal framework relating to commercial transactions, as well as new incentives to invest in shipping to transport goods on behalf of the state. In reducing some of the risks and subsidizing some of the costs associated with inter-regional distribution, the state had only its own interests in view, but its actions nevertheless created conditions conducive to the further development of market trade."[8] Urbanization and increasing rural prosperity created growing demand for goods and services, which led to the development of new urban (and in some cases, rural) industries, particularly the manufacture of ceramics and textiles.[9] The economic growth and new opportunities to be found in the city undoubtedly attracted many who aimed to improve their economic and perhaps even social position. The wealthy businessman, the skilled artisan, and even the impoverished, low-skilled day-laborer each hoped to take advantage of the economic possibilities the city had to offer.

In spite of these advantages, many of those who left the village, particularly low-skilled laborers, might nonetheless have found themselves even more vulnerable in the city when faced with periods of generalized food shortage or individualized impoverishment caused by some personal misfortune. Cities had no institutionalized systems for poor relief, but instead depended upon the generosity of benefactors.[10] Fortunate individuals could perhaps also turn to personal patrons in times of need.[11] Yet this type of poor relief was not for everyone. Those without

6. Scheidel, "Demography," 79.
7. Ibid., 80.
8. Morley, "Distribution," 589.
9. Kehoe, "Production," 559–566. See also Scheidel, "Demography," 85.
10. Garnsey, *Famine and Food Supply*, 82–84.
11. Ibid., 84–85.

civic status or patrons found themselves particularly vulnerable in times of want. As Morley states,

> Urban poverty is in general likely to be more severe than rural poverty; the city poor had no direct access to the means of subsistence, no source of food other than the market, theft, or charity. The burden fell particularly heavily on recent arrivals: the decision to migrate separated them from traditional social structures like kinship and patronage, whereas longer-established residents might have succeeded in building alternative social networks. It is conceivable, though unprovable, that the shame of poverty might be aggravated by being cut off from the traditions of rural life, idealized within Roman culture; it would take time for the migrant to become acclimatized to alternative sets of values, advertised on tombstones, that celebrated industriousness and skill.[12]

While some urban residents undoubtedly found improved economic security by moving to the city, countless others slipped into poverty. My contention in this chapter is that the Pauline Christian assemblies were structured to provide an alternative social subsistence strategy for those who were otherwise without a social support network in the city.

Care for the Poor in the Pauline Mission

Objections might be raised at this point. Can we even be sure that Paul considered care for the poor to be an important component of his missionary efforts? Paul's view that the parousia was imminent and that the status of being "in Christ" would save believers from the wrath of God on that day may suggest that he was not especially concerned with establishing long-term communal arrangements. If anything, the behavioral norms he advanced reflect only a temporary, interim ethic for an age that he believed was quickly being brought to completion. According to this logic, Paul saw no need to establish lasting communities that would provide ongoing alternative subsistence insurance for their poor members. Moreover, the fact that economic matters and instructions about caring for the poor appear relatively infrequently in Paul's writings might also confirm that economic concerns were not a major point of emphasis for him.

---

12. Morley, "Poor in the City of Rome," 38.

Regarding the first objection it should be pointed out that Paul devotes extensive space in every letter to ethical issues, and it is impossible to separate Paul's theological discourse from his moral instruction. Paul's practice was to engage in moral reasoning by drawing out the ethical implications of his gospel. Even in the Letter to the Romans, the most systematically theological of his writings, the ethical discussion of chapters 12–15 forms a crucial component of the letter and may even be his ultimate goal for the composition. It is also problematic in my view to assume that because Paul viewed the parousia as imminent, his exhortations for moral behavior were therefore merely provisional. Why should we not believe that the behavioral norms that govern those in Christ prior to the parousia would also govern the new creation after the parousia when Christ's lordship is fully consummated? Finally, we must admit that it is impossible to know with certainty the time frame that Paul actually had in mind regarding the coming of the end, if indeed he had any at all. While indications seem to suggest that he believed it would happen soon, his ultimate uncertainty about the timing of this event raises doubts that he would have considered his ethical instructions as merely temporary.

Regarding the second objection Bruce W. Longenecker has in my view persuasively argued that Gal 2:10 indicates that care for the poor was indeed at the very heart of Paul's preaching and missionary agenda.[13] At the conclusion of a paragraph in which Paul reviews the chronology of his visits to Jerusalem and his meetings with the leaders of the church (specifically James, Cephas, and John, whom he refers to as "pillars" (στῦλοι) in v. 9), Paul states in v. 10, "They asked only one thing, that we remember the poor, which was actually what I was eager to do."[14] The pillars' request that Paul "remember the poor" is usually understood as being geographically and ethnically restricted to the Jerusalem Jewish Christians, with "the poor" referring either to an impoverished subgroup within the church or perhaps to the entire church, which was collectively known as "the poor." This meeting with the "pillars," therefore, marks the beginning of Paul's collection project.[15] Longenecker argues, however, that there is no reason to believe that this request was geographically or ethnically limited. It was not until the fourth century CE that Christian interpreters understood this verse to have such restrictions; prior to that,

---

13. Longenecker, *Remember the Poor*, especially 135–219.
14. μόνον τῶν πτωχῶν ἵνα μνημονεύωμεν, ὃ καὶ ἐσπούδασα αὐτὸ τοῦτο ποιῆσαι.
15. 1 Cor 16:1–4; 2 Cor 8 and 9; and Rom 15:22–33.

interpreters including Tertullian assumed that to "remember the poor" was generally applicable throughout Paul's ministry.[16] Drawing on the earlier work of Leander Keck and Richard Bauckham, Longenecker then debunks the claim that the later Palestinian Jewish Christians referred to as the "Ebionites" descended from the earliest Christian community in Jerusalem, which had originally assumed the name, "the poor," as a primarily religious designation.[17] Moreover, in the larger rhetorical context of Gal 2:1–10, Longenecker shows that "remember the poor" is linked closely with Paul's references to the gospel in vv. 2 and 5 and concludes that

> from 2:2 through 2:10, then, Paul has constructed a discursive web in which the phrase "remember the poor" in 2:10 is expected to be heard within the overarching parameters of apostolic efforts to tease out the full implications of the gospel. In Paul's reconstruction of the late-40s meeting, the Jerusalem leadership is depicted as uncompromising in its view that "remembering the poor" is not to be discarded in Paul's mission to the gentiles. On the contrary, remembering the poor is to be an essential feature of that mission to spread the gospel, not least among the gentiles.[18]

Longenecker continues by stating, "The Jerusalem leadership of the Jesus-movement agreed not only that circumcision is non-essential across the spectrum of Jesus-groups but also that care for the poor is essential in all incarnations of Jesus-groups, not simply among the Jewish followers of Jesus."[19] In my view this is a very persuasive analysis. The Jerusalem leaders were legitimately concerned that without circumcision gentile Jesus groups might very well become disconnected from the movement's Jewish origins and its distinctive moral system based on the Israelite covenant. The commitment to remember the poor emerged in that context as a way for gentile Christian groups to preserve that connection and embody a distinctively Jewish identity without the burden of circumcision and Torah observance. For Paul, therefore, care for the poor was not merely an issue of secondary importance pertaining to "ecclesial polity,"

---

16. Longenecker, *Remember the Poor*, 159–70.
17. Ibid., 173–76.
18. Ibid., 189–90.
19. Ibid., 203.

but rather "an intrinsic part of the good news to the Greco-Roman world" which he made his life's work to proclaim.[20]

The Model of Care for the Poor in the Pauline Communities

If remembering the poor was then in fact central to Paul's mission, an important follow-up question is how this concern was structured, organized, and implemented in his churches. In an important work, which at the time of its publication drew valuable attention to the neglected subject of Paul and poverty, Justin J. Meggitt argued that the predominant practice of the Pauline groups was "economic mutualism."[21] This is similar to what I described in the previous chapter as "sacrificial sharing" among the poor in which those who were equally impoverished agreed to make even greater sacrifices for the collective well-being. In the Jesus groups of rural Galilee, I observed examples in the Gospels that suggest that Jesus did promote this survival strategy occasionally as a temporary, stopgap measure, but I argued that more prominent, and presumably more reliable, was Jesus's strategy of calling upon the relatively wealthy, either traditional village patrons or those newly recruited, to fulfill their economic responsibilities to the poor. Meggitt acknowledges that while almsgiving and hospitality were occasionally practiced in Paul's churches, "economic mutualism" was by far more common, and that "vertical" reciprocal relationships between the wealthy and the poor did not contribute in any meaningful way to the alleviation of hunger in Paul's assemblies.[22] Meggitt's argument is based on the premise that the vast majority of the participants in Paul's assemblies, and even Paul himself, belonged to the lower classes, which lived right at the level of basic subsistence.

To support this conclusion, Meggitt enters a long-standing debate among scholars regarding the socioeconomic level of the Pauline congregations, specifically challenging the so-called New Consensus, represented by scholars, such as Wayne Meeks, Gerd Theissen, and Abraham J. Malherbe, who have argued that Paul's churches attracted neither the social elite classes nor the destitute but were composed mainly of a cross-section of the broad middle in Roman society.[23] A couple of brief

20. Ibid., 198.
21. Meggitt, *Paul, Poverty, and Survival*, 163–78.
22. Ibid., 158.
23. Theissen, "Social Setting," 69–119; Malherbe, *Social Aspects*, 71–91; and

quotations serve to illustrate their position. Theissen, for example, states, "It can be said that Hellenistic primitive Christianity was neither a proletarian movement among the lower classes nor an affair of the upper classes. On the contrary, what is characteristic for its social structure is the fact that it encompassed various strata—and thus various interests, customs, and assumptions."[24] Similarly Meeks claims that "the extreme top and bottom of the Greco-Roman social scale are missing from the picture. It is hardly surprising that we meet no landed aristocrats, no senators, no *equites*, nor (unless Erastus might qualify) decurions. But there is also no specific evidence of people who are destitute—such as the hired menials and dependent handworkers; the poorest of the poor, peasants, agricultural slaves, and hired agricultural laborers, are absent because of the urban setting of the Pauline groups."[25] Meggitt challenges the New Consensus on a number of points. First, assuming that the majority of the population in the cities of the Roman Empire lived at the level of basic subsistence, Meggitt claims that it is implausible to think that Paul's churches would have been better off economically; in fact, as a marginal group they were even more likely to be impoverished. According to Meggitt, "Paul and the Pauline churches shared in this general experience of deprivation and subsistence. Neither the apostle nor any members of the congregations he addresses in his epistles escaped from the harsh existence that typified life in the Roman Empire for the non-elite."[26] Second, New Consensus scholars often point to Paul's statement in 1 Cor 1:26: "Consider your own call, brothers and sisters: not many of you were wise by human standards, not many were powerful, not many were of noble birth" as evidence that while not numerous there were at least some who had elevated social status.[27] Meggitt, however, cites epigraphic evidence indicating that the term translated "well-born" (εὐγενεῖς and its cognates) was often applied to slaves and freedmen, perhaps reflecting wishful thinking and social aspirations more than reality.[28] Third, regarding Erastus, mentioned by Paul in Rom 16:23 as "the treasurer of the city" (ὁ οἰκονόμος τῆς πόλεως) and identified by some with the *aedile*

Meeks, *First Urban Christians*, 51–73.

24. Theissen, "Social Setting," 106.

25. Meeks, *First Urban Christians*, 73.

26. Meggitt, *Paul, Poverty, and Survival*, 75.

27. Βλέπετε γὰρ τὴν κλῆσιν ὑμῶν, ἀδελφοί, ὅτι οὐ πολλοὶ σοφοὶ κατὰ σάρκα, οὐ πολλοὶ δυνατοί, οὐ πολλοὶ εὐγενεῖς.

28. Meggitt, *Paul, Poverty, and Survival*, 104.

named Erastus of the "Corinthian Inscription" and therefore a member of the decurial class,[29] Meggitt points out that his name was too common to assume that the Erastus of Rom 16:23 was the same individual as the officeholder of the inscription, and also that the title was often applied to lower-level, even enslaved, civic functionaries and therefore not necessarily an indication of the elite status of an elected official.[30] Meggitt further argues that details often taken as evidence of wealth in the Pauline assemblies (for instance, the possession of a house used as a meeting place for the Christian assembly, references to services rendered to Paul or to the churches, and the ability to travel) do not necessarily indicate a level of wealth above basic subsistence.[31]

Meggitt's work has drawn sharp criticism among Pauline scholars.[32] A key point of contention is that by defining 99 percent of the population as "poor," Meggitt has created a category that is far too large and homogenous to be meaningful.[33] While Meggitt is undoubtedly right to emphasize that the majority of the ancient population was susceptible to shortfall and faced regular concerns about subsistence, he overstated his case by paying insufficient attention to the gradations of economic means among the non-elite. His thesis provides little room for people who, though not a part of either the local or imperial aristocracies, would have nonetheless been considered relatively wealthy by the standards of their neighbors. Meggitt's study is prone to false dichotomies—such as urban/rural and working-class/leisure-class—which cannot do justice to the complexity of ancient society. Certainly the ancient agrarian economy was far less complex than modern economies, yet even within a relatively simple system, countless factors, both natural and artificial, would have led to differing levels of economic security, even among the working classes. Moreover, archaeology has shown that contrary to Meggitt's assumption, rich and poor would have been in close contact with one another in the cities of the Roman Empire, judging from the

---

29. Theissen, "Social Stratification," 75–83.

30. Meggitt, *Paul, Poverty, and Survival*, 138–41.

31. Ibid., 128–135.

32. See, for example, the exchanges in *JSNT* (2001): Theissen, "Social Structure," 65–84; Martin, "Review Essay," 51–64; Meggitt, "Response to Martin and Theissen," 85–94; and Theissen, "Social Conflicts," 371–91.

33. A potential point of criticism of which Meggitt himself is aware (*Paul, Poverty, and Survival*, 5).

domestic architecture uncovered in Ostia, Pompeii, and Herculaneum.[34] These and other considerations raise serious doubts about the general validity of Meggitt's attempt to divide the population of the empire into two clear categories: the elite rich and the hungry poor.

As I discussed in chapter 1, Walter Scheidel and Steven J. Friesen have persuasively argued for an "income distribution" scale that effectively refutes this binary view of the Roman Empire's economic structure.[35] According to Scheidel and Friesen, below the elite 1.5 percent of the population which controlled up to 25 percent of the gross domestic product, between 6 and 12 percent of the population (what they refer to as the "middling" segment of Roman society) also controlled up to 25 percent of the GDP, thus creating a significant population block that enjoyed not only food security but also substantial discretionary income—between 2.4 and ten times the level of basic subsistence.[36] In a series of studies prior to his collaboration with Scheidel, Friesen had already argued for a more nuanced view of the "poor" in Roman society by proposing a seven-tiered "poverty scale" that allowed for gradations of wealth among the non-elite population.[37] Though speculative, Friesen's scale provided a helpful tool for imagining the relative wealth of participants in the Pauline assemblies with a great deal more precision than is possible with Meggitt's two-tiered model of rich and poor. Friesen's first three economic categories (PS1–PS3) included people of the social elite at both the imperial and local levels. These three divisions constituted no more than 3 percent of the population and correspond essentially to the social and economic elites of Meggitt's model. Friesen's more significant contribution was that he differentiates four economic groupings among the non-elite. In the fourth tier (PS4), Friesen includes those who through various means were able to acquire a relatively substantial surplus: some traders, merchants, artisans, army veterans, and (I would add) some relatively affluent working farmers. These people did not possess wealth enough to match the level of the civic aristocracy, let alone the imperial aristocracy, but their wealth was sufficient to insure that they would not likely face subsistence concerns, even in times of generalized food shortage. In Friesen's view, this group constituted about 7 percent of the population.

34. Balch, "Pompeiian Houses," 27–46.
35. Scheidel and Friesen, "Size of the Economy."
36. Ibid., 84–85.
37. Friesen, "Poverty in Pauline Studies," 323–61; Friesen, "Demography of the Pauline Mission," 351–70.

Twenty-two percent fell into Friesen's fifth grouping (PS5), constituted by those who had sufficient resources to provide stability and a reasonable expectation of remaining above subsistence level and included smaller-scale merchants, traders, shopowners, regular wage earners, artisans, and some farm families. Forty percent of the population, those categorized as (PS6), lived at the level of subsistence and probably fell below that line on a fairly regular basis. According to Friesen, this grouping would have included small farm families, artisans employed by others, the owners of small shops and taverns, and laborers. Finally, 28 percent of the population, the grouping designated as PS7, were chronically below subsistence level. This group included some farm families, unattached widows and orphans, the disabled, beggars, unskilled day laborers, and prisoners. In his recent collaboration with Scheidel, Friesen altered his earlier poverty scale by expanding the size of the "middling" segment of the population (his original PS4) from 7 percent of the population to between 6 and 12 percent (the second number representing the most optimistic calculations) and shrinking somewhat from 68 percent to between 55 and 60 percent the number who lived at or below basic subsistence (his original PS6 and PS7 groups).[38]

Precision is impossible, of course, when attempting to estimate the economic levels of the population of the Roman world, yet exact figures are unnecessary. These scholars have persuasively challenged the binary view that imagines Roman society to have been divided between the 1 percent wealthy and the 99 percent who lived at the level of basic subsistence. Regardless of the actual percentages of the population that belonged to each economic grouping and how much wealth they actually controlled, these studies provide a solid basis for supposing that the non-elite population was not uniformly poor, and that some of these families possessed enough wealth that they not only were safe from personal subsistence concerns but also enjoyed a substantial level of discretionary income. Even so, a second important conclusion from these studies is that the majority of the population did indeed live at the level of basic subsistence—not the 99 percent as Meggitt supposed, but

38. Bruce W. Longenecker has also entered this discussion in recent years. In 2009, Longenecker offered a critique of Friesen's poverty scale and proposed among other points that Friesen's PS4 group (which Longenecker renames, "ES4"—"economy scale") constituted 17 percent of the population as opposed to Friesen's 7 percent ("Economic Middle"). In 2010, Longenecker adopted the results of the collaboration between Scheidel and Friesen and accepts their optimistic 12 percent view of the "middling" sector of Roman society (*Remember the Poor*, 49).

still a very significant 55 to 60 percent who were chronically vulnerable in times of food shortage and personal misfortune, while up to 28 percent fell below subsistence. Thus this model provides a helpful way forward in the debate between the supporters of the "old consensus" and the "new consensus" regarding the economic makeup of the Pauline churches. With proponents of the "new consensus" Scheidel and Friesen's model makes plausible the claim that relatively wealthy individuals of non-elite status numbered among the participants in the Pauline churches. With the proponents of the "old consensus," however, this model also suggests that the majority of the members of Paul's churches lived at subsistence level and were therefore vulnerable to food insecurity.

In light of these conclusions, I contend in this chapter that instead of the model of "economic mutualism" proposed by Meggitt, care for the poor in Paul's churches revolved around the benevolent activity of the relatively wealthy members of those congregations. In this way, care for the poor in Paul's urban churches resembled the traditional practice of rural communities in which the village patron felt a sense of communal obligation to care for the needs of his poor neighbors. This traditional model became an alternative subsistence strategy in urban settings where the natural communal bonds of village society were lacking. Thus, in Paul's churches, relatively wealthy non-elites needed to be persuaded that it was their responsibility to look after the needs of the poor in these groups. In the pages that follow, I look at evidence from the Pauline letters that suggests that this was the predominant model of care for the poor practiced in these churches, and I also look at the rhetorical strategies and theological ideas that Paul used to cultivate a sense of moral obligation in the relatively wealthy church members to provide for the poor.

Care for the Poor in the Pauline Letters

Paul's Collection Project

Paul's commitment to caring for the poor is perhaps best illustrated in the collection, a project he organized with the churches of Galatia, Macedonia, and Achaia to "share their resources with the poor among the saints at Jerusalem."[39] This effort was clearly important to Paul. We

---

39. κοινωνίαν τινὰ ποιήσασθαι εἰς τοὺς πτωχοὺς τῶν ἁγίων τῶν ἐν Ἰερουσαλήμ (Rom 15:27).

might guess that he proposed it to the churches and persuaded them to participate during his initial missions in Galatia, Macedonia, and Achaia in 51 CE. He then mentions the project in his Letter to the Romans, probably composed in 55 or 56 CE. Furthermore, while Paul's pledge to "remember the poor" (Gal 2:10) should not, as I discussed above, be limited exclusively to the collection, the project does indeed reflect this more generalized concern; so it is possible that Paul was developing the idea as early as his meeting with the Jerusalem Christian leaders, which took place perhaps in 48 CE.[40] Regardless of the exact details, it is clear that this was a sustained effort that occupied his attention for at least five years and possibly even longer. Admittedly, Paul's collection is somewhat different from the main focus of this study, which is to see Christian care for the poor as a local alternative subsistence strategy, but Paul's reflection on the collection does illustrate the model in which the relatively wealthy are called upon to take a leading role in the effort, and also exemplifies the ideological rationale that Paul used to legitimize care for the poor among his hearers.

Paul states explicitly that the collection was for the "poor,"[41] but scholars debate whether addressing physical need was Paul's main goal for the project.[42] Some, for example, argue that Paul was motivated primarily by what he saw as the collection's eschatological significance; the contribution of the gentile Christians to the poor of the church in Jerusalem represented to him the fulfillment of prophetic texts such as Isa 2:2–4, Mic 4:1–2, and Isa 60:5 which speak of the eschatological pilgrimage of the nations to Zion.[43] Others argue that Paul saw the collection as an obligation, either because the Jerusalem leaders imposed it upon him and his gentile churches[44] or because the norm of reciprocity demanded repayment for the spiritual services offered by the Jewish church in Jerusalem to Paul's gentile converts.[45] Still others argue that Paul had an ecumenical purpose for the collection in that he hoped with the offering to repair the

40. Longenecker, *Remember the Poor*, 338–44.

41. Rom 15:26.

42. See Downs for a concise survey and categorization of scholarly proposals for Paul's view of the significance of the collection project (*Offering of the Gentiles*, 3–26).

43. For examples of this view see: Munck, *Paul and the Salvation of Mankind*, 282–308; Georgi, *Remembering the Poor*; and Nickle, *The Collection*, 129–42.

44. For examples of this view, see Holl, "Der Kirchenbegriff des Paulus"; and Berger, "Almosen für Israel."

45. Joubert, *Paul as Benefactor*.

rift between the Jewish and gentile segments of the church.[46] In contrast to these primarily theological arguments, some scholars maintain that Paul was motivated primarily by concern for the needy Jewish Christians in Jerusalem.[47] Finally, Downs himself argues that Paul understood the collection according to two dominant metaphors: Collection as Worship and Collection as Harvest.[48] According to Downs, "Paul's attempt to frame the collection as an act of corporate worship offered to God functions to subvert the values of patronage and euergetism by depicting an alternate mode of benefaction, one that brings glory, praise, and thanksgiving to God rather than to human benefactors."[49] In other words, by emphasizing that God was not only the source but also the recipient of the offering, Paul hoped to minimize the potential manifestation of exploitation and dominance between the gentile and Jewish Christians that was commonplace in the typical Greco-Roman patronage relationship.

In my view, each of these arguments has merit, and it seems very likely that Paul found multiple, interlocking layers of meaning in the collection effort.[50] Considering Paul's apocalyptic worldview, it would not be surprising if he attached eschatological significance to the collection, though there is no explicit evidence for this in his discussions of the collection in 1 Cor 16:1-4; 2 Cor 8-9; and Rom 15:22-32. On the other hand, Paul does use the language of obligation in Rom 15:22-33 which suggests that conventional assumptions about the norm of reciprocity may have influenced his thinking. Reciprocity theory also helps to explain how the exchange of benefits between the gentile Christians and Jerusalem could have worked to foster unity between the two branches of the church: the exchange of gifts serves to preserve friendship between two parties which might otherwise be in conflict with one another.[51] Downs's argument is particularly helpful in that it allows for seeing the basic structural similarity between the collection and Greco-Roman pat-

---

46. For examples see Cullmann, "The Early Church"; and Wedderburn, "Paul's Collection."

47. For examples see Horrell, "Paul's Collection"; and Meggitt, *Paul, Poverty, and Survival*, 158-61.

48. Downs, *Offering of the Gentiles*, 120-60.

49. Ibid., 158.

50. I do concur with Downs, however, that there is little evidence to support the view of Holl that the collection represented a sort of tax imposed by the Jerusalem leaders on the gentile congregations (*Offering of the Gentiles*, 161).

51. Gouldner, "Norm of Reciprocity," 174-75.

terns of patronage and benefaction, while at the same time drawing attention to the theological and behavioral differences that emerge when it is seen as an act of worship to God. In short, Downs's work demonstrates that Paul's theological reflection on the collection should not be separated from the tangible effects of the collection as a real act of benevolence. Paul was not only concerned about meeting the needs of the poor. He also wanted to restore and preserve unity between the branches of the church that would likely be further disrupted if the gentile Christians conceived of the collection according to the conventional assumptions of patronage and benefaction. Paul hoped his distinctive theological vision for the collection would serve both goals: Christian unity and care for the poor. In short, my point here is that regardless of the theological meaning that Paul attributed to the collection, it was, at its root, an act of benevolence designed to meet the real and tangible needs of the poor. It was an alternative subsistence strategy.

If the collection was an alternative subsistence strategy, what form did it take? In Meggitt's view, the collection project is the most notable example of the economic mutualism practiced by the Pauline Christian assemblies. He writes:

> *It was in no sense an individual or unilateral undertaking for any of those involved.* Paul emphasizes that *all* the members of the churches were contributors as, indeed, were *all* the communities (we hear of no exceptions). It was not intended to be the work of a few wealthy members or congregations. And it was premised on the assumption of mutual interdependence. It was not a one-off act of charity. *The material assistance given was understood as a something that would, in time, be returned, when the situation was reversed."*[52]

Meggitt is correct that the collection was "mutual" in that whole groups, not individuals, undertook it. Moreover, reciprocity theory would suggest that Meggitt is also correct that one effect of the collection was the establishment of a reciprocal relationship in which the Jerusalem Christians would be bound to assist the gentile assemblies if they were to experience food shortage at some future time.[53]

Meggitt's larger argument, however, is less persuasive because it is based on the premise that there were no wealthy participants in the

---

52. Meggitt, *Paul, Poverty, and Survival*, 159 (italics original).
53. Ibid.

Pauline assemblies. In Meggitt's estimation Paul's churches practiced economic "mutualism" because they were just as poor and economically insecure as the Jerusalem Christian community. But as we have seen, the income distribution scale of Scheidel and Friesen posits that between 6 and 12 percent of the overall population of the empire enjoyed a level of wealth that was well above basic subsistence. I see no reason to doubt that a similar percentage of relatively affluent, non-elite individuals and households populated Paul's churches. Conversely, the rest of the participants in Paul's churches who lived at or below subsistence level had little if any discretionary income. It is my argument here that Paul appealed primarily to the relatively wealthy in his churches to bear the bulk of the burden for the collection for the poor in Jerusalem. We see several pieces of evidence for this when we examine Paul's extended reflection on the collection in 1 Cor 16:1–4; 2 Cor 8 and 9; and Rom 15:22–33. I will first discuss direct indicators that Paul was addressing the relatively wealthy, then I will examine the arguments Paul develops to persuade this group of Christians to participate in the project.

Three items in passages where Paul discusses the collection suggest that he expected the relatively wealthy in his churches to be the primary contributors to the project. First, in 1 Cor 16:1–4, Paul gives practical advice about saving for the offering so that the givers will be prepared when he arrives and no further collections will be necessary. Paul writes: "On the first day of every week, each of you is to put aside and save whatever extra you earn, so that collections need not be taken when I come."[54] The NRSV translates the ambiguous phrase, ὅ τι ἐὰν εὐοδῶται, as "whatever extra you earn," in order to convey the sense of uncertainty and good fortune implied in the passive subjunctive form of the verb εὐοδόω.[55] Paul appears to be addressing here those who might legitimately hope for weekly earnings beyond the minimum necessary to sustain life. This would certainly apply to Scheidel's and Friesen's "middling" group and perhaps also to *some* of the 8 to 19 percent who lived slightly above subsistence with incomes that fell somewhere between 1 and 2.4 times basic subsistence.[56] On the contrary, the majority who lived right at subsistence or below that line, either temporarily or chronically, could not anticipate

---

54. κατὰ μίαν σαββάτου ἕκαστος ὑμῶν παρ' ἑαυτῷ τιθέτω θησαυρίζων ὅ τι ἐὰν εὐοδῶται, ἵνα μὴ ὅταν ἔλθω τότε λογεῖαι γίνωνται (1 Cor 16:2).

55. Cf. the KJV which conveys this idea with the translation, "as God hath prospered him."

56. Scheidel and Friesen, "Size of the Economy," 82–84.

having a surplus in any given week and therefore should be excluded from Paul's instruction here. It is also noteworthy that Paul mentions in 1 Cor 16:1 that he had given the same instructions to the Galatian churches, which indicates that it was Paul's regular practice for organizing the collection to recruit the relatively wealthy in his churches as the primary participants in the project.

A second clue that this was Paul's practice is found in 2 Cor 8 and 9 in passages where he emphasizes the "abundance" of those who participate in the giving. In 2 Cor 8:13–15 Paul writes:

> I do not mean that there should be relief for others and pressure on you, but it is a question of a fair balance between your present abundance and their need, so that their abundance may be for your need, in order that there may be a fair balance. As it is written, 'The one who had much did not have too much, and the one who had little did not have too little.'[57]

Paul is clear that the goal is not to place an unnecessary burden on those who give but rather that they will be persuaded to give out of their abundance. In the context of subsistence, this means that those with περίσσευμα, "abundance" (NRSV) or "plenty" (NIV) are individuals whose economic surplus provided them with immunity from personal subsistence concerns as well as with some level of discretionary income that could be given to those in need. Paul's words in 2 Cor 9:6–15 also emphasize the abundance of the relatively wealthy who are to bear the brunt of the collection effort.[58] In vv. 6 and 7, Paul assumes that the Corinthian givers are able to decide for themselves (ἕκαστος καθὼς προῄρηται τῇ καρδίᾳ) how much they will give, and that they have the ability to "sow bountifully" (ὁ σπείρων ἐπ'εὐλογίαις) if they choose to do so. Paul then states that God "is able to provide [them] with every blessing in abundance, so that by always having enough of everything, [they] may share

---

57. οὐ γὰρ ἵνα ἄλλοις ἄνεσις, ὑμῖν θλῖψις, ἀλλ᾽ ἐξ ἰσότητος. ἐν τῷ νῦν καιρῷ τὸ ὑμῶν περίσσευμα εἰς τὸ ἐκείνων ὑστέρημα, ἵνα καὶ τὸ ἐκείνων περίσσευμα γένηται εἰς τὸ ὑμῶν ὑστέρημα, ὅπως γένηται ἰσότης, καθὼς γέγραπται, Ὁ τὸ πολὺ οὐκ ἐπλεόνασεν, καὶ ὁ τὸ ὀλίγον οὐκ ἠλαττόνησεν.

58. Interpreters debate whether the text segments represented by 2 Cor 8 and 9 originally appeared as one letter or portions of two. Resolution of this point is unnecessary for my purposes here since my only concern is to establish that Paul expected the relatively wealthy in the Corinthian church to bear the primary responsibility in the collection effort and not the chronology of the project.

abundantly in every good work."⁵⁹ Paul here makes a theological claim that would have been at right at home in the thinking of the formerly pagan Corinthian Christians, but he adds an important twist: God has blessed them with material abundance with the express purpose (ἵνα) of enabling them to give generously to those in need. Similarly in v. 11, Paul writes, "You will be enriched in every way so that you can be generous on every occasion."⁶⁰ Again, Paul's point is that Corinthian abundance is a gift from God, given so they could be generous toward others. For those living at or below subsistence level, however, giving to the collection project would have caused an excessive burden (θλῖψις),⁶¹ a scenario that Paul clearly intended to avoid. The contribution of the Macedonian Christians to the collection is a case in point. Paul describes their condition in 2 Cor 8:2 as one of "extreme poverty" (ἡ κατὰ βάθους πτωχεία), suffered in the midst of a "severe ordeal of affliction" (ἐν πολλῇ δοκιμῇ θλίψεως). Paul's language here seems to reflect a situation of what I have referred to as "conjunctural poverty," a presumably short-term crisis (perhaps some kind of persecution that accompanied their initial reception of Paul and his gospel, described in 1 Thess 1:6) that caused them to fall temporarily below subsistence level. Yet, in spite of their own economic need, the Macedonian Christians "voluntarily" (αὐθαίρετοι) gave "according to their means" (κατὰ δύναμιν) and "even beyond their means" (καὶ παρὰ δύναμιν).⁶² That Paul was reluctant to allow them to do so is indicated by the fact that they had to "beg [him] earnestly for the privilege of sharing in this ministry to the saints."⁶³ Paul clearly did not expect "the poor" to participate in the collection project, but only those who had been blessed by God with abundance and who therefore enjoyed a sufficient level of personal economic security and a measure of discretionary income.

Paul also discusses the collection in Rom 15:22–33 and here again offers clues that it was the relatively wealthy in the churches of Achaia and Macedonia who were the primary participants in this project. This passage appears near the conclusion to the Letter to the Romans, and

---

59. δυνατεῖ δὲ ὁ θεὸς πᾶσαν χάριν περισσεῦαι εἰς ὑμᾶς, ἵνα ἐν παντὶ πάντοτε πᾶσαν αὐτάρκειαν ἔχοντες περισσεύητε εἰς πᾶν ἔργον ἀγαθόν (2 Cor 9:8).

60. ἐν παντὶ πλουτιζόμενοι εἰς πασαν ἁπλότητα (2 Cor 9:11). I follow the NIV in this verse which takes the εἰς as introducing a purpose clause.

61. 2 Cor 8:13.

62. 2 Cor 8:3.

63. μετὰ πολλῆς παρακλήσεως δεόμενοι ἡμῶν τὴν χάριν καὶ τὴν κοινωνίαν τῆς διακονίας τῆς εἰς τοὺς ἁγίους (2 Cor 8:4).

Paul's primary purpose is to announce his plan for a future visit to Rome and from there a missionary effort into Spain (vv. 23–24). First, however, he must travel to Jerusalem "in a ministry (διακονῶν) to the saints" (v. 25). At this point, Paul takes the opportunity to explain the collection project, its recipients, participants, and purpose. I will return below to what Paul says here about the reason for giving as I discuss the ways Paul tried to motivate the participants in this project. For now, I want to focus simply on the terminology that Paul used to describe this effort. As I noted above, in v. 25, Paul calls the collection διακονῶν, "ministries" or "services" to the saints in Jerusalem. In v. 26, Paul refers to the collection as an act of κοινωνίαν, "sharing" or "fellowship."[64] But in v. 27, Paul uses the term λειτουργῆσαι, "to serve" or "to minister."[65] This term, in both its noun and verb forms, is relatively rare in the New Testament and is typically used in reference to one's "service" or "worship" of God.[66] In the wider Greco-Roman context, λειτουργία and λειτουργέω commonly referred to the services performed by the decurial class on behalf of their cities.[67] Cities of the Roman world depended upon the personal wealth of the elite class rather than on public funds for the construction of infrastructure, urban amenities, and public religious observances. While ostensibly "voluntary," public expectations for the generosity of the local wealthy class were enormous, so that such service was essentially obligatory.[68] Paul discusses contributions to the collection in a similar manner when he claims that the Achaians and Macedonians "owe" (ὀφείλουσιν) their monetary contribution to the saints of Jerusalem in exchange for the spiritual services rendered to them (v. 27). Paul's use of the terminology of urban benefaction once again suggests that he expected the relatively wealthy of his gentile assemblies to play the primary role in the collection.

If Paul's appeal to support the collection was mainly to those in his congregations who fell within the 6 to 12 percent of the population that enjoyed income and wealth that put them comfortably above subsistence

---

64. εὐδόκησαν γὰρ Μακεδονία καὶ Ἀχαΐα κοινωνίαν τινὰ ποιήσασθαι εἰς τοὺς πτωχοὺς τῶν ἁγίων τῶν ἐν Ἰερουσαλήμ (Rom 15:26).

65. εὐδόκησαν γὰρ καὶ ὀφειλέται εἰσὶν αὐτῶν. εἰ γὰρ τοῖς πνευματικοῖς αὐτῶν ἐκοινώνησαν τὰ ἔθνη, ὀφείλουσιν καὶ ἐν τοῖς σαρκικοῖς λειτουργῆσαι αὐτοῖς (Rom 15:27). Paul also uses the same term in 2 Cor 9:12 in his discussion of the collection there.

66. BDAG, 590–91.

67. Strathmann, "λειτουργέω, λειτουργία, κτλ.," 216–19.

68. Veyne, *Bread and Circuses*, 10–11.

level, what kinds of arguments did he make to convince them of the merits of this project? Paul employs three interrelated strategies in support of the collection, which appeal to the cultural value of honor and shame, the norm of reciprocity, and to Christ as an example of generous giving.

First, Paul appeals to the givers' concern for honor and shame. By encouraging the Corinthians to make preparations before his arrival "so that collections need not be taken when I come" (1 Cor 16:2), Paul appears to be making space for the Corinthians to preserve their honor. The idea is that he is giving them fair warning so that they will take it upon themselves to follow through on their commitment to avoid any awkwardness if they were to be unprepared when he arrives. Paul also appeals to the Corinthians' honor in 2 Cor 8 and 9 when he compares their level of participation with that of the Macedonian Christians, who, though impoverished, had insisted upon participating in the project and giving generously well beyond their means (2 Cor 8:1–5). In this highly agonistic cultural environment, competition for honor shaped not only interpersonal relationships between men and families, but also relationships between communities, voluntary associations, cities, and even provinces. By highlighting the extreme generosity of the Macedonian Christians, Paul hoped to appeal to the Corinthians' competitive spirit so they would follow through with their commitment, which was clearly now in jeopardy. He makes this point explicitly in 2 Cor 9:1–5. Paul says here that he has been "boasting" (καυχῶμαι) about the Corinthians and their "zeal" (ζῆλος) for the project, which in turn had stirred the Macedonian Christians to action (v. 2). But now, concerned for the state of the collection in Corinth, he plans to send "the brothers" (τοὺς ἀδελφούς), ahead of his own arrival in Corinth, to prove that his previous "boasting" (τὸ καύχημα) had not been "empty" (κενωθῇ) in this matter (v. 3). Paul wanted to avoid a situation in which he and the Corinthians would "be humiliated" (καταισχυνθῶμεν) by the Corinthians lack of preparedness when he arrived accompanied by representatives from the Macedonian churches (v. 4). The vocabulary of honor and shame is obvious in this passage and represents Paul's attempt to exploit a fundamental cultural value to motivate the Corinthians to put forward a strong showing in the project. Since they excel in every other spiritual gift, Paul hopes for the sake of their honor, not to mention his own, that they will excel also in this (2 Cor 8:7).

Paul also appeals to the norm of reciprocity. This cultural value was closely connected with honor and shame. Failure to reciprocate appropriately shamed both the giver and the receiver. The norm of reciprocity demands balance in the exchange relationship: a benefit must be returned for a benefit given. As Marshall Sahlins has shown, "generalized reciprocity," in which there may be some form of imbalance (perhaps the good that is returned is different in kind or delayed in time), characterizes exchange within kinship groups or among close village neighbors.[69] Details in Paul's reasoning in 2 Cor 8 and 9 and Rom 15 indicate that he assumes this cultural norm. In 2 Cor 8:13–14, for instance, Paul writes, "I do not mean that there should be relief for others and pressure on you, but it is a question of a fair balance between your present abundance and their need, so that their abundance may be for your need, in order that there be a fair balance."[70] Paul makes two assumptions here. First, in a society of limited goods and wealth, it is only right that the ones presently enjoying material abundance would meet the needs of the poor. Second, the Corinthians' financial contribution to the collection is part of an exchange relationship in which the saints in Jerusalem also contribute to the Corinthians in areas where they are lacking. Justin Meggitt argues that Paul imagines here a potential future situation in which economic conditions are reversed and the Jerusalem Christians reciprocate by meeting the economic needs of the Corinthians.[71] But in Rom 15:27, Paul identifies the spiritual nature of the benefits that the Jerusalem church has given to the Christians of Macedonia and Achaia. Speaking of the contribution to the collection Paul writes, "They were pleased to do this, and indeed they owe it to them; for if the Gentiles have come to share in their spiritual blessings, they ought also to be of service to them in material things."[72] In one sense, Paul envisions a form of balanced reciprocity in these passages. The collection is one side of an equal exchange between two parties. Yet, the fact that they are different in kind—a material benefit as reciprocation for a spiritual benefit—indicates that Paul may be thinking in terms of generalized reciprocity, a form of exchange that defines a close kinship relationship between the two parties. In fact, nurturing a sense of kinship between gentile Christian and Jewish Christian brothers

---

69. Sahlins, "Sociology of Primitive Exchange."

70. οὐ γὰρ ἵνα ἄλλοις ἄνεσις, ὑμῖν θλῖψις, ἀλλ' ἐξ ἰσότητος, ἐν τῷ νῦν καιρῷ τὸ ὑμῶν περίσσευμα εἰς τὸ ἐκείνων ὑστέρημα, ἵνα καὶ τὸ ἐκείνων περίσσευμα γένηται εἰς τὸ ὑμῶν ὑστέρημα, ὅπως γένηται ἰσότης.

71. Meggitt, *Paul, Poverty, and Survival*, 160–61.

72. εὐδόκησαν γὰρ καὶ ὀφειλέται εἰσὶν αὐτῶν. εἰ γὰρ τοῖς πνευματικοῖς αὐτῶν ἐκοινώνησαν τὰ ἔθνη, ὀφείλουσιν καὶ ἐν τοῖς σαρκικοῖς λειτουργῆσαι αὐτοῖς (Rom 15:27).

and sisters was most likely an important aspect of Paul's vision for this project. But not only are the Corinthians obligated to contribute as reciprocation for the spiritual benefits that they had already received from the saints in Jerusalem, Paul also promises additional, future benefits from God as a result of their giving. In 2 Cor 9:10 Paul writes: "He who supplies seed to the sower and bread for food will supply and multiply your seed for sowing and increase the harvest of your righteousness."[73] Though speaking metaphorically in this verse, Paul seems to be saying that God will continue to bless them materially so that the mutually beneficial relationship of giving and receiving might continue.

Last, Paul makes a christological argument to persuade the reluctant Corinthian givers. Paul's arguments based on honor and on the norm of reciprocity would have been completely at home in the larger social and cultural context of first-century Mediterranean society. Even Paul's theological argument that the Corinthians would be blessed by God as a result of their generosity would have sounded familiar to a formerly pagan audience. But Paul's point in 2 Cor 8:9 makes his reasoning in this passage distinctly Christian and offers the Corinthians perhaps the most compelling reason for generous giving to the project. Paul reminds the Corinthians of "the generous act [grace] of our Lord Jesus Christ, that though he was rich, yet for your sakes became poor, so that by his poverty you might become rich."[74] Perhaps this was a harder sell, but Paul's point here is that ultimately the motive for Christian giving is to follow the example of Christ himself, who voluntarily became poor so that others might be rich. As we have seen in this section, Paul certainly believed that the Corinthians would receive benefits, both spiritual and material, from their generous contributions to the project. Yet, even if the individual giver received nothing in return, a greater social good (alleviation of poverty) could be achieved which would compensate for the giver's own sacrificial gift.

Though the collection project does not exactly fit the congregationally based alternative subsistence strategy of the Christians for which I am arguing, we do see in Paul's treatment of the project principles and arguments he also employed when encouraging local Christian assemblies to care for the poor. Paul relied primarily upon the more affluent in his

---

73. ὁ δὲ ἐπιχορηγῶν σπόρον τῷ σπείροντι καὶ ἄρτον εἰς βρῶσιν χορηγήσει καὶ πληθυνεῖ τὸν σπόρον ὑμῶν καὶ αὐξήσει τὰ γενήματα τῆς δικαιοσύνης ὑμῶν (2 Cor 9:10).

74. τὴν χάριν τοῦ κυρίου ἡμῶν Ἰησοῦ Χριστοῦ, ὅτι δι' ὑμᾶς ἐπτώχευσεν πλούσιος ὤν, ἵνα ὑμεῖς τῇ ἐκείνου πτωχείᾳ πλουτήσητε.

congregations, those representing the 6 to 12 percent of the population who were relatively immune from personal subsistence concerns, to bear the main financial burden in the project and made a variety of arguments to encourage this behavior.

Care for the Poor in the Observance of the Lord's Supper

While the collection project reveals Paul's concern for the poor on an interregional level, his discussion of the Corinthian Christians' observance of the Lord's Supper in 1 Cor 11:17-34 demonstrates his commitment to the poor also at the local level of the house churches. There are many uncertainties when interpreting the specific details of this passage, but some basic points are clear. Among the Corinthian Christians, division between rich and poor manifested itself when the community gathered for fellowship and worship. Paul addresses the problem from the perspective of the poor and takes their side in it. His solution is to instruct the wealthy to change their behavior by sharing with the needy during the Lord's Supper. Based on what Paul says in this passage, not only do we see his concern for the poor, but we may also conclude that the communal meal surrounding the Lord's Supper played a key role in the alternative subsistence strategy of the Pauline churches.

Beginning in 1 Cor 11:2, Paul deals with problems related to the communal gatherings of the house church in Corinth. In 1 Cor 11:2-16, Paul addresses the issue of head coverings for the women who were prophesying in the assembly and commends the church for remembering and maintaining the traditions that he had passed on to them on this issue.[75] Then in 11:17-34 Paul turns to the topic of the Lord's Supper and this time says, "I do not commend you" (οὐκ ἐπαινῶ, v. 17); on this matter, they had not kept the "tradition," namely, the words of institution which Paul reminds them of in 11:23-26. In the large unit that follows in 1 Cor 12-14, Paul deals with the topic of spiritual gifts and their use in the assembly and offers his view that prophecy is preferable to glossolalia because it does more to edify the church than speaking in tongues, which, at least in the case of the Corinthians, tended to be more for the benefit of the individual Christian and an indicator of spiritual status. How Paul became aware of the question about head coverings is uncertain. His

---

75. Ἐπαινῶ δὲ ὑμᾶς ὅτι πάντα μου μέμνησθε καί, καθὼς παρέδωκα ὑμῖν, τὰς παραδόσεις κατέχετε (1 Cor 11:2).

treatment of spiritual gifts in 12:1 begins with a περὶ δὲ clause, which in 1 Cor signals Paul's response to the items in the letter that the church had sent to him. It is possible that the letter addressed head coverings as well, even though he does not introduce the topic in his standard way in 11:2.[76] The problem of divisions in the Lord's Supper, on the other hand, is something that Paul has heard about (rather than reading about it in the letter), perhaps from those who had visited him from Chloe's household (1:11). If these visitors were Chloe's slaves, then the division between rich and poor becomes all the more poignant as they reported first hand their poor treatment by the wealthier Christians in Corinth.[77]

In 11:17-22, Paul states the problem: he has heard that when they "come together" (συνερχομένων) as a church there are "divisions" (σχίσματα) among them. The divisions, it becomes clear as the paragraph proceeds, are between the rich and the poor, and the rich are to blame. Ostensibly, they gather to eat the "Lord's Supper" (κυριακὸν δεῖπνον), but the reality is that they do just the opposite: each "goes ahead" (προλαμβάνει) with his "own supper" (τὸ ἴδιον δεῖπνον) with the result that the poor one "goes hungry" (ὃς μὲν πεινᾷ) while the rich one "becomes drunk" (ὃς δὲ μεθύει). The heart of the issue is selfish disregard from the rich for their poor and needy brothers and sisters in Christ. Because of this selfish behavior, Paul says that their "meetings do more harm than good."[78] It would be better in his opinion if they did not even gather at all.

Paul is clear in this paragraph about the basic problem, but reconstructing the background scenario is difficult because of the lack of specific detail, though interpreters have offered a number of plausible suggestions that fall into two main categories, with some variations in each. One possibility is to take the verb προλαμβάνει (v. 21) in a temporal sense with the idea that the rich had the luxury of gathering early, and that by the time the poor (the free poor and slaves who were engaged in manual labor and had no control of their work schedules) arrived, the rich had already overindulged, and there was nothing left for the late arrivals.[79] Another possibility is to take the prefix προ- as an intensifier, rather than as indicator of time; thus the translation could be "devours" or "consumes."[80] In this case, the problem is that the wealthy and the poor

76. Fee, *First Corinthians*, 492.
77. Ibid., 537 n.31.
78. NIV; οὐκ εἰς τὸ κρεῖσσον ἀλλ' εἰς τὸ ἧσσον συνέρχεσθε (11:17).
79. Bailey is a representative of this traditional view (*Paul*, 318).
80. Winter, "Lord's Supper." Garland (*1 Corinthians*, 540-41), Fee (*First Epistle to*

are eating at the same time, but not together. The rich have their own food, but the poor have to fend for themselves and end up hungry as a result. Gerd Theissen expands upon this scenario and imagines that the wealthy provide the elements for the Lord's Supper, which they share with the poor, but prior to the ritual meal the wealthy eat their own food together with their peers in a manner reflecting the social stratification of the society at-large.[81] In Roman society, the table represented distinctions of social status, so it seemed perfectly natural to the wealthy Corinthian Christians that they would eat a greater quantity of better quality food even in the presence of poor fellow Christians without feeling bothered to share with them. Jerome Murphy-O'Connor imagines this spatially in the context of the typical Roman upper-class house: the wealthy would eat together in the dining room, the *triclinium*, but since this room could accommodate only a few, the poor would gather together outside, in the *atrium*.[82] While there may be an element of truth in each of these scenarios, Paul's lack of specificity does not allow for a firm conclusion. Nevertheless, the key point again remains clear. Wealthy Corinthian Christians were showing contempt for their needy brothers and sisters, not simply by humiliating those who had nothing (καταισχύνετε τοὺς μὴ ἔχοντας), but by ignoring their basic needs, allowing them to go hungry even though they had plentiful resources to share if they had only chosen to do so.

Before giving guidelines for a solution to the problem, Paul offers a christological rationale to show that the wealthy Corinthians' behavior was utterly opposed to the spirit of the Lord's Supper that they had gathered to observe. In 11:23-26, Paul reminds the Corinthians of the traditional words of institution. This paragraph has been the subject of extensive scholarly discussion that not only examines Paul's view of the theological significance of the Lord's Supper but also compares Paul's version of the tradition with that which is found in the Synoptic Gospels. As important as these issues are in other contexts, they are only secondary to my purposes here. Why does Paul remind the Corinthians of these traditional words, words that they undoubtedly knew well and probably even recited regularly as they gathered for the Lord's Supper? Paul's main point was to show that their *behavior* at the Lord's Supper was an utter

---

the Corinthians, 540-41), and Thiselton (*First Epistle to the Corinthians*, 863) also accept this view with variations.

81. Theissen, *Social Setting*, 145-74.
82. Murphy-O'Connor, *St. Paul's Corinth*, 158-61.

contradiction of what they had ostensibly gathered to remember. The Lord's Supper is a remembrance of the ultimate example of sacrificial sharing and self-giving. The meal was a memorial to Jesus offering his life for his disciples. Yet, the wealthy Corinthian Christians had done just the opposite by eating "their own meals" (τὸ ἴδιον δεῖπνον) and leaving their poor brothers and sisters needy and hungry. Paul's point is theological (specifically christological) to be sure, but his purpose is not simply doctrinal in the sense that he only wanted to instruct them in the proper understanding of theological matters. Rather, his point was to correct their attitudes and behaviors. In short, Paul appeals to Christ's example of self-giving to condemn the selfishness of the wealthy Corinthian Christians and shame them into changing their ways.

Paul continues in the next paragraph by explaining the consequences of eating the Lord's Supper in a manner that dishonors the tradition of which he has just reminded them. He says that "whoever eats the bread or drinks the cup of the Lord in an unworthy manner will be answerable for the body and blood of the Lord."[83] He then says that "all who eat and drink without discerning the body, eat and drink judgment against themselves."[84] A common popular interpretation of "unworthily" (ἀναξίως) in v. 27 focuses on one's inner sinfulness as a reason to abstain from the Lord's Supper, but in the context here, "unworthily" clearly refers to the disregard the wealthy were showing the poor by not sharing with them during the meal. Likewise, "without discerning the body" (μὴ διακρίνων τὸ σῶμα) in v. 29 is often taken as a lack of reverence for the communion elements by not recognizing that the body and blood of the Lord are in the bread and the wine. But again, in light of the larger context, it seems that "not discerning the body" refers instead to the wealthy Corinthians not paying attention to the body of Christ, the church, particularly the needs of their poor brothers and sisters. Because of their behavior at the Lord's Supper, in Paul's estimation, they are already experiencing the judgment of God, evidenced in the fact that "many" were becoming "weak and ill" (πολλοὶ ἀσθενεῖς καὶ ἄρρωστοι) and that "some" had even "died" (κοιμῶνται ἱκανοί, v. 30). In these things they were being "disciplined by the Lord" (ὑπὸ τοῦ κυρίου παιδευόμεθα) so that they would not "be condemned with the world" (ἵνα μὴ σὺν τῷ κόσμῳ κατακριθῶμεν)

---

83. ὃς ἂν ἐσθίῃ τὸν ἄρτον ἢ πίνῃ τὸ ποτήριον τοῦ κυρίου ἀναξίως, ἔνοχος ἔσται τοῦ σώματος καὶ τοῦ αἵματος τοῦ κυρίου (1 Cor 11:27).

84. ὁ γὰρ ἐσθίων καὶ πίνων κρίμα ἑαυτῷ ἐσθίει καὶ πίνει μὴ διακρίνων τὸ σῶμα (1 Cor 11:29).

in the final judgment (v. 32). To avoid the Lord's judgment, Paul tells them to "examine yourselves" (δοκιμαζέτω δὲ ἄνθρωπος ἑαυτὸν) in v. 28 and then later says, "if we judge ourselves, we would not be judged."[85] Again the point here is that the wealthy Corinthians need to examine and judge (and then correct) how they treat the poor when they share meals together as the church.

In the first sentence of the final paragraph of the discussion, Paul instructs them on what they need to do. He states simply: "So then, my brothers and sisters, when you come together to eat, wait for one another."[86] The imperative ἐκδέχεσθε in this sentence allows for more than one interpretation. The NRSV translates the term as "wait for," which lends itself to the temporal reconstruction mentioned above in which the poor were arriving late to a meal and finding nothing left to eat. The NIV translates the term loosely as "you should all eat together," but this may convey Paul's meaning more accurately nonetheless. Some commentators favor interpreting ἐκδέχομαι in this context as "receive" with the connotation of "welcome" or "entertain."[87] Thus, Paul is instructing the wealthy to show hospitality to the poor. They should welcome the needy as honored guests and insure that they are well-fed, even though they should not expect to be repaid in the same way as when they entertain their social and economic peers. This is an act of sharing and self-giving that is true to the example of Jesus himself.

The final sentence of the passage may be the most difficult to interpret. Paul writes, "If you are hungry, eat at home, so that when you come together, it will not be for your condemnation."[88] This is typically interpreted as a concession to the elitist behavior of the wealthy Christians; Paul offers a compromise by allowing them to continue to enjoy private meals with their social peers, but only in their own houses and not as part of the Christian gathering.[89] Another possibility is that in allowing this exception Paul is actually expressing sarcasm;[90] he is not condoning their behavior at all but rather shaming them with it. In both interpretations,

---

85. εἰ δὲ ἑαυτοὺς διεκρίνομεν, οὐκ ἂν ἐκρινόμεθα (1 Cor 11:31).

86. ὥστε, ἀδελφοί μου, συνερχόμενοι εἰς τὸ φαγεῖν ἀλλήλους ἐκδέχεσθε (1 Cor 11:33).

87. See Fee, *First Corinthians*, 568; Garland, *1 Corinthians*, 554–55; and Winter, *After Paul Left Corinth*, 151–52.

88. εἴ τις πεινᾷ, ἐν οἴκῳ ἐσθιέτω, ἵνα μὴ εἰς κρίμα συνέρχησθε (1 Cor 11:34).

89. Theissen, *Social Setting*, 164. See also Fee, *First Corinthians*, 568.

90. Bartchy, "Undermining Ancient Patriarchy," 75.

"at home" (ἐν οἴκῳ) refers to the private houses of the wealthy, and the idea is that they should host banquets in their own houses if that is what they really want to do. Suzanne Watts Henderson, however, has argued that ἐν οἴκῳ refers not to private houses but to the house in which the Corinthian church met.[91] Thus, when Paul says, "If anyone is hungry, let him eat in the house," he is not telling them to eat on their own before coming together as the church.[92] Instead, he is saying that the hungry should be fed when the church gathers in the house where they meet.[93] This is an attractive option. The ambiguity of Paul's language in this sentence allows for it on grammatical grounds. Moreover, it solves the problem of why Paul would offer a concession after having written so forcefully against their behavior in the preceding verses. Admittedly, it is conceivable that Paul really did not care about the needs of the poor and that he merely wanted to protect the sanctity of the Lord's Supper when he told them to have their meals at home. But in light of his expressed concern for the poor in Gal 2:10 as well as his prolonged efforts in organizing the collection project for the poor in Jerusalem, it seems likely that his objective in this context was also to insure that the wealthy in Corinth assumed the responsibility of providing for their poor Christian brothers and sisters.

The shared meal common meal, during which the Christians observed the ritual of the Lord's Supper, was most likely, therefore, the focal point of the alternative subsistence strategy practiced by the Pauline house churches. In this practice, we can see the familiar pattern. The community expected their wealthier members to invite their poor Christian brothers and sisters into their homes to feed them and meet their basic physical needs, in much the same way as the rural patron in village communities. Thus, the Christian practice of care for the poor followed a traditional model, but they were innovative in forming small associations in urban settings among those who were not related by blood but who had become siblings based upon their common identity in Christ.

Care for the Poor in the Letter to the Romans

We also see examples of concern for the poor in Paul's letter to the Romans. The historical context of this letter has been the subject of extensive

---

91. Henderson, "If Anyone Hungers."
92. εἴ τις πεινᾷ, ἐν οἴκῳ ἐσθιέτω (1 Cor 11:34, my translation).
93. Henderson, "If Anyone Hungers."

discussion in the history of the interpretation.[94] In two important respects, Romans is clearly different from the other genuine Pauline letters. First, while Paul is fairly transparent regarding the occasion and purpose in his other letters, this is not the case with Romans. Scholars have identified a number of clues that seem to reflect Paul's reason for writing, but none stands out above the rest as his primary purpose. Second, in Romans Paul offers what seems to be a comprehensive and systematic exposition of his gospel and its implications for Christian faith and practice, pieces of which we find in his other letters but never as systematically. As a result of these distinctive features, I agree with commentators who suggest that Paul probably had multiple and overlapping reasons for writing Romans. In light of Rom 14:1—15:13, one of Paul's goals must have been to promote unity between Jewish and Gentile Christians in Rome. Paul's thorough explanation of justification and its implications for law observance make sense under this scenario. On the other hand, Paul's plan for a mission to Spain and his hope that the church will partner with him in this effort (Rom 15:24) also seem to be an important reason for writing. In this scenario, his thorough exposition of the gospel can be explained by the need to insure that he and the church are "on the same page" before they partner together in mission. Whatever Paul's specific reasons for writing, the fact remains that he has written a letter that provides us with a comprehensive and systematic summary of his gospel. More specifically in my view, the gospel we find in Romans is what Paul presented orally to the other churches in his initial evangelistic work with them. This gospel provided the premise from which he could then reason when dealing with specific problems in those churches when he addressed them in letters. The fact that Paul did not start the church in Rome made it necessary for him to articulate his gospel in writing so that he could have the same basis for continued theological reflection and moral reasoning with this church. All this is to say that in Romans we find not only a systematic exposition of Paul's gospel but also ethical exhortations that in most cases would have been generally applicable in all of Paul's churches. Paul's instructions about care for the poor fall into this category of general guidelines in the Letter to the Romans and may be taken as demonstrating the usual patterns of the alternative subsistence strategy of his churches.

94. See Schreiner for a survey of scholarly theories regarding Paul's purpose in this letter (*Romans*, 10–23).

Beginning in Rom 12:1, Paul turns to a concluding section of exhortation in which he presents to the church in Rome the ethical demands of the gospel which he has just laid out in the first eleven chapters of the letter. Rather than an addendum casually tacked on at the end, the instructions of Rom 12:1—15:13 convey the logical conclusion to the content of chapters 1–11; in the first part Paul of the letter deals with the "indicative" of the gospel and now in this concluding section its "imperative."[95] According to James D. G. Dunn, by the end of chapter 11, Paul has "effectively redrawn the boundaries of the people of God—the one God of Jew and Gentile," and now in Rom 12–15 he formulates a new "rule of life" for the new people of God.[96] Rom 12:1–2 provide the transition between these two sections in the letter, picking up on themes that Paul introduced earlier while also serving as the "heading" for the sections that follow.[97] In these introductory verses Paul sets Christian ethics in a cultic context by urging the Roman Christians to: "present your bodies as a living sacrifice, holy and acceptable to God, which is your spiritual worship."[98] Paul's point here is that the everyday behaviors and social interactions of Christians—toward fellow brothers and sisters in Christ, toward nonbelievers, toward persecutors, and even toward magistrates and the Roman state—should be offered as sacred acts of worship to God. This is similar to the cultic language that Paul uses to describe the collection[99] and indicates the theological orientation of Paul's ethics. Paul's words here remind his readers of the effects of the Christ-event that he previously outlined for them. Once enslaved to sin (Rom 1:18—3:20), they have now been justified through faith in Christ (Rom 3:21—4:25), which means that they have been reconciled to God and liberated from the power of sin, having died with Christ in baptism and raised to walk in the newness of life, which is a life lived in the power of the Spirit (Rom 5:1—8:31). Yet Paul goes on to exhort them: "Do not be conformed to this world, but be transformed by the renewing of your minds, so that you may discern what is the will of God—what is good and acceptable and perfect."[100] In Paul's view, Christians live in the tension of the "now"

95. Schreiner, *Romans*, 640.
96. Dunn, *Romans 9–16*, 705.
97. Moo, *Romans*, 748.
98. παραστῆναι τὰ σώματα ὑμῶν θυσίαν ζῶσαν ἁγίαν εὐάρεστον τῷ θεῷ τὴν λογικὴν λατρείαν ὑμῶν (Rom 12:1).
99. Observed in Downs, *Offering of the Gentiles*, 120–60.
100. μὴ συσχηματίζεσθε τῷ αἰῶνι τούτῳ, ἀλλὰ μεταμορφοῦσθε τῇ ἀνακαινώσει τοῦ

and "not yet"; they have experienced the redemptive work of Christ but still wait for the culmination of their salvation which is yet to come. Thus, in v. 2 Paul affirms that the power of God is at work transforming them and renewing their minds but also acknowledges that the process of discerning the good, acceptable, and perfect will of God requires their own acts of intentional obedience. To follow the ethical instructions that Paul outlines in the next four chapters, therefore, requires not simply a change of behavior but also a renewal of the mind to overcome the deeply ingrained cultural assumptions that reinforce the behavioral patterns of a fallen world. With its focus on need as the primary consideration, the practice of care for the poor in the Pauline assemblies required strange new behaviors as well as a new mindset to support them. While Paul seems to focus on specific issues confronting the church in Rome in his instructions in Rom 14:1—15:13, Rom 12:3—13:14 are general guidelines for Christian conduct that are applicable regardless of context.[101] It is in this section that we see a few short instructions that address care for the poor in the Christian assemblies of Rome.

We see the first set of instructions pertaining to care for the poor in Paul's discussion of spiritual gifts (χαρίσματα) in Rom 12:3–8. Paul begins with the basic principle that Christians should not think of themselves more highly than they ought but should rather be "sober" (εἰς τὸ σωφρονεῖν) in their judgment (v. 3), especially with respect to their spiritual gifts. There are two reasons for this: First, since gifts comes from God (v. 3), they provide no basis for claims of personally acquired honor. Second, the gifts are given by God to individuals for the benefit of the church, not for their own personal glory (v. 4). In Christ, Paul says, "individually, we are members of one another."[102] This exhortation to humility and concern for the body would be especially pertinent to the relatively affluent who might normally have been inclined to leverage their wealth, through acts of patronage and benefaction, for the sake of their personal honor. Paul hoped that a humble assessment of the source of their wealth (it is from God) and its proper use (it is for the benefit of the body) would curb these errors.

After encouraging the Christians in Rome to have a correct understanding of the source and proper use of their gifts (vv. 3–5), Paul then

---

νοὸς εἰς τὸ δοκιμάζειν ὑμᾶς τί τὸ θέλημα τοῦ θεοῦ, τὸ ἀγαθὸν καὶ εὐάρεστον καὶ τέλειον (Rom 12:2).

101. Moo, *Romans*, 747.

102. τὸ δὲ καθ' εἷς ἀλλήλων μέλη (Rom 12:5).

mentions seven specific gifts, all of which seem to be related to Christian leadership (vv. 6–8). Paul's list is not comprehensive but rather includes "representative" examples,[103] which he may have seen as especially useful for illustrating the general ethical principle he stated in vv. 3–5. Three of the gifts Paul mentions relate to care for the poor. Paul's exhortation in v. 7 to those gifted for service (εἴτε διακονίαν ἐν τῇ διακονίᾳ) may have the sense of financial assistance, particularly in light of the fact that Paul uses variations of the same term when referring to the collection in Rom 15:25 and in 2 Cor 8 and 9.[104] The most obvious reference to care for the poor is v. 8, in which Paul says that the "giver" should do so "generously" (ὁ μεταδιδοὺς ἐν ἁπλότητι). The term, ὁ μεταδιδοὺς, can be understood to mean the one who oversees and disburses the benevolence funds of the assembly, but the context in this passage favors the idea of one who gives generously out of his or her own personal wealth.[105] Dunn adds that more than simply "giving," the context favors the sense of "sharing" in that the wealthy member gives for the benefit of the church as a whole.[106] The term ἁπλότητι is also open to interpretation.[107] The usual translation in this verse is "generously," which places the emphasis on the sacrificial nature of the wealthy person's giving. On the other hand, the more literal meaning of the term in other contexts is "in simplicity." If that is the sense Paul has in mind in this passage, the idea could be that the giver should have no ulterior motive, such as honor-seeking. Finally, in v. 9, Paul refers to the one who shows mercy (ὁ ἐλεῶν ἐν ἱλαρότητι). Acts of mercy could take many forms, including care for the sick or the emotionally distressed, but Paul's exhortation to do so ἐν ἱλαρότητι ("cheerfully") parallels his statement about a "cheerful giver" in 2 Cor 9:7 and may therefore suggest an economic connotation in this context as well.[108] Regardless of the nuances of Paul's vocabulary in this passage, we see again in these verses a model of care for the poor that is reflected elsewhere in his letters. In this passage, Paul appeals to the relatively wealthy Christians in his churches to give to the needy from the surplus wealth they enjoyed. By exhorting them to give "in simplicity" and "cheerfully," Paul wants them to give to

103. Schreiner, *Romans*, 655.

104. Ibid., 657.

105. Dunn, *Romans*, 730; Fitzmyer, *Romans*, 648; Moo, *Romans*, 768; Schreiner, *Romans*, 659.

106. Ibid.

107. See Schreiner (*Romans*, 659) for discussion.

108. Ibid., 660.

the needy without harboring the usual reservations about whether or not these poor members were deserving of assistance. And, even though Paul emphasizes their corporate responsibility to the needy in his reflections on the body in vv. 4 and 5, it appears to fall to the relatively wealthy among them to bear the brunt of the financial burden in doing so.

Instructions related to care for the poor appear also in Rom 12:9–13. In these verses, Paul gives a series of short exhortations in the form of participial phrases that are loosely connected under the heading "Let love be genuine."[109] In the verses that follow Paul identifies several tangible behaviors by which Christians should demonstrate this "genuine love."[110] In v. 10, Paul writes: "Love one another with mutual affection."[111] Here Paul uses familial terms (φιλαδελφίᾳ, φιλόστοργοι) to describe Christian love. This is consistent with his regular practice of using sibling language to convey his vision of the church as a surrogate family.[112] As we saw in the previous chapter, Jesus also used familial language to support his alternative subsistence strategy in rural Galilee. Paul has a similar goal here. As I noted previously, the subsistence ethic of the rural village, the "moral economy of the peasant," was based upon the notion that the village community was structured along the lines of extended kinship relations. Such close relations among villagers allowed for "generalized" forms of reciprocity while also sustaining the commitment of the village as a whole to insure that the basic food needs of everyone in the community were met. Here again, we see Paul's attempt to transfer this traditional, rural ethic into a new urban context by shaping the vision of the church as a family. In the second part of v. 10, Paul makes the ironic statement: "Outdo one another in showing honor."[113] The Christians in Rome certainly would have understood the idea of competition for honor conveyed by the words in this sentence, and the idea of "outdo one another in *seeking* honor" would have sounded perfectly normal to them.

---

109. ἡ ἀγάπη ἀνυπόκριτος (Rom 12:9). The NRSV supplies the imperative verbs in this section, but commentators agree that Paul's intent in this passage is prescriptive and not simply descriptive (Dunn, *Romans*, 739; Moo, *Romans*, 775; Schreiner, *Romans*, 663–64).

110. The entire unit extends to 12:21, but since Paul's style of using of participles rather than imperative verbs in vv. 9–13 changes in v. 14, it seems legitimate to focus on 12:9–13 as a distinct sub-unit.

111. τῇ φιλαδελφίᾳ εἰς ἀλλήλους φιλόστοργοι.

112. Hellerman, *Ancient Church as Family*, 92–127.

113. τῇ τιμῇ ἀλλήλους προηγούμενοι.

But Paul here inverts the familiar by telling them to "outdo one another in *showing* honor." Again, Paul is shaping a vision of the church as a family in which honor attributed to the individual accrues to the assembly as a whole. These general principles in vv. 9–10 provide the ideological support for the specific exhortations to care for the poor that follow in v. 13.

In the first part of v. 13, Paul writes, "Contribute to the needs of the saints."[114] Three items are noteworthy here. First, κοινωνοῦντες conveys the ideas of "sharing" and "holding in common." In the New Testament, forms of this term frequently reflect economic sharing, with noteworthy examples found in Acts 2:42–47 and 4:32–35 to describe the practice of the Jerusalem church as they shared their material resources.[115] Second, Paul once again emphasizes need (ταῖς χρείαις) as the basic criterion for wealthier Christians to decide when and with whom they would share their resources. Third, Paul encourages sharing among the members of the Christian assembly (τῶν ἁγίων) and not generally to the needy in the city of Rome. The exclusive character of Christian care for the poor should not be taken as a lack of compassion for the poor in general, but rather represents the only realistic and practical means of addressing the ubiquitous problem of poverty, particularly by a group that held no political power or influence. The early Christians organized small communities in urban settings, on the model of the rural village, to provide an alternative means of subsistence insurance for those who joined them. In the second part of v. 13, Paul makes a related exhortation: "Extend hospitality to strangers."[116] The term διώκοντες more literally conveys the idea of "pursue" and may reflect Paul's idea that believers should take the initiative in pursuing opportunities to show hospitality to strangers.[117] Hospitality was a significant cultural value in ancient Greco-Roman society and included the provision of meals and lodging and perhaps occasionally the sort of legal protection that a patron might offer. Commentators generally envision "strangers" in this context as Christian missionaries or Christian travelers from other cities.[118] But in light of the economic conditions of the Roman Empire in the first century that I outlined in chapter 1, I would suggest that foreigners in need of hospital-

---

114. ταῖς χρείαις τῶν ἁγίων κοινωνοῦντες.
115. Discussed in the following chapter.
116. τὴν φιλοξενίαν διώκοντες.
117. Schreiner, *Romans*, 666.
118. Dunn, *Romans*, 744; Fitzmyer, *Romans*, 655; Moo, *Romans*, 780; Schreiner, *Romans*, 666.

ity might also include those who traveled to Rome for economic reasons, either because they had fallen on hard times and had no other choice, or because they were already relatively well-off and sought additional opportunities for economic advancement and upward social mobility. In spite of the possibilities offered by the city, such moves were inherently risky, particularly for those who came from rural communities with a strong social network. Such individuals might now find themselves even worse off in the city if their prospects failed to improve. In Rome and other cities with a Christian presence, Christian assemblies offered an alternative subsistence strategy in response to these kinds of conditions.

Care for the Poor in the Letter to the Philippians

To conclude this chapter, I now briefly consider one other Pauline text, the Letter to the Philippians, that may address care for the poor, though the evidence here is not as direct as we have seen previously. But whether or not Paul is writing specifically about care for the needy in these passages, he does promote in Philippians the relational values upon which the alternative subsistence strategy of his churches rested and for this reason are relevant to my topic here.

In Phil 2:1–5, Paul writes:

> If then there is any encouragement in Christ, any consolation from love, any sharing in the Spirit, any compassion and sympathy, make my join complete: be of the same mind, having the same love, being in full accord and of one mind. Do nothing from selfish ambition or conceit, but in humility regard others as better than yourselves. Let each of you look not to your own interests, but to the interests of others. Let the same mind be in you that was in Christ Jesus.[119]

Paul here encourages the Christians in Philippi to cultivate attitudes and behaviors that will strengthen the unity of their fellowship. Peter Oakes has argued that instead of the peaceful conditions that readers typically imagine for the Philippian congregation, this church was actually

---

119. Εἴ τις οὖν παράκλησις ἐν Χριστῷ, εἴ τι παραμύθιον ἀγάπης, εἴ τις κοινωνία πνεύματος, εἴ τις σπλάγχνα καὶ οἰκτιρμοί, πληρώσατέ μου τὴν χαρὰν ἵνα τὸ αὐτὸ φρονῆτε, τὴν αὐτὴν ἀγάπην ἔχοντες, σύμψυχοι, τὸ ἓν φρονοῦντες, μηδὲν κατ'ἐριθείαν μηδὲ κατὰ κενοδοξίαν ἀλλὰ τῇ ταπεινοφροσύνῃ ἀλλήλους ἡγούμενοι ὑπερέχοντας ἑαυτῶν, μὴ τὰ ἑαυτῶν ἕκαστος σκοποῦντες ἀλλὰ [καὶ] τὰ ἑτέρων ἕκαστοι. τοῦτο φρονεῖτε ἐν ὑμῖν ὃ καὶ ἐν Χριστῷ Ἰησοῦ.

experiencing significant discord, principally with regard to its economic situation and division between rich and poor.[120] Oakes notes that suffering and unity are the prominent themes in the letter to the Philippians and argues that the suffering was mainly economic in nature, and that the call to unity was an exhortation to the wealthy to care for the poor.[121] So, when Paul says: "Let each of you look not to your own interests, but to the interests of others," he is admonishing the wealthy to provide for the needy. And once again Paul appeals to the example of Christ, in the Christ Hymn of Phil 2:6–11, as the supporting rationale for the practice of care for the poor. This is consistent with his strategy in 2 Cor 8:9 as well as in 1 Cor 11:23–26. In each case, Paul offers the example of Christ, who gave his own life on the cross, as a model for the wealthy to follow, encouraging them to give of themselves and their resources to provide for the needy among them.

Conclusion

In this chapter, I have argued that an important function of Paul's urban house churches was to provide for their members an alternative subsistence strategy modeled after the patterns of the rural village. Just as the village functioned with its "moral economy," so Paul's churches functioned to meet the needs of those who temporarily fell below subsistence level, whether as a result of general food shortage or personal misfortune. Even though caring for the poor was considered to be the collective responsibility of the Pauline assemblies, it was the wealthier members who, in a manner similar to the village patron, assumed the bulk of this responsibility. Paul articulated several theological ideas in support of this alternative subsistence strategy designed to alleviate the concerns of these wealthier members about the propriety of giving to the poor. For example, by using sibling language he encouraged the believers to see themselves as a new kind of family that would practice a generalized form of reciprocity. He also sought to curtail the exploitative and abusive features of Greco-Roman patronage and benefaction by helping his converts imagine their gifts to the poor as offerings to God in the context of worship. Most important, Paul offered the example of Christ as a model of self-giving, sacrificial love to inspire the wealthier members

---

120. Oakes, *Philippians*, 212.
121. Ibid., 77–102.

to similar acts of generosity. Both in Paul's model of care for the poor as well as in the theological ideas he articulated to support it, we see parallels with the ideas and practices recommended by Jesus in rural Galilee two decades earlier. In the next chapter we will see a similar continuity of thought and practice of Christian care for the poor in the Luke-Acts.

CHAPTER 4

Care for the Poor in Luke-Acts

In the previous chapter I argued that Paul promoted an alternative subsistence strategy that resembled the traditional practices of the agrarian village by encouraging wealthier members to assume responsibility for the economic well-being of the community in a manner similar to that of the rural patron. In this we see continuity with Jesus, who earlier in the Galilean countryside sought to bolster the traditional strategies which were being disrupted by economic development during the time of Herod Antipas. In this chapter, I turn to Luke-Acts and argue that Luke also aimed to promote an alternative subsistence strategy in the urban Christian assemblies for which he wrote. Furthermore, like Jesus and Paul, Luke developed a supporting ideology to persuade those who might otherwise be reluctant to give generously, tailoring his message to address the specific concerns of his late first-century audience.

Luke-Acts is important for this study for a number of reasons. Not only does this lengthy composition constitute the largest block of material in the New Testament, but it also represents the work of a second-generation Christian deeply influenced by both the Jesus and the Pauline traditions. Moreover, even casual readers are struck, particularly in the uniquely Lukan material, by the prominence of economic matters in Luke-Acts. Some interpreters have seen in Luke's work the beginning of a change in the economic beliefs and practices of the early Christians.[1] According to this view, the earliest followers of the Jesus movement were uniformly poor (either because they were themselves destitute or because they renounced their wealth upon joining the movement) and practiced economic mutualism in an egalitarian social structure. By contrast, in

1. See, for example, Oakman, "Countryside in Luke-Acts," 176–79; and Schottroff and Stegemann, *Hope*, 67–120.

Luke–Acts better-off members are permitted to hold on to their wealth provided that they voluntarily give alms to the poor. In Luke's world, the church is becoming more stratified, both socially and economically, and the radical call to renunciation has been relaxed in order to accommodate an increasingly affluent membership. It is my contention here, however, that what we see in Luke-Acts does not in fact depart so dramatically from the earlier practices of Jesus and Paul. As we have seen, they also called upon the relatively wealthy in their communities to care for the poor, not by giving away the entirety of their wealth, but by generously giving from their surplus. Luke-Acts is important, therefore, not only for its extensive use of economic themes, but also because it reflects a basic continuity with earlier forms of Christian care for the poor.[2]

Background Issues in Luke-Acts

Before proceeding to the substance of this chapter, it is necessary first to state my assumptions regarding certain background issues in the interpretation of Luke-Acts. Though the authorship of the Gospel and Acts is anonymous, I see little reason to doubt the traditional ascription and for the sake of convenience will refer to the author as Luke. Nevertheless, the author's actual identity has little bearing on my argument in this chapter. The author declares that he carefully investigated trustworthy sources for the story of Jesus,[3] and I assume that he used the same methodology in his reporting on the early church in Acts, regardless of whether or not he was actually a traveling companion and close associate with Paul.[4] I take the Gospel and Acts to be two volumes of a unified narrative in which overarching themes can be traced.[5] Identifying the genre of Luke's composition has been notoriously difficult given that the first volume has

---

2. See Wilson, *For I Was Hungry*, for a similar analysis of the Gospel of Matthew on the issue of subsistence concerns and access to food.

3. ἔδοξε κἀμοὶ παρηκολουθηκότι ἄνωθεν πᾶσιν ἀκριβῶς καθεξῆς σοι γράψαι (Luke 1:3).

4. Interpreters debate the authenticity of the so-called "we sections" in Acts (16:10–17, 20:5–15, 21:1–18, 27:1—28:16). These passages imply that the author was traveling with Paul and therefore an eyewitness to events described in those sections of the narrative.

5. The unity of Luke-Acts remains a contested issue. See for example the debate between Johnson ("Literary Criticism of Luke–Acts") and Rowe ("Unity of Luke-Acts"). For the literary connections in Luke-Acts see Tannehill, *Narrative Unity*, vols. 1–2.

certain features of the ancient biography (βίος) while the second resembles ancient history (ἱστορία).⁶ By ancient standards, however, Luke was a reliable historian and intended to be read as such, but this should not obscure the fact that he was also a Christian writer who artfully shaped his story to highlight key theological themes for the spiritual edification of his readers.⁷

While the majority of interpreters accept a date of composition in the 70s or 80s CE, this is not a universally held position.⁸ Based on the fact that Acts reports neither Paul's execution (traditionally dated to around 64 CE) nor the fall of Jerusalem, some argue that the conscientious historian Luke would surely have included these watershed moments in Christian history had he written after these events.⁹ On the other end of the spectrum, Richard Pervo suggests a date between 110 and 120 CE.¹⁰ In Pervo's view, the canonical Acts should not be read as a reliable historical account of the early years of the Christian movement but rather as a story meant to "edify and entertain" its readers.¹¹ In my view a date in the 70s or 80s best fits the evidence. A date of composition prior to Paul's execution seems implausible considering Luke's clear reliance on the Gospel of Mark, and if we acknowledge that Luke was also a theologian, it is not difficult to imagine why he would have chosen to exclude these events: his basic goal was to narrate the progress of the gospel to the "ends of the earth,"¹² not Paul's death or the fall of Jerusalem. A late date in the early second century on the other hand seems unlikely in light of the way Luke depicts political conditions in his narrative. Because

---

6. For discussion see Parsons and Pervo, *Rethinking*, 20–44; Talbert, *Genre of Luke–Acts*; Alexander, *Preface to Luke's Gospel*; Palmer, "Acts"; Downing, "First Reading," 91–109; Pervo, *Profit with Delight*.

7. See Marshall, *Luke*, 21–76; and Green, *Theology of the Gospel of Luke*, 16–21.

8. This traditional view of critical scholars is based primarily on two assumptions: 1) that Luke used the Gospel of Mark (believed to have been written sometime either just before or after 70 CE) as a source for his own Gospel, and 2) that Jesus' prophecy about the fall of Jerusalem (Luke 21:20-4) seems to include specific details of the actual event. Both points require a post-70 date for Luke–Acts. For a presentation of this view see, Fitzmyer, *Luke*, 1:53–57.

9. See for example, Bock, *Luke*, 1:16–18.

10. Pervo, *Acts*, 5.

11. Ibid., 122. More recently, Pervo has made the point that while Acts should be generically classified as "historiography," one should not take this to mean that its reports are "factual" (*Acts*, 15).

12. ἔσεσθέ μου μάρτυρες . . . ἕως ἐσχάτου τῆς γῆς (Acts 1:8).

of the implications of Luke's historical context for my argument in this chapter, let me briefly expand upon this last point.

In Luke-Acts, Christians face no persecution at the hands of the Roman authorities. Jesus and Paul, of course, stand trial before Roman governors, yet both Pilate and Festus declare that the accused had "done nothing deserving of death."[13] Luke depicts Roman authorities generally as moderate and conscientious rulers who aspire to uphold the rule of law, even if they are occasionally ignorant and clumsy in their dealings with the Christians.[14] Roman centurions fare even better in Luke's narrative, frequently appearing as being favorably disposed toward the Christians or even as positive examples of Christian discipleship.[15] Luke's generally favorable presentation of the Roman Empire may perhaps be explained by the apologetic purpose of his composition and the church's need to establish a *modus vivendi* under the empire because of the delay of the Parousia.[16] Another possibility is that Luke was actually highly critical of the Roman Empire and offered a devastating yet veiled critique of Roman imperial rule.[17]

In my view, the best explanation is that Luke did in fact write during a period of relative peace and stability in the Roman world, at a time when the Christians were not yet targeted as an illegal religious association by the imperial authorities. The period of the Flavian emperors fits this description. After the traumatic end of the Julio-Claudian dynasty and the eighteen-month period of civil war from 68 to 70 CE following the death of Nero, the emperor Vespasian rose to power and quickly restored order and stability in the empire. Good government continued throughout the short reign of his son, Titus, and though Domitian fares poorly among ancient historians, modern interpreters have tended to view his reign more favorably.[18] Moreover, no evidence exists for Roman persecution

---

13. οὐδὲν ἄξιον θανάτου ἐστὶν πεπραγμένον αὐτῷ (Luke 23:25); μηδὲν ἄξιον αὐτὸν θανάτου πεπραχέναι (Acts 25:25).

14. Luke depicts Pilate (Luke 23:1–25), Felix (Acts 23:23—24:27), and Festus (Acts 25:1—26:32) as being reluctant to condemn Jesus and Paul, but also facing serious political constraints that require them to act contrary to their sense of justice. Likewise, Gallio in Corinth refused to condemn Paul and his fellow missionaries because the conflict lay in Jewish, rather than Roman, law (Acts 18:12–17).

15. See Luke 7:1–10, 23:47 and Acts 10:1–48, 22:25–26, 24:23, 27:1–3, and 27:43.

16. See Conzelmann, *Theology of St. Luke*, 137–49.

17. See Kuhn, *Kingdom according to Luke and Acts*, especially 263–74.

18. See Wells, *Roman Empire*, 166–67.

of the Christians during this period, the claims of the historian Eusebius notwithstanding.[19] Brent Shaw has persuasively argued that it was not until the early decades of the second century that "there emerged an official consciousness in the Roman ruling élite of a distinctive group of people named Christians."[20] The Neronian persecution, in Shaw's estimation, is therefore a myth, an anachronism retrojected by Tacitus into his account, a move explained by the growing awareness of (and concern about) the Christians among Tacitus's contemporaries in the Roman upper class.[21] Luke-Acts reflects a period when Roman authorities were not yet able to distinguish Christians from Jews, a dynamic which is consistent with the fact that the primary conflict in Luke's narrative centers on the religious debate involving the increasing gentile constituency of the Jesus movement and its relationship with Judaism. It seems likely, therefore, that Luke-Acts was composed sometime in the 70s or 80s under the Flavian rulers.

Even though the Roman world enjoyed relative peace and continued economic expansion during the Flavian period, this did not eliminate poverty. Rome's fundamentally agrarian economy would continue to experience food shortages, and those living at the level of basic subsistence would continue to turn to a variety of traditional survival strategies. But as I argued in chapter 1, the expanding economy of the Pax Romana and the resulting upward mobility enjoyed by some segments of the population may have undermined these traditional strategies by disrupting the social networks upon which the poor had formerly relied in times of want. A village patron might decide to cultivate new relationships with affluent urbanites rather than fulfill his responsibilities to the poor of his home village. Likewise, a poor farmer might try his luck in the city, hoping for new opportunities, only to discover when he gets there that he has no social network to turn to when tough times hit. No matter how affluent a society becomes, poverty persists, and alleviating it is generally not so much a lack of resources but rather an insufficient infrastructure for distributing assistance and, perhaps more important, a lack of will to do

19. Eusebius, *Hist. eccl.* 3.17.
20. Shaw, "Myth of the Neronian Persecution," 97. A key example of this "emerging consciousness" can be seen in Pliny's correspondence with the emperor Trajan on the Christians, which should be dated sometime during his provincial governorship in Bithynia-Pontus between 111 and 113 CE.
21. Ibid.

so. Luke-Acts represents another example of an early Christian response to these issues.

Finally, let me say a word about Luke's purpose and the recipients of his two-volume composition. Luke dedicates his work to a "most excellent Theophilus."[22] Interpreters have offered a number of theories regarding the identity of this individual and the nature of his relationship with Luke.[23] Whatever the situation may have been, Luke did not write for Theophilus alone; Theophilus stands for "the Christian readers of Luke's own day and thereafter."[24] The honorific title, "most excellent," may suggest that Theophilus was a person of some wealth and possibly of elevated social standing.[25] It is also likely that Theophilus was a Christian, which seems to be the implication of Luke's statement of purpose in the last sentence of the prologue, "so that you may know the truth concerning the things about which you have been instructed."[26] Fitzmyer interprets this verse as indicating that Theophilus had already learned and accepted the basic tenets of the Christian faith and now needed further instruction; thus, he is best viewed as a "catechumen or neophyte."[27]

The nature of "the truth" (τὴν ἀσφάλειαν) in this context lends itself to a number of possible interpretations. Perhaps Theophilus remained doubtful about the core doctrines[28] he had accepted and needed further convincing of their truthfulness. Or maybe some form of opposition had caused him to rethink his faith commitment.[29] Or possibly Luke hoped to create an explanatory context so that the historical facts concerning the origins of the Christian movement might not be misinterpreted.[30] In

22. κράτιστε Θεόφιλε (Luke 1:3; cf. Acts 1:1).

23. See Fitzmyer, *Luke*, 1:299–300, for a brief overview of the discussion. Traditionally, Theophilus was thought to have been Luke's patron who provided the financial backing for the publication of his work, but this is uncertain and probably anachronistic. Others have supposed that the name is symbolic and refers to any "friend of God." The designation "most excellent," however, suggests that Theophilus was an actual person (Bock, *Acts*, 52).

24. Fitzmyer, *Luke*, 1:300.

25. Ibid.

26. ἵνα ἐπιγνῷς περὶ ὧν κατηχήθης λόγων τὴν ἀσφάλειαν (Luke 1:4).

27. Fitzmyer, *Luke*, 1:301.

28. For example, the "necessity" (δεῖ, Luke 9:22 and *passim*) of the suffering and death of the Christ.

29. Bock, *Luke*, 1:65.

30. Danker, *Jesus and the New Age*, 25. For example, it was especially important to Luke to be able to lay out clearly the course of events leading to Jesus' crucifixion to

my view, Joel Green is probably correct that Luke's goal was to instruct his readers not only in the basic doctrines of the Christian faith but also in the consequences of these truths for their own lives as disciples.[31] In other words, Luke's purpose was the formation of disciples who not only believed but also put into practice what had been proclaimed by Jesus and the apostles about the kingdom of God and its good news for the poor.[32]

To accomplish this purpose, Luke wrote an "orderly account" (ἀνατάξασθαι διήγησιν), trying his own hand at what his predecessors had undertaken.[33] The term, διήγησις, refers to a "longer narrative composed of a number of events" in which the proper arrangement of these events is the key challenge facing the author.[34] Luke claims to have done this "accurately" (ἀκριβῶς) and "in order" (καθεξῆς), which Johnson takes to mean that he has drawn "connections between events, so that a thread of purpose runs through his entire narrative."[35] Joel Green makes a similar point when he says that Luke "has 'ordered' the events of his narrative so as to bring out their significance, to persuade Theophilus."[36] Similarly, Robert Tannehill states: "Telling a story involves 'narrative rhetoric.' The narrator constructs a narrative world which readers are invited to inhabit imaginatively, a world constructed according to certain values and beliefs. These values and beliefs are intended to be appealing and convincing . . . The message of Luke-Acts is not a set of theological presuppositions but the complex reshaping of human life, in its many dimensions, which it can cause."[37] As Tannehill emphasizes here, Luke wrote a story in which distinctive beliefs and values prevail. Though, as we will find, many of these values ran counter to those of Roman imperial society, they are perfectly consistent and appropriate within the narrative world that Luke

---

show that he did nothing to deserve this punishment but willingly accepted it as the will of God.

31. Green, *Luke*, 21–25.

32. The "kingdom of God" (τὴν βασιλείαν τοῦ θεοῦ) is the subject of proclamation throughout Luke-Acts, and Luke concludes his narrative on this note (Acts 28:30–31). The proclamation of the coming kingdom is summed up as "good news for the poor" (εὐαγγελίσασθαι πτωχοῖς) in Jesus's sermon in Nazareth which sets the agenda for his mission (Luke 4:18).

33. Luke 1:1.

34. Tannehill, *Narative Unity*, 1:10.

35. Johnson, *Luke*, 6.

36. Green, *Luke*, 36.

37. Tannehill, *Narrative Unity*, 1:8.

has created. In short, Luke's story provides the essential framework for the peculiar way of life practiced by the Christian community for whom he wrote.[38]

Later in the chapter, I will examine elements of Luke's story that served to reinforce his model of care for the poor. But first, what was that model? In the following section I examine Luke's summary statements in Acts 2:42–47 and 4:32–35 to detect what seems to be Luke's vision for how the Christian communities represented by his readers should care for the poor among them.

Luke's Model of Care for the Poor

The summary statements in Acts 2:42–47 and Acts 4:32–35 provide an obvious starting point for understanding Luke's vision of Christian care for the poor. A distinctive feature of Luke's literary style, summaries appear throughout Luke-Acts, not only to provide transitions between blocks in Luke's narrative,[39] but also "to generalize and thus make the experience of individuals normative."[40] The summaries in Acts 2:42–47 and 4:32–35 are especially important in this regard. Appearing as they do near the beginning of the book, these statements not only describe the noteworthy features of the fellowship of the earliest church in Jerusalem but also provide a reference for Christian communal life at various later points in the Acts narrative.[41] But if Tannehill's general point is correct, Luke's goal was more than simply providing an antiquarian description of primitive Christian care for the poor; he wanted to shape Christian

---

38. Similarly, Esler uses the work of Peter Berger and Thomas Luckmann (*Social Construction of Reality*) to argue that Luke's purpose was to provide "legitimation" for new converts (*Community and Gospel*, 16–23). Esler writes, "Luke creates a symbolic universe which orders history in such a way as to provide a past, present and future for his Christian contemporaries. He links them with their predecessors and successors in a meaningful totality" (19). Pervo as well describes Acts as a "legitimating narrative" by which he means that the goal of the author was to make "a case by telling a story (or stories), rather than by means of a treatise or dialogue" (*Acts*, 21).

39. Johnson, *Acts*, 9.

40. Schnabel, *Acts*, 175.

41. In spite of Conzelmann's doubts about the historicity of these summaries (*Acts*, 24), I follow Bartchy ("Community of Goods," 309–18) and assume the basic genuineness of these descriptions of early Christian communal behavior.

values and behaviors of his own times by recommending a similar pattern of behavior for his readers.[42]

In Acts 2:42–47, Luke describes the ongoing unity of mind and purpose (ὁμοθυμαδὸν)[43] that marked the earliest days of the Christian community. Rather than go their separate ways after the profound religious experience of Pentecost, the Christians remained together and formed an intimate fellowship. Christian initiation brought the convert into a new community that transcended kinship ties and ethnic allegiances.[44] The Christians continually devoted themselves (ἦσαν δὲ προσκαρτεροῦντες) to ongoing religious instruction (τῇ διδαχῇ ἀποστόλων), to a common life and mission (τῇ κοινωνίᾳ), to regular table fellowship (τῇ κλάσει τοῦ ἄρτου), and to devotional practices (ταῖς προσευχαῖς).[45] An important tangible expression of the Christians' unity was their sharing of possessions and provision for the poor. Luke reports that the "believers were together and had all things in common."[46] Commentators frequently note here an allusion to Hellenistic ideals about friendship and the proverb that states, "friends hold all things in common."[47] Luke's point seems to be that what his audience had known only as a utopian aspiration, the Christians put into actual practice. Luke goes on to state that they "would sell their possessions and goods and distribute the proceeds to all, as any had need."[48] The term that the NRSV translates as "possessions" (κτήματα) can also be understood as "landed property,"[49] which would be consistent with Luke's more specific statement in Acts 4:34. Whatever the case may be, the practice seems to have been that those who owned some surplus above subsistence—whether possessions, property, or other forms of wealth—voluntarily responded and gave indiscriminately ("to all," πᾶσιν), with "need" (χρείαν) being the only criterion.[50] It is also important to note

42. Tannehill, *Narrative Unity*, 1:8.

43. Acts 2:46

44. Bartchy, "Community of Goods," 313–14.

45. Acts 2:42.

46. πάντες δὲ πιστεύοντες ἦσαν ἐπὶ τὸ αὐτὸ καὶ εἶχον ἅπαντα κοινά (Acts 2:44).

47. Johnson, *Acts*, 59. See Plato, *Resp.* 449C and Aristotle, *Eth. nic.* 1168B. See also Mealand, "Community of Goods," 96–99; and Mitchell, "Social Function of Friendship," 255–72.

48. καὶ τὰ κτήματα καὶ τὰς ὑπάρξεις ἐπίπρασκον καὶ διεμέριζον αὐτὰ πᾶσιν καθότι ἄν τις χρείαν εἶχεν (Acts 2:45).

49. BDAG, 572.

50. See Moxnes, *Economy of the Kingdom*, 94–96, for a discussion of the priority

that it was in the context of these very human relational activities that the believers continued to experience the presence of God. Luke says that "everyone was filled with awe" because of the "wonders and signs done through the apostles" and that the "Lord added to their number those who were being saved."[51]

Acts 4:32–35 presents a similar picture. In this summary statement, Luke shows that the Christians continued in their unity, in spite of the fact that the initial enthusiasm of Pentecost had now given way to persecution at the hands of the Jewish authorities.[52] In response, the Christians gathered together for prayer, were filled with the Holy Spirit, and continued to speak "the word of God with boldness."[53] Once again, Luke emphasizes the intimacy of their fellowship and communal sharing. He says that "the whole group of those who believed were one in heart and soul, and no one claimed private ownership of any possessions, but everything they owned was held in common."[54] Luke takes special note that care for the poor was a priority for the Christians, so much so that he is able to say that "there was not a needy person among them."[55] Here, commentators typically see an allusion to Deut 15:4–5: "There will, however, be no one in need among you, because the Lord your God is sure to bless you in the land that the Lord your God is giving you as a possession to occupy, if only you will obey the Lord your God by diligently observing this entire commandment that I command you today." The LXX uses the term ἐνδεής ("one in need"), a word that appears only here in the New Testament, strongly suggesting that Luke is indeed making a connection to this Old Testament passage. We see a parallel here with Acts 2:44 and its hints of the Hellenistic ideal of friendship. Just as the Christians now practiced what had previously been a utopian aspiration in Hellenistic thought, they were also fulfilling what had previously been only an eschatological hope for Israel. As in the Acts 2 summary, the practice was that the wealthier members voluntarily sold lands and houses and brought

---

that Luke places on human need.

51. ἐγίνετο δὲ πάσῃ ψυχῇ φόβος, πολλά τε τέρατα καὶ σημεῖα διὰ τῶν ἀποστόλων ἐγίνετο (Acts 2:43); ὁ δὲ κύριος προσετίθει τοὺς σῳζομένους καθ'ἡμέραν ἐπὶ τὸ αὐτό (Acts 2:47).

52. Acts 4:1–22.

53. τὸν λόγον τοῦ θεοῦ μετὰ παρρησίας (Acts 4:31).

54. Τοῦ δὲ πλήθους τῶν πιστευσάντων ἦν καρδία καὶ ψυχὴ μία καὶ οὐδὲ εἷς τι τῶν ὑπαρχόντων αὐτῷ ἔλεγεν ἴδιον εἶναι ἀλλ' ἦν αὐτοῖς ἅπαντα κοινά (Acts 4:32).

55. οὐδὲ γὰρ ἐνδεής τις ἦν ἐν αὐτοῖς (Acts 4:34).

the proceeds to the apostles who distributed it to those in need.[56] Once again, Luke depicts the distribution as being indiscriminate, with need (χρείαν) being the only criterion.

Interpreters have debated exactly what model of communal sharing Luke depicts in these summaries. Brian Capper argues that Luke's statement that the early Christians "had all things in common" should be taken literally as indicating the sale of possessions, deposit into a common purse, and general distribution by which the daily needs of all were met—a pattern of communal sharing that they could have learned from Essene communities.[57] Other interpreters have concluded that the phrase, "had all things in common," does not necessarily demand the idea of a communal purse. Fitzmyer comments: "The sense of the clause is not clear. It could mean that the early Christians pooled all that they owned, or it could mean that they remained owners of property, which they put to the common use of others."[58] Similarly, Lüdemann states about 4:32–35: "We do not have to presuppose that the owners sold *all* their possessions, so that the difference from v. 32 would simply be one between *the surrender of possessions* (vv. 34–35) and *resignation of the right to possessions*."[59]

Two considerations support this view that Luke presents a model of sharing in which relatively affluent Christians retain private ownership of their wealth and possessions but voluntarily provide for those in need out of their abundance. First, commentators note that the imperfect form of the verbs in the summaries (ἐπίπρασκον, διεμέριζον, ἔφερον, ἐτίθουν) suggests a recurring practice in which landowners would sell their properties when occasions of need arose, rather than a one-time donation of all their assets into a general church fund.[60] Second, Luke's follow-up narrative in 4:36—5:11 also implies that it was customary for benefactors to sell and donate only a portion of their property to the community in response to poverty. In 4:36–37, Barnabas serves as a positive illustration of Luke's model of communal sharing, but there is no indication that he

---

56. ὅσοι γὰρ κτήτορες χωρίων ἢ οἰκιῶν ὑπῆρχον, πωλοῦντες ἔφερον τὰς τιμὰς τῶν πιπρασκομένων καὶ ἐτίθουν παρὰ τοὺς πόδας τῶν ἀποστόλων, διεδίδετο δὲ ἑκάστῳ καθότι ἄν τις χρείαν εἶχεν (Acts 4:34–35).

57. εἶχον ἅπαντα κοινά (Acts 2:44) and ἦν αὐτοῖς ἅπαντα κοινά (Acts 4:32); Capper, "Palestinian Cultural Context," 324–35.

58. Fitzmyer, *Acts*, 272.

59. Lüdemann, *Early Christianity*, 61 (author's emphasis). For a similar view see, Lindemann, "Beginnings of Christian Life in Jerusalem," 202–18.

60. Lindemann, "Beginnings of Christian Life in Jerusalem," 207.

sold all his possessions; Luke says only that he sold one field and placed the money at the feet of the apostles. Likewise, in the episode involving Ananias and Sapphira, Peter states explicitly that the property remained under their control all along (5:4), which suggests that they had the freedom to give as much or as little as they personally determined. Thus, the evidence points to a situation along the lines of what Lindemann has described: "The idea is therefore obviously not that there was a common purse with common access, rather that those who held extra wealth beyond what was necessary for living sold that off in favor of those in need."[61] It appears, then, that the model that Luke puts forward in the summary statements of Acts 2:42–47 and Acts 4:32–35 relies primarily upon the generosity of the relatively wealthy.

In this way, the practice of care for the poor described by Luke resembles what James Scott has shown regarding the traditional practices of the peasant village.[62] According to Scott, subsistence is regarded as a moral right of every individual in a peasant society. Luke's emphasis that the early Christian community was most concerned about meeting human need (χρείαν, 2:45 and 4:35) indicates the same concern. Scott also observes that because subsistence is a fundamental right of all, providing for the needs of the poor is the moral obligation of the peasant community as a whole. Accordingly, this requires that the community have a sense of unity and a shared moral framework. Luke's statements that the "believers were together" (2:44) and that they were "one in heart and soul" (4:32) indicate that the first Jerusalem Christians had the same sort of ethos necessary to sustain the obligation to provide for the needy among them. Finally, in Scott's model, the relatively wealthy in the peasant community bear the brunt of the obligation to provide for the subsistence needs of those whose resources fail them. Those who do so, who conform to the social pressure created by the ethic of unity in the village, are praised as good patrons. In fact, according to Scott, disparity between the rich and poor is generally not resented so long as the wealthy are seen as doing their duty for the needy. Those, on the other hand, who hoard their wealth in the face of the need incur the negative judgments of the community. As we have seen, this fits with much of what Luke reports in the summaries of chapters 2 and 4.[63] The implication of the relevant

---

61. Ibid.
62. See chapter 1 in this study.
63. Specifically, 2:45; 4:32, 34–35; and 4:36—5:11.

verses seems to be that the relatively wealthy disposed of their surplus for the sake of meeting the needs of the poor. This provides the explanation for the favorable report concerning Barnabas (4:36–37), who by selling a field and donating the money played the part of a good patron in the peasant moral economy.[64] Such a scenario may also provide the explanation for the negative example of Ananias and Sapphira. We are not told specifically what their sin was. One attractive suggestion is that they attempted to acquire honor from the community, befitting a sacrifice that they had not actually been willing to make.[65] From the standpoint of the peasant moral economy, however, a more straightforward reading may perhaps be offered: Luke wants to show the severity of the harm done to the community when the affluent hoard their surplus wealth while fellow community members go hungry. This in Luke's view is a moral violation of the highest order, and in the context of the narrative consequently incurs the severest of penalties.

In Luke's summaries in Acts 2:42–47 and 4:32–35, therefore, we find a description of an alternative subsistence strategy designed to benefit those negatively affected by the social and economic disruption caused by Roman imperial rule, even though this was, in general, a period of overall peace and prosperity. As Jesus and Paul did, Luke also promoted a strategy in which relatively wealthy members in the Christian community took it upon themselves to provide for the needs of those who occasionally found themselves in need, thus assuming the position traditionally filled by the rural village patron. This was a strategy that was not only employed by the earliest Christian community in Jerusalem as described by Luke, but also one that Luke hoped to promote among the Christian churches of his own day.

Yet, relatively wealthy Christians in Luke's audience were unlikely to embrace this alternative subsistence strategy easily, so Luke had to do more than simply recommend the practice. He also needed to provide ideological support for behavior that would have seemed irresponsible and culturally unacceptable to many of his readers. In the section that follows, I look briefly at the story that Luke tells and the rationale it provides for his alternative subsistence strategy. In this story, Luke creates a world for his readers in which generosity to the poor makes sense, thereby validating the attitudes and behaviors that he recommends to them.

64. Bartchy, "Community of Goods," 315.
65. Ibid., 316; see also Ascough, "Benefaction Gone Wrong."

Luke's Ideological Support for Christian Care for the Poor

Luke-Acts is the story of the fulfillment of Israel's eschatological expectations in the person of Jesus of Nazareth.[66] For Luke, Jesus was the long-awaited Davidic Messiah through whom God had intervened in history for the redemption of Israel. Luke, then, relates not the origins of a new religious movement or belief system, but rather the culmination of Israel's long-held hopes and aspirations. Yet, Luke's story was not for Israel alone. The climax of Israel's history also represented the hope of the world as the promise to Abraham that his descendants would be a "blessing to the nations" finds fulfilment in Jesus.[67] Luke's story, therefore, has deep roots in the traditions of Israel but moves beyond these traditions by relating the surprising final chapters represented in the death and resurrection of Israel's messiah. C. K. Barrett offers a helpful way of understanding what was involved in this process in his claim that Luke wrote the church's "first New Testament."[68] Even though Luke did not refer to his composition this way, this is essentially what he accomplished by providing a dramatic conclusion, in parts 2 and 3 (the Gospel and Acts), to the story of Israel as found in the Septuagint.

As the announcement of God's intervention through Jesus the Messiah for the redemption of Israel, Luke's story is good news for the poor. The "poor" in Luke-Acts are not only the economically needy—though they of course would be included in this designation—but also those who are oppressed, powerless, and on the margins of their society. They are the humble ones who depend solely on the benevolent power of God for their well-being. The story of God's intervention in Israel's history in the coming of Jesus the Messiah is good news because of the "great reversal" this brings.[69] The poor are lifted up and receive the blessings of God, while the rich and powerful are humbled. Just as the poor are not only the economically needy, so also the "rich" include those who find themselves in positions of power and affluence because they stand opposed to the purposes of God. Johnson adds that the term "rich" in Luke's narrative "connotes . . . a sense of arrogance that does not require the visitation of God."[70] These categories, however, are not always what they might ap-

66. Moessner and Tiede, "Introduction," 1–8.
67. Dahl, "Story of Abraham," 139–158.
68. Barrett, "First New Testament."
69. González, *Luke*, 5–8; Esler, *Community and Gospel*, 187–97.
70. Johnson, *Luke*, 108.

pear to be on the surface. In Luke-Acts, the Roman authorities are not the only, or even the primary, representatives of the "rich." The rich also include some religious leaders who undoubtedly would have thought of themselves as being on the side of God and therefore numbered among the "poor." Ultimately, it is Satan himself who is God's chief opponent in Luke-Acts, and in Luke's vision of reality it is primarily from Satan's power that all people need liberation. In other words, Luke's story of the death and resurrection of Israel's Messiah is ultimately the story of liberation from oppressive spiritual powers that are manifested in a variety of ailments afflicting God's people in Luke-Acts: demon possession, physical illness, exclusion on the basis of cultic rules, religious persecution, political abuse, and economic need.

Three passages that appear early in the Gospel illustrate these themes and provide a paradigm for the idea of the great reversal in Luke's subsequent narrative. First, Mary's response to the announcement from the angel Gabriel that she would give birth to the Messiah, traditionally referred to as the Magnificat, expresses these ideas.[71] In this song Mary praises God, saying, "He has shown strength with his arm; he has scattered the proud in the thoughts of their hearts. He has brought down the powerful from their thrones, and lifted up the lowly; he has filled the hungry with good things, and sent the rich away empty."[72] Mary's song draws upon older Israelite traditions, such as the songs of Miriam (Exod 15:21), Deborah (Judg 5:2–31), and Hannah (1 Sam 2:1–10).[73] But in Luke's story it is now in the announcement of the birth of the Messiah that these ancient hopes of Israel are finally coming to fulfillment. A second example is found in Luke 4:16–30, a passage that describes Jesus's synagogue sermon in Nazareth and that Luke presents as the archetype of the message that Jesus proclaimed throughout Galilee. After reading from the scroll of Isaiah,[74] Jesus announced that he had been anointed by the Spirit of the Lord "to proclaim good news to the poor . . . to proclaim freedom for the prisoners and recovery of sight for the blind, to set the oppressed free, to proclaim the year of the Lord's favor."[75] Commentators often see an allu-

---

71. Luke 1:46–55.

72. Ἐποίησεν κράτος ἐν βραχίονι αὐτοῦ, διεσκόρπισεν ὑπερηφάνους διανοίᾳ καρδίας αὐτῶν. καθεῖλεν δυνάστας ἀπὸ θρόνων καὶ ὕψωσεν ταπεινούς, πεινῶντας ἐνέπλησεν ἀγαθῶν καὶ πλουτοῦντας ἐξαπέστειλεν κενούς (Luke 1:51–53).

73. Horsley, *Liberation of Christmas*, 108.

74. The quotation is a conflation of Isa 58:6 and 61:1–2.

75. εὐαγγελίσασθαι πτωχοῖς . . . κηρύξαι αἰχμαλώτοις ἄφεσιν, καὶ τυφλοῖς

sion in this last clause to the year of Jubilee (Lev 25:8-55), the celebration every fiftieth year when debts would be forgiven and ancestral properties would be returned to their rightful owners.[76] An economic dimension may be part of what Luke has in mind here, but it is not limited simply to that. Johnson rightly comments that: "Rather than picturing Jesus' work in terms of a political or economic reform, Luke portrays his liberating work in terms of personal exorcisms, healings, and the teaching of the people."[77] Last, in the blessings and woes of Luke 6:20-26 we see another passage which emphasizes these themes.[78] Following a pronouncement of blessing upon those who are poor, hungry, hated, and excluded, Jesus pronounces a set of corresponding woes upon the rich, comfortable, and socially well-placed. The first group should anticipate a future reward, the second group, future punishment.

These passages are important because they establish, early in the Gospel, a theme that appears over and over again throughout Luke-Acts every time the humble, the weak, the sinner, the demon possessed, the sick, and the poor are lifted up and find salvation because "the kingdom of God has come near."[79] This eschatological hope is rooted ultimately in the experience of Israel's Messiah. What appeared to be the failed mission of a messianic pretender who suffered a humiliating defeat on a cross came to be recognized as the very plan and victory of God when Jesus was raised from the dead. Implicit in the eschatological great reversal is the idea that current cultural values and the present ways of the world will be overturned and a new way of life established. In Acts 17:6, Paul and his companions are accused by the Jews of Thessalonica of "turning the world upside down" (τὴν οἰκουμένην ἀναστατώσαντες). In the context of Luke's narrative, this is clearly a false accusation. As Luke presents the story, Paul had simply been "explaining and proving" in the synagogue

ἀνάβλεψιν, ἀποστεῖλαι τεθραυσμένους ἐν ἀφέσει, κηρύξαι ἐνιαυτὸν κυρίου δεκτόν (Luke 4:18-19, NIV).

76. Danker, *Jesus and the New Age*, 107.

77. Johnson, *Luke*, 81.

78. Luke 6:20-26//Matt 5:3-12 is Q material, but the absence of the "woes" in Matthew raises the question of whether Luke 6:24-26 was in Q or whether these verses represent Luke's special material (L). Resolving this question is not important for my purposes. The key point is that in the "blessings and woes" Luke focuses on good news for the poor and the reversal that the resulting reversal for the wealthy and powerful. For discussion of the sources of the Beatitudes see Fitzmyer, *Luke*, 1:627-37; Nolland, *Luke*, 1:280-81; and Bock, *Luke*, 1:549-53.

79. "Ἤγγικεν ἐφ'ὑμᾶς ἡ βασιλεία τοῦ θεοῦ (Luke 10:9).

that the "Messiah had to suffer and rise from the dead" and that "Jesus was this Messiah."[80] From Luke's perspective, it was not the actions of Paul or his fellow missionaries, but rather the violent response of their opponents that led to the disturbance in the city; the Christians were not agents of civil disobedience. Yet, on another level, the accusation is completely accurate. The Christians' good news to the poor—the coming of Jesus the Messiah—is indeed an earth-shaking message, not necessarily as a call for political revolt or the overthrowing of empires, but as the proclamation of an alternative set of cultural norms and their corresponding behaviors. In his two-volume composition, therefore, Luke provides his readers with a narrative framework, one governed by the overarching story of God's intervention in Jesus the Messiah, in which these alternative values and patterns of life now make sense. It is a story, in other words, in which care for the needy makes sense as an acceptable pattern of behavior for the relatively wealthy among Luke's readers.

Luke's Redefinition of Prodigality

As we have seen, the relatively wealthy were critical to the success of the early Christians' alternative subsistence strategy. While the Christian movement probably counted no members from among the top 2 percent of the population (the senatorial, equestrian, and decurial orders), it is likely that Luke's audience included some Christians of non-elite social status who nevertheless possessed above-average wealth. These Christians belonged to what Scheidel and Friesen have referred to as a "middling" class, 6 to 12 percent of the population who enjoyed incomes that were 2.4 to 10 times basic subsistence.[81] New Testament interpreters have drawn similar conclusions about Luke's church. Halvor Moxnes, for example, argues that Luke's audience included some wealthy freedmen.[82] Beyond freedmen, Luke's community may also have included relatively wealthy peasants living in cities, affluent craftsmen, merchants, traders, and centurions. Though personal aspirations for entering the Roman elite orders were perhaps far-fetched in most cases, this class of upwardly-mobile families certainly would have entertained such hopes for later

---

80. διανοίγων καὶ παρατιθέμενος ὅτι τὸν χριστὸν ἔδει παθεῖν καὶ ἀναστῆναι ἐκ νεκρῶν καὶ ὅτι οὗτός ἐστιν ὁ χριστὸς Ἰησοῦς ὃν ἐγὼ καταγγέλλω ὑμῖν (Acts 17:3).

81. See the discussion in chapter 1 above.

82. Moxnes, "Patron-Client Relations," 267.

generations in the family line. In light of these longer-term goals, they would have continued to amass wealth and would have been inclined to emulate the cultural values and behavioral patterns of the elite classes.

One elite behavior emulated by the relatively wealthy was charitable giving in the form of patronage and benefaction. The Roman elite class eagerly sought opportunities to give generously because doing so was considered an indication of one's noble character.[83] To be recognized and honored as a benefactor was to accrue social capital well-worth the financial investment. Following the example of their elite counterparts, wealthy non-elites also sought opportunities for euergetism in an effort to establish their social superiority. The early Roman imperial period was a time when increasing numbers of people experienced a phenomenon called "status dissonance."[84] This refers to the discrepancy between one's low social status and relative affluence. The rigid social hierarchy of the Roman Empire made it impossible for most of the newly rich to attain elite social status. Many provincial landowners without Roman citizenship, some freedmen, and many who engaged in commerce (a disreputable occupation according to traditional Roman values) may have enjoyed significant wealth but not an elevated social status to go with it. For these types of people in particular, benefaction was an activity of the elite class that they attempted to emulate in hopes of increasing their personal honor. Various types of *collegia*, or voluntary associations (organized according to occupation, ethnicity, religion, or even neighborhood affiliation) were a prominent feature of Mediterranean society under the Roman Empire.[85] These groups often provided burial services for their members as well as opportunities for social interaction and the sharing of common meals.[86] Though constituted by individuals of humble social status, *collegia* nevertheless tended to be structured hierarchically and were often patronized by their wealthier members.[87] Similarly, John H. D'Arms has shown that wealthy freedmen often held the title of *sevir Augustalis* in cities throughout the empire.[88] The college of *Augustales* provided opportunities for

83. Veyne, *Bread and Circuses*, 101–31.
84. Meeks, *First Urban Christians*, 16–23.
85. See Harland for an overview of the variety of associations, their composition, and their activities in Greco-Roman society (*Associations, Synagogues, and Congregations*, 25–112).
86. Garnsey and Saller, *Roman Empire*, 156–59.
87. Ibid., 157.
88. D'Arms, *Commerce and Social Standing*, 121–48.

benefaction to those who, because of their formerly slave status, were barred from membership in the civic decurion. Thus, the institution of the college of *Augustales* emerged as a response to a changing society in which freedmen were often wealthy and prominent.[89] In this way, the voluntary association provided an important avenue by which the relatively affluent, non-elite person could act as a benefactor and be honored for doing so.

Considering this larger trend, it would not be surprising if freedmen and other wealthy non-elites also saw Christian assemblies as opportunities for providing benefaction. If so, would they be able to practice benefaction in the traditional way, or would they have to adopt a different set of values and behaviors in the Christian context? Halvor Moxnes thinks so and argues that Luke advocated a new form of patronage that eschewed the reciprocity ethic in order to remove the power dimension inherent in the patron-client relationship.[90] Considering the cultural context, however, it seems unlikely to me that Luke could have expected Christian patrons to give without any hope that they would be repaid in some way, if not financially, then at least with the promise of being honored as a good and generous patron. There is no hint, for example, that Barnabas lorded his generosity over the church, but it is also clear that he enjoyed the respect and esteem of his fellow Christians and that he emerged as a natural leader in the community, in part at least, because of his generosity.

For Luke, the main difference between Christian and Greco-Roman patterns of patronage consisted not in whether one should expect a return on one's generosity, but in how to determine the worthiness of the recipients of one's generosity. The poor, as such, were not the objects of benefaction in Greco-Roman society.[91] This is not to say that the poor never received gifts from the wealthy, but when they did, it was because they were citizens of a city or members of a voluntary association to which a benefactor made a general donation and not because they were poor.[92] In contrast, the Christian community considered the poor to be worthy recipients of generosity precisely because of their *need*, a concern reflected in Acts 2:45 and Acts 4:35. It is not surprising, then, that Luke found it

---

89. Ibid.
90. Moxnes, "Patron-Client Relations," 264.
91. Hands, *Charities and Social Aid*, 74–75.
92. Ibid.

necessary to deal with objections to his economic program, considering that he was promoting what were basically rural, non-elite values in a social context in which urban values were dominant. To address these concerns, Luke needed to define what constitutes virtuous generosity in the context of the Christian community. In doing so, he challenged the traditional norms and assumptions of the wider Greco-Roman society which were reflected in the moral tradition of Hellenistic philosophy.

The Hellenistic moral philosophers devoted a significant amount of attention to the topics of patronage and benefaction because of their political ramifications. In the era of the late Republic, for example, this discussion took place in the context of frequently violent clashes between leading men, some of whom were referred to as *populares* because they solicited political support from the lower classes by means of generous gifts and promises of favorable legislation. In contrast the *optimates* professed disdain for these popular strategies and jealously guarded their power in the senate by insisting upon a more traditional approach to politics. Under the early empire, the emperor, who claimed to be the foremost benefactor, restrained elite giving.[93] Giving improperly could challenge the emperor's prerogative. Thus, the popular philosophers' praise of virtuous generosity had a conservative tendency designed to curtail nontraditional and potentially explosive claims to political power. I briefly survey here three writers on this subject in order to exemplify the standard view of virtuous generosity in the society of Luke's day. I begin with Aristotle and then examine the similar ideas of Cicero and Seneca, Aristotle's intellectual heirs.

Aristotle considered the type of giving appropriate to the virtuous free man, ἐλευθεριότητος ("liberality"), to be the mean between the extremes of ἀνελευθερία ("illiberality" or "stinginess") and ἀσωτία ("prodigality" or "wastefulness"). It is the distinction between liberality and prodigality that I want to focus on here because of its particular relevance to Luke's attempt to redefine these concepts. According to Aristotle, the liberal man gives in such a way as to demonstrate the virtue of his character and for no other reward than this. This means that he "will give to the right people, and the right amount, and at the right time."[94] In contrast to the virtuous man, the prodigal "gives to the wrong people and not for the

---

93. Veyne, *Bread and Circuses*, 292–419.

94. καὶ ὁ ἐλευθέριος οὖν δώσει τοῦ καλοῦ ἕνεκα καὶ ὀρθῶς, οἷς γὰρ δεῖ καὶ ὅσα ἕπεται τῇ ὀρθῇ δόσει (*Eth. nic.* 4.1.12).

nobility of giving but from some other motive."⁹⁵ Furthermore, prodigals are those who

> being indifferent to nobility of conduct are careless how they get their money, and take it from anywhere; their desire is to give, and they do not mind how or where they get their means of giving. Hence even their giving is not really liberal; their gifts are not noble, nor given for the nobility of giving, nor in the right way; on the contrary, sometimes they make men rich who ought to be poor, and will not give anything to the worthy, while heaping gifts on flatterers and others who minister to their pleasures. Hence most prodigal men are profligate; for they spend their money freely, some of it is squandered in debauchery; and having no high moral standard they readily yield to the temptation to pleasure.⁹⁶

Aristotle notes that prodigality is often associated with debauchery in the popular mind, but he insists that more fundamentally, the prodigal is guilty of one particular vice: "wasting his resources" (τὸ φθείρειν τὴν οὐσίαν) by giving indiscriminately.⁹⁷ Aristotle concedes that prodigality is preferable to illiberality because of the prodigal's natural tendency toward openhandedness. Nevertheless, his generosity is not virtuous because he fails to discriminate sufficiently with regard to the amount, purpose, and, especially, the recipients of his benefaction.

Similarly, Cicero insists that virtuous benefactors should show utmost care in their acts of generosity, for "when generosity is not indiscriminate giving, it wins most gratitude and people praise it with more enthusiasm because goodness of heart in a man of high station becomes the common refuge of everybody."⁹⁸ In other words, prodigals aim simply

---

95. ὁ δὲ διδοὺς οἷς μὴ δεῖ, ἢ μὴ τοῦ καλοῦ ἕνεκα ἀλλὰ διά τιν' ἄλλην αἰτίαν, οὐκ ἐλευθέριος ἀλλ'ἄλλος τις ῥηθήσεται (*Eth. nic.* 4.1.14).

96. ἅμα δὲ καὶ διὰ τὸ μηδὲν τοῦ καλοῦ φροντίζειν ὀλιγωρός καὶ πάντοθεν λαμβάνουσιν, διδόναι γὰρ ἐπιθυμοῦσι, τὸ δὲ πῶς ἢ πόθεν οὐδὲν αὑτοῖς διαφέρει. διόπερ οὐδ'ἐλευθέριοι αἱ δόσεις αὐτῶν εἰσίν, οὐ γὰρ καλαί, οὐδὲ τούτου ἕνεκα, οὐδὲ ὡς δεῖ, ἀλλ' ἐνίοτε οὓς δεῖ πένεσθαι, τούτους πλουσίους ποιοῦσι, καὶ τοῖς μὲν μετρίος τὰ ἤθη οὐδὲν ἂν δοῖεν, τοῖς δὲ κόλαξιν ἢ τιν' ἄλλην ἡδονὴν πορίζουσι πολλά. διὸ καὶ ἀκόλαστοι αὐτῶν εἰσὶν οἱ πολλοί, εὐχερῶς γὰρ ἀναλίσκοντες καὶ εἰς τὰς ἀκολασίας δαπανηροί εἰσι, καὶ διὰ τὸ μὴ πρὸς τὸ καλὸν ζῆν πρὸς τὰς ἡδονὰς ἀποκλίνουσιν (*Eth. nic.* 4.1.34–35).

97. Ibid., 4.1.5

98. Temeritate enim remota gratissima est liberalitas, eoque eam studiosius plerique laudant quod summi cuiusque bonitas commune perfugium est omnium (Cicero, *Off.* 2.16 [63]).

to please the recipient and earn his praise, while liberals contribute to causes with lasting value and significance. Cicero continues:

> There are, in general, two classes of those who give largely: the one class is lavish, the other the generous. The lavish are those who squander their money on public banquets, doles of meat among the people, gladiatorial shows, magnificent games, and wild-beast fights—vanities of which but a brief recollection will remain, or none at all. The generous, on the other hand, are those who employ their own means to ransom captives from brigands, or who assume their friends' debts or help in providing dowries for their daughters, or assist them in acquiring property or increasing what they have.[99]

In Cicero's view, the *liberalis* should consider not only the appropriateness of the gift but also the worthiness of his recipients. He states:

> The third rule laid down was that in acts of kindness we should weigh with discrimination the worthiness of the object of our benevolence; we should take into consideration his moral character, his attitude toward us, the intimacy of his relations to us, and our common social ties, as well as the services he has hitherto rendered in our interest. It is to be desired that all these considerations should be combined in the same person; if they are not, then the more numerous and the more important considerations must have the greater weight.[100]

In Cicero's view, a virtuous benefactor gives in moderation and is careful to consider the moral worthiness of his beneficiaries.

Seneca also advises his readers to be discerning when choosing the recipients of benefaction. For example, he says that "on the one hand, benefits ought not to be showered upon the mob, and on the other, it is not right to be wasteful of anything, least of all benefits; for, if you

---

99. Omnio duo sunt genera largorum quorum alteri prodigi, alteri liberales: prodigi qui epulis et viscerationibus et gladiatorum muneribus, ludorum venationumque apparatus pecunias profundunt in eas res quarum memoriam aut brevem aut nullam omnino sint relicturi; liberales autem qui suis facultatibus aut captos a praedonibus redimunt aut aes alienum suscipiunt amicorum aut in filiarum collocationem adiuuant aut opitulantur vel in re quaerenda vel augenda (Cicero, *Off.* 2.16 [55–56]).

100. Tertium est popositum ut in beneficentia dilectus esset dignitatis; in quo et mores eius erunt spectandi, in quem beneficium conferetur, et animus erga nos et communitas ac societas vitae et ad nostras utilitates official ante collata; quae ut concurrant omnia, optabile est; si minus, plures causae maioresque ponderis plus habebunt (Cicero, *Off.* 1.14 [45]).

eliminate discernment in giving them, they cease to be benefits, and will fall under any other name you please."[101] In his "The Fortunate Life" Seneca provides a nice summary of the popular ethos concerning generosity:

> He will give of it either to good men or to those whom he will be able to make good men; choosing the most worthy after the utmost deliberation, he will give of his wealth, as one who rightly remembers that he must render account no less of his expenditures than of his receipts; he will give of it only for a reason that is just and defensible, for wrong giving is no other than a shameful waste; he will have his pocket accessible, but it will have no hole in it—a pocket from which much can appear and nothing can drop. Whoever believes that giving is an easy matter, makes a mistake; it is a matter of great difficulty, provided that gifts are made with wisdom, and are not scattered at haphazard and by caprice. To this man I do a service, to that one make return; this one I succour, this one I pity; I supply this other one because he does not deserve to be dragged down by poverty and have it engross him; to some I shall not give although they are in need, because, even if I should give, they would still be in need; to some I shall proffer my help, upon certain ones even thrust it. In this matter I cannot afford to be careless; never am I more careful to register names than when I am giving.[102]

To sum up, in the popular moral tradition, generosity was praised and was regarded as a key component of social life. However, the moralists also assumed that generosity should be practiced with the wisdom and discretion befitting a virtuous man. Thus, virtuous benefaction involves giving worthy gifts to worthy people. Prodigality, on the other hand,

---

101. nam nec in vulgum effundenda sunt, et nullius rei, minime beneficiorum, honesta largitio est; quibus si detraxeris iudicium, desinunt esse beneficia, in aliut quodlibet incident nomen (Seneca, *Ben.* 1.2.1).

102. Donabit—quid erexistis aures, quid expeditis sinum?—donabit aut bonis aut eis quos facere poterit bonos, donabit cum summo consilio dignissimos eligens, ut qui meminerit tam expensorum quam acceptorum rationem esse reddendam, donabit ex recta et probabili causa, nam inter turpes iacturas malum munus est; habebit sinum facilem, non perforatum, ex quo multa exeant et nihil excidat. Errat si quis existimat facilem rem esse donare: plurimum ista res habet difficultatis, si modo consilio tribuitur, non casu et impetu spargitur. Hunc promereor, illi reddo; huic succurro, huius misereor; illum instruo dignum quem non deducat paupertas nec occupatum teneat; quibusdam non dabo quamuis desit, quia etiam si dedero erit defuturum; quibusdam offeram, quibusdam etiam inculcabo. Non possum in hac re esse neglegens; numquam magis nomina facio quam cum dono (Seneca, *Vit. beat.*, 23.5—24.1).

consists in indiscriminate giving—the wrong things at the wrong time to the wrong kinds of people.

Whom did the ancient moralists consider to be worthy? According to each of these three writers, a worthy recipient was one who practiced the virtues. But this presupposes a certain level of wealth and status, thus making virtue, by definition, an elite affair and generally beyond the reach of the lower classes, not to mention those who would be classified as the "poor" (πτωχοί). As a result of their Stoic inclinations, Cicero and Seneca tended to articulate somewhat more egalitarian views, expressing the assumption that any human as an innately rational being has the potential for virtue. Nevertheless, economic constraints effectively limited virtue to those who had the leisure for such a pursuit. In fact, according to Cicero, the noble sort of reciprocal relationship under discussion in his *On Duties* is only fully achieved in virtuous friendship:

> But of all the bonds of fellowship, there is none more noble, none more powerful than when good men of congenial character are joined in intimate friendship; for really, if we discover in another that moral goodness on which I dwell so much, it attracts us and makes us friends to the one in whose character it seems to dwell. And while ever virtue attracts us and makes us love those who seem to possess it, still justice and generosity do so most of all. Nothing, moreover, is more conducive to love and intimacy than compatibility of character in good men; for when two people have the same ideals and the same tastes, it is a natural consequence that each loves the other as himself.[103]

Thus, while theoretically possible for a non-elite person to achieve virtue and thereby be worthy to receive the generosity of another, these writers would have thought this to be a rare occurrence.

I argue that Luke knows the attitudes associated with popular moral philosophy, enters the discussion, and offers the Christian community a new definition of virtuous generosity. In doing so, he holds on to one part of the popular definition of prodigality, namely, its associations with

---

103. Sed omnium societatum nulla praestantior est, nulla firmior quam cum viri boni moribus similes sunt familiaritate coniuncti; illud enim honestum quod saepe dicimus, etiam si in alio cernimus, tamen nos movet atque illi in quo id inesse videtur, amicos facit. Et quamquam omnis virtus nos ad se allicit facitque ut eos diligamus in quibus ipsa inesse videatur, tamen iustitia et liberalitas id maxime efficit. Nihil autem est amabilius nec copulatius quam morum similitudo bonorum; in quibus enim eadem studia sunt, eaedem voluntates, in iis fit ut aeque quisque altero delectetur ac se ipso (Cicero, *Off.* 1.17 [53–56]).

licentiousness. But he rejects what Aristotle saw as primary: prodigality as the indiscriminate spending of one's resources. Luke would have agreed with this to a point, but where the Greco-Roman moralists emphasized the importance of evaluating the moral worthiness of a recipient, Luke offers a new criterion: in the Christian community, human need, and not the achievement of virtue, should determine a recipient's worthiness.

Luke's redefinition of these concepts is illustrated in the parable of the prodigal son, which could legitimately be called the parable of the prodigal father, if judged by contemporary social values. This parable is particularly significant for what it indicates about proper social relations in the Christian community. Traditionally, scholars as well as laypeople, have read this parable as an allegory that emphasizes the sinner's repentance and God's forgiveness.[104] N. T. Wright sees the parable of the prodigal son as Jesus's retelling of the story of Israel in exile and its moment of return.[105] Others have resisted allegorical readings in favor of what this parable suggests for social relations in the Christian community. Kenneth Bailey and Richard Rohrbaugh, for example, have both analyzed the story in light of Mediterranean social values, drawing attention to the manner in which Luke depicts an alternative set of values for his readers.[106] For my purposes, the resolution to this debate is not crucial. Consistent with what seems to be the intent of the other parables of Jesus, a reading of this story that emphasizes social relations in the Christian community is most natural. However, if the parable was indeed meant to be read allegorically, the implication remains that Luke intended his audience not only to relate to the younger son, but also to model the actions of the father, who represents God. Moreover, I have been working with the assumption in this chapter that Luke created a narrative world in the Gospel and Acts that supports the values of an alternative community. Whether understood as an allegory or a more straightforward story about social relations, the parable of the prodigal son holds a key place in Luke's strategy of a creating a narrative world in which particular social and economic values make sense.

Based on the commonly held attitudes described above, Luke's audience would have undoubtedly recognized the prodigal behavior of the younger son, and it appears that Luke intended to confirm this

104. For this view see Nolland, *Luke*, 2:789.

105. Wright, *Jesus and the Victory of God*, 125–44. Similarly, see Bailey, *Jacob and the Prodigal*, 195–201.

106. Bailey, *Poet and Peasant*; Rohrbaugh, "Dysfunctional Family," 141–64.

perception. For example, when Luke writes that the younger son "scattered his property in dissolute living" (15:13) he uses the word ἀσώτως, the term employed by Aristotle and other Hellenistic moralists but used only here in the New Testament.[107] The complaint of the elder brother in v. 30 also reinforces the view that his brother had acted immorally: "this son of yours who has devoured your property with prostitutes."[108] Luke clearly does not whitewash the younger son's lack of virtue and even considers his behavior worthy of censure. It seems that Luke has intentionally retained a negative assessment of prodigality and its association with debauchery, and in doing so affirms the commonly held view of his audience reflected in the Greco-Roman moral tradition.

But in light of contemporary moral assumptions, Luke's audience would also have recognized a second prodigal in this story—the young man's father.[109] To begin with, the father's willingness to grant his son's original request for his share of the inheritance, with no apparent hesitation mentioned in the text, suggests his lack of discretion; he is generous to a fault.[110] This is especially true if one considers that this act would have had serious consequences not only for his own financial condition but also for the economic viability of the entire family and, as a result, for its social standing in the village community. Rohrbaugh observes:

> We can now say that much more is at stake here than losing and gaining an errant son, traumatic as that event would be. The wellbeing and future of an entire extended family is at stake. Its honour and place in the village, its social and economic networks, even its ability to call on neighbours in times of need are all at issue. If the family were to lose its "place," no one would marry its sons or daughters, patrons would disappear, and the

107. The noun form, ἀσωτία, is found only in three places in the New Testament: Eph 5:18; Titus 1:6; and 1 Pet 4:4.

108. ὁ υἱός σου οὗτος ὁ καταφαγών σου τὸν βίον μετὰ πορνῶν.

109. David A. Holgate has also argued that Luke engaged with the Greco-Roman moral tradition in the parable of the Prodigal Son on the topic of virtuous generosity (*Prodigality, Liberality, and Meanness*). But Holgate's interpretation differs from my own in a key way in his view that the father represents "liberality," and thus the "mean between the extremes" of the younger son's "prodigality" and the elder son's "meanness." Crucial to my argument is that the father would also have been seen by Luke's readers as acting in a prodigal manner, and that this is part of Luke's redefinition of the concept. Moreover, rather than an example of "meanness," the elder brother in fact represents the sort of discretion that was admired in virtuous generosity.

110. Luke 15:12. On this point see Scott, *Hear then the Parable*, 111; see also Rohrbaugh, "Dysfunctional Family," 151.

family would be excluded from the necessary economic and social relations. Families that do not maintain solidarity with neighbours are quickly in trouble.[111]

Also noteworthy is the father's shameful reception of his returning son: "but while he was still far off, his father saw him and was filled with compassion; he ran and put his arms around him and kissed him."[112] As Bailey has observed, a Mediterranean man would not have run in public.[113] Moreover, in the eyes of the village community, the expected response would have been for the father to give the son a beating, thus partially restoring the honor he had lost as a result of his son's shameful behavior.[114] Finally, the father's prodigality is best illustrated in the celebration he prepares. He lavishes his son with a great feast, killing the fattened calf. He gives him his finest robe. He puts a ring on his finger. In short, the father's giving is like that observed by Aristotle: prodigals tend to "make rich, those who should be poor."[115] From the perspective of Greco-Roman moral values, both the father and younger son are deserving of moral censure for their foolish and wasteful use of resources.

Luke's depiction of the third major character in this parable, the older brother, also fits into the contemporary discussion of the distinction between prodigality and virtuous generosity. From a Greco-Roman perspective, it is the older son alone in the story who demonstrates any sense of economic morality. He is the voice of virtuous discrimination. He says to his father,

> Listen! For all these years I have been working like a slave for you, and I have never disobeyed your command; yet you have never given me even a young goat so that I might celebrate with my friends. But when this son of yours came back, who has devoured your property with prostitutes, you killed the fatted calf for him!"[116]

---

111. Rohrbaugh, "Dysfunctional Family," 149.

112. ἔτι δὲ αὐτοῦ μακρὰν ἀπέχοντες εἶδεν αὐτὸν ὁ πατὴρ αὐτοῦ καὶ ἐσπλαγχνίσθη καὶ δραμὼν ἐπέπεσεν ἐπὶ τὸν τράχηλον αὐτοῦ καὶ κατεφίλησεν αὐτόν (Luke 15:20).

113. Bailey, *Poet and Peasant*, 180–82.

114. Rohrbaugh, "Dysfunctional Family," 156.

115. οὓς δεῖ πένεσθαι, τούτους πλουσίους ποιοῦσι (*Eth. nic.* 4.1.35).

116. Ἰδοὺ τοσαῦτα ἔτη δουλεύω σοι καὶ οὐδέποτε ἐντολήν σου παρῆλθον, καὶ ἐμοὶ οὐδέποτε ἔδωκας ἔριφον ἵνα μετὰ τῶν φίλων μου εὐφρανθῶ· ὅτε δὲ ὁ υἱός σου οὗτος ὁ καταφαγών σου τὸν βίον μετὰ πορνῶν ἦλθεν, ἔθυσας αὐτῷ τὸν σιτευτὸν μόσχον (Luke 15:29–30).

Though his complaint was clearly self-serving—he was bitter that his father had not lavished more upon him—the Greco-Roman moralists, nevertheless, would have approved of his reasoning: his younger brother was undeserving because of his egregious lack of virtue, but he himself had proven worthy by means of loyalty and service to his father. In short, Luke's audience would undoubtedly have been able to discern the exemplars of virtue and vice as defined by contemporary moral standards. But as Luke tells the story, it becomes clear that he has intentionally upended these conventional expectations.

As I discussed above, the younger son does indeed remain a picture of vice to the extent that he squandered his resources in immoral behaviors, but in Luke's narrative he also quickly becomes an object of compassion rather than contempt. The concrete way Luke depicts his humiliation and hunger evokes pity and sympathy: "He would gladly have filled himself with the pods that the pigs were eating; and no one gave him anything."[117] Accordingly, Luke depicts the father not as a prodigal spendthrift but rather as one motivated to give freely out of compassion for his son's great need. For example, Luke emphasizes the son's neediness in v. 14 when he writes that: "there was a severe famine in the whole country, and he began to be in need."[118] In v. 17, the son considers the fact that his father's laborers have plenty of food but that he is "dying of hunger."[119] Upon his return, the father in v. 24 and again in v. 32, graphically assesses his son's dire condition of need: he "was dead and is alive again; he was lost and is found!"[120] This statement is understood typically as a reference to the spiritual condition of the sinner, but in the context of the story, these words refer to the vulnerability of the son outside of the protective embrace of the family and the larger village community. As for the elder son, while his stance toward his brother and father would have seemed perfectly legitimate from the perspective of contemporary moral reasoning, in the context of the parable, he appears petty and ungracious, hardly a model of virtue for Luke's audience.

In sum, Luke enters the contemporary discussion on the morality of giving and receiving in his telling of the parable of the prodigal son. By no means, however, does he offer an endorsement of the popular view. Luke

---

117. καὶ ἐπεθύμει χορτασθῆναι ἐκ τῶν κερατίων ὧν ἤσθιον οἱ χοῖροι, καὶ οὐδεὶς ἐδίδου αὐτῷ (Luke 15:16).

118. ἐγένετο λιμὸς ἰσχυρὰ κατὰ τὴν χώραν ἐκείνην, καὶ αὐτὸς ἤρξατο ὑστερεῖσθαι.

119. ἐγὼ δὲ λιμῷ ὧδε ἀπόλλυμαι.

120. οὗτος ὁ υἱός μου νεκρὸς ἦν καὶ ἀνέζησεν.

instead issues a devastating critique, perhaps directed especially toward the relatively wealthy in his audience, who would have seen their prospects for upward social mobility as contingent upon being regarded by their peers and superiors as virtuous men. Individuals such as the "most excellent Theophilus" may have feared that giving indiscriminately to the needy within the Christian assembly would mark them as prodigals and therefore open to censure, something they could ill afford if they had aspirations for social advancement. In the story of the prodigal son, Luke offers a new, broader definition of virtuous generosity that was intended to alleviate such concerns. Living lavishly and engaging in immoral behavior remains a vice as far as Luke is concerned; however, giving generously to those in need, regardless of their moral condition, should no longer be classified as prodigality according to Luke's redefinition of the concept.

This emphasis on need rather than on a recipient's virtue constituted the most important difference between the economic morality espoused by Luke and that of the Greco-Roman moralists. It can also be repeated at this point that Luke's focus on human need corresponds with the values of the peasant economy. Luke's redefinition of liberality and prodigality, therefore, constituted part of his effort to create an alternative subsistence strategy in which an urban-based group adopted rural peasant values. Seen in this light, Luke's strategy was both conservative and innovative: conservative, in that it was an effort to re-create traditional social relations, innovative because it was a response in a new social setting (the city) to the negative effects of imperial rule.

Examples of Redefined Liberality in Luke-Acts

Even beyond this parable, one quickly notices that lavish, seemingly indiscriminate, giving is a major theme in the Gospel and Acts. Luke positively depicts numerous examples of those who, according to contemporary moral standards, would have been considered prodigal in the way they distributed their resources. In this final section, I will briefly examine six passages, four of which are found only in Luke's composition. These six units can also be grouped into three pairings, each of which offers both a negative and positive example of the redefined economic morality advanced in the parable of the prodigal son. Depending on one's frame of reference, these stories can be read differently. Read from the perspective of Greco-Roman morality, one might see examples of virtuous discrimination in these stories, but in Luke's hands they become examples of hardheartedness and illiberality. Likewise, what might seem like examples of prodigality and wastefulness become models of virtuous generosity. Much depends upon whether Luke's readers have begun to adopt the values he advances as natural and virtuous in light of the narrative world he has created for them.

The first grouping pairs the story of the rich man and Lazarus (Luke 16:19–31) and the parable of the great feast (Luke 14:15–24). I consider these two texts together because of the element of feasting that is prevalent in each. The rich man and Lazarus is a story of reversal, which, as Johnson has observed, is a perfect narrative expression of the Lukan blessings and woes of 6:20, 26.[121] The "rich man" dressed in fine purple clothing and "feasted sumptuously every day."[122] By contrast, Lazarus was "poor," was covered in sores, and "longed to satisfy his hunger with what fell from the rich man's table."[123] It is worth noting that the expression, ἐπιθυμῶν χορτασθῆναι, parallels what Luke says about the younger son in 15:16 who "would have gladly filled himself (ἐπεθύμει χορτασθῆναι) with the pods that the pigs were eating." In each case the expression serves to emphasize in a very graphic way the concrete reality of the needy person's hunger. In this story, Luke shines the spotlight on Lazarus's need and offers no assessment of his personal virtue.

From the standpoint of contemporary Greco-Roman economic morality, there would have been nothing unusual or morally questionable about the rich man's way of life. In ancient urban society, the poor would always have been underfoot, and their presence generated little reflection about the reasons for their condition other than the assumption that it was a necessary consequence of their own moral inadequacy, or perhaps more graciously, simply their lot in life. In fact, the morally questionable act would have been to give to one such as Lazarus. But from the standpoint of the moral economy of the peasant, living lavishly in the face of human need would have caused resentment.[124] In a traditional village society, such sentiments would have exerted a powerful pressure on the rich to conform to social expectations, but in a period of

---

121. Johnson, *Luke*, 255–56.

122. ἄνθρωπος πλούσιος . . . εὐφραινόμενος καθ' ἡμέραν λαμπρῶς (Luke 16:19).

123. πτωχὸς . . . ἐπιθυμῶν χορτασθῆναι ἀπὸ τῶν πιπτόντων ἀπὸ τῆς τραπέζης τοῦ πλουσίου (Luke 16:21).

124. Moxnes, *Economy of the Kingdom*, 89.

social and economic change during the Pax Romana, the poor were able to exert less and less moral pressure on their wealthy neighbors to help meet their subsistence needs. The local wealthy had new outlets for social relations and were therefore less dependent upon the esteem of their immediate neighbors.

This scenario fits the situation of the rich man in Luke's story. He was apparently a Jew who knew the Law and the Prophets (Luke 16:29–31), so the obligation to care for the poor would have been familiar to him. But he had apparently begun to ignore the economic demands of his traditional law observance, perhaps for the sake of social advancement that would have required adopting a new set of economic values. From the rich man's perspective, giving to Lazarus would be judged as prodigal behavior and could jeopardize his aspirations for social advancement, but in the world of Luke's story, the opposite is the case. Such blatant disregard for the needs of others destines one for torment in the world of the dead, while it is the poor man, in contrast, who is drawn up to father Abraham after his death (v. 22). In Luke's view, the needy are the primary beneficiaries of the promises to Abraham, which were being fulfilled in the ministry of Jesus, the Christ.[125]

Jesus tells the parable of the great feast in the home of a Pharisee who has invited him for table fellowship on a Sabbath day. What might appear to a modern reader as a simple gesture of generous hospitality was actually an occasion for displaying and seeking honor.[126] Luke tells us, for example, that Jesus saw that the guests chose "places of honor" (τὰς πρωτοκλισίας) as they arrived for the feast (v. 7). Likewise, the host invited those from whom he could expect to be repaid (γένηται ἀνταπόδομά): his friends, brothers, relatives, and rich neighbors (v. 12).[127] The host likely had several goals for this feast: to bring honor to himself, to create and nurture beneficial social relations, and perhaps also to repay others who had benefited him in the past. In his choice of guests he was undoubtedly discerning, inviting those who would enhance his reputation by their presence. In this way, he exhibits the qualities of virtuous generosity as defined by the Greco-Roman moralists. But instead of this socially acceptable behavior, Jesus recommends actions that must have

125. See Dahl, "Abraham," 139–58 for the role of Abraham in Luke-Acts.

126. For discussion see Bartchy, "Historical Jesus and Honor Reversal," 175–83.

127. Moxnes notes that Luke uses the technical vocabulary of the reciprocity ethic (ἀνταπόδομα), a clue that he is engaging with and challenging the customary morality of his day (*Economy of the Kingdom*, 129).

sounded careless and prodigal when he tells the host to invite the "poor," the "crippled," the "lame," and the "blind."[128]

This theme of irresponsible generosity continues in the parable itself (14:16–24). The story begins with the host initially acting in a thoroughly conventional manner. He invites his peers and presumably does so for the usual reasons. He hopes to nurture his social network, increase his prestige and power by putting others in his debt, and gain honor from his display of well-placed generosity. But very quickly the parable departs from the expected story-line. Prepared perhaps to hear about the pleasant outcome of a great feast, Luke's audience instead is presented with an unhappy ending: the invited guests refuse the host's invitation. Though the excuses seem legitimate, the host is humiliated by the rejection of his peers. He must now find a way to deal with this unexpected turn of events and restore a measure of the honor he has lost.

In chapter 2, I argued that this parable has a plausible social setting in the village renewal movement promoted by the historical Jesus. Galilee was experiencing social and economic change as a result of Herod Antipas's efforts to integrate the region into the wider Roman economy. With the building of Sepphoris and Tiberias, the rural wealthy found new opportunities for social advancement. Part of Jesus's village revitalization effort was to curb this trend by encouraging the local wealthy to resist the allure of the city and to remain committed to their home villages. In Jesus's context, the point of this parable may have been to warn the rural wealthy of the potential danger of turning to the city and adopting its values. Jesus wanted this class of individuals to consider what would happen if their overtures to the urban elites were rebuffed. In rejecting the village, were they not, like the host in the parable, putting themselves at risk of being rejected by the city, thereby finding themselves rootless and isolated? It is better, Jesus says in effect, to remain in the village and to enjoy the honor of being a generous giver in times of food shortage than to fail in the city. In Luke's context, however, the question may have been a little different: once in the city, how should a moderately wealthy man respond when his overtures to the elite class are rejected? Such a scenario is quite plausible if one considers that some of Luke's audience may have included freedmen, relatively wealthy rural peasants, merchants, traders, and perhaps even soldiers and centurions—people of moderate wealth who nevertheless lacked the markers of elevated social status.

---

128. πτωχούς ... ἀναπείρους ... χωλούς ... τυφλούς (Luke 14:13–14).

According to Jesus's parable, the way to salvage one's honor in such a situation is to invite those who would not refuse the invitation, namely, the poor, disabled, blind, and lame. To do so, of course, would not have impressed the original invitees. Such an act would have sealed the fate of the host as excluded from their elite company. But in the context of the parable, the point seems to be, what does it matter now? If a wealthy man's aspirations for social advancement in the city are suddenly and unexpectedly thwarted, what more could be lost by giving generously to those deemed unworthy? Moreover, by inviting the poor, he would accomplish at least part of what he set out to do originally: host a great feast and be honored for his generosity. It is also interesting to note that upon hearing the excuses from the originally invited guests, the host "became angry" (τότε ὀργισθείς) and sent out his slave to invite those who could not repay him (v. 21). How should his anger be interpreted? This could suggest that part of the host's motive in inviting the poor was to get back at those who had shunned him. If so, then perhaps in Luke's view the simple fact that the wealthy in the Christian community give to the poor was more important than their motives for doing so. Moreover, Luke may be expressing a sort of realism about how the disappointed aspirations of a class of relatively wealthy social climbers could be channeled in a positive direction, if being slighted by the elites motivated them to give generously to a new group that would be more than happy to accept their benefaction.

A comparison between the story of the rich ruler (Luke 18:18-30) and the story of Zacchaeus (Luke 19:1-10) reveals a similar concern to redefine the concepts of prodigality and virtuous generosity. Scholars generally agree that Luke intended to draw a comparison between these two figures.[129] Luke has redacted his source to make the wealthy man a "ruler" (ἄρχων, v. 18) who was "very rich" (πλούσιος σφόδρα, v. 23) rather than simply a man who had "many possessions" (κτήματα πολλά) as Mark describes him (10:22). Luke does this presumably for the sake of establishing a parallel with Zacchaeus, who is a "chief tax collector" (ἀρχιτελώνες, 19:2). Both men then are in positions of power, and both are presumably Jewish. In the case of the rich ruler, Luke portrays him as being righteous with regard to the law, having observed all its requirements since his youth (18:21). Zacchaeus, on the other hand, is referred to as a "sinful man" (ἁμαρτωλῷ ἀνδρί, 19:7), which suggests that

---

129. Johnson, *Luke*, 285, 287; Evans, *Luke*, 660.

he was not a foreigner to the covenant but rather one who had fallen away from its careful observance. Both men had also embraced opportunities for advancement, available to them because of their great wealth. Both, therefore, would have been attuned to the social values of the elite class and aware of the need to conform to contemporary notions of virtue. This need to conform would have precluded them from being overly concerned with the conditions of the subordinate classes. Thus, both men seem to have been straddling two different worlds. Each, by necessity, had distanced himself from his roots among the people in order to be acceptable to the ruling class. In Luke's narrative, Jesus challenges both to reconsider the course they have taken.

To the rich ruler Jesus says, "You still lack one thing. Sell everything you have and give to the poor, and you will have treasure in heaven. Then come, follow me."[130] Luke tells readers that upon hearing this, the ruler "became very sad, for he was rich."[131] From the perspective of Greco-Roman economic morality, Jesus's instructions would have seemed like a foolishly indiscriminate use of one's resources. Choosing to follow Jesus likely meant the end of the rich man's aspirations for social advancement. In fact, his decision constituted a choice between two different communities and a competing set of values. And rather than "enter the kingdom of God" (τὴν βασιλείαν τοῦ θεοῦ εἰσπορεύονται, v. 24), the man chose to remain at the margins of elite society. Considering all that has come before in Luke's narrative, it is quite clear to readers that the man made the wrong choice. Better to be regarded as a foolhardy spendthrift and inherit the kingdom of God than to exercise economic virtue and be excluded.

In contrast, Zacchaeus seems to have no doubt about what he should do. Without even being asked by Jesus, Zacchaeus volunteers to give half his possessions to the poor and to make a fourfold restitution to anyone whom he had defrauded (19:8). One might assume that when Zacchaeus promises to make repayment, he is vowing to cease lining his own pockets by exacting more from the population than had been stipulated by the Romans. However, this is not explicitly stated in the text. Alternatively, it could be that Zacchaeus is in fact promising to use his position to mitigate the burden of Roman taxation itself. If this is the case, it might be analogous to the parable of the Dishonest Steward, which I discussed in chapter 2. There I proposed interpreting the parable

---

130. "Ἔτι ἕν σοι λείπει· πάντα ὅσα ἔχεις πώλησον καὶ διάδος πτωχοῖς, καὶ ἕξεις θησαυρὸν ἐν τοῖς οὐρανοῖς, καὶ δεῦρο ἀκολούθει μοι (Luke 18:22).

131. περίλυπος ἐγενήθη· ἦν γὰρ πλούσιος σφόδρα (Luke 18:23).

in a straightforward manner as Jesus encouraging retainers to use their position to aid members of the subordinate class by means of deceptive practices. It is possible that Zacchaeus promises something similar here: to use his position to create a veiled, indirect form of tax resistance. If so, with such an act of insubordination Zacchaeus not only jeopardizes his social position, he risks severe punishment as well. At the very least, Zacchaeus acts in a prodigal manner by giving half his possessions to the poor.

For the final comparison, I return to the examples of Barnabas (Acts 4:36–37) and Ananias and Sapphira (Acts 5:1–11) mentioned earlier in this chapter. As I discussed above, Luke presents Barnabas as an ideal patron of the Jerusalem church whose actions demonstrate the workings of the alternative subsistence strategy that he outlined in Acts 2:42–47 and 4:32–35. In response to human need, Barnabas sold a field that he owned and brought the money to the community, laying it at the feet of the apostles.[132] Enough has been said to this point to make clear that Barnabas's action would have been morally questionable from the perspective of Greco-Roman values. But one particular element of Barnabas's actions can be pointed out for brief comment here. Not only does Barnabas give to a questionable group, needy followers of Jesus of Nazareth, but he also relinquishes his authority over what he gives. If a virtuous benefactor is careful to choose recipients who are morally worthy, what does it say about one who trusts others to make that decision for him? This would seem to be the very antithesis of prudent generosity, but in Luke's narrative Barnabas is praised as an ideal exemplar whom Luke hopes other wealthy Christians will follow.

Ananias and Sapphira, on the other hand, who were more prudent in their benefaction, face the severest of penalties for their wise use of resources and virtuous generosity. Cicero praises the virtuous man for giving freely after, of course, doing the necessary homework to determine the worthiness of his recipients. Even then, in Cicero's view, one should be prudent about how much he gives. It is not virtuous, for example, to give so much of one's property to strangers that his kin suffer the consequences later.[133] One should protect his capital so that he is able to give freely on a repeated basis. Cicero writes:

---

132. ὑπάρχοντος αὐτῷ ἀγροῦ πωλήσας ἤνεγκεν τὸ χρῆμα καὶ ἔθηκεν πρὸς τοὺς πόδας τῶν ἀποστόλων (Acts 4:37).

133. Cicero, *Off.* 1.14 [44].

> We should have a care for our personal property, for it is discreditable to let it run through our fingers; but we must guard it in such a way that there shall be no suspicion of meanness or avarice. For the greatest privilege of wealth is, beyond all peradventure, the opportunity it affords for doing good, without sacrificing one's fortune.[134]

Is it possible that Ananias and Sapphira had such advice in mind when they gave a portion of what they sold to the Christian community while keeping back the rest?[135] Their behavior is certainly defensible in light of the assumptions surrounding virtuous generosity. In the context of Luke's narrative, however, this act is a violation of the ethos of the community. The term used by Luke, ἐνοσφίσατο, is found in Greek literature with the meaning of "to deprive, rob" in the active form and "to put aside for oneself" or "keep back . . . in a type of skimming operation" in the middle voice.[136] This is consistent with what Scott has shown regarding the peasant moral economy, namely, that it is not so much disparities of wealth that are resented but rather hoarding one's surplus while others go without. This helps explain why Luke uses the terminology of theft to refer to property that Ananias and Sapphira owned and over which they technically had control. As members of the community, the moral claims of the needy overrode the moral right of Ananias and Sapphira to retain their surplus wealth. Furthermore, such behavior tends to evoke the condemnation of one's poor neighbors, who in a variety of ways apply negative social pressure to bring about conformity to the communal ethos. A story about two wealthy hoarders being struck dead would appear to function in a similar, albeit extreme, manner.

To sum up, in these three sets of passages, Luke provides both positive and negative examples of his redefinition of prodigality and virtuous generosity. From the standpoint of Greco-Roman economic morality, the rich man who failed to provide for Lazarus, the rich ruler, and Ananias and Sapphira all acted in a conventional, morally defensible manner. In the context of Luke's narrative of God's intervention and the resulting

---

134. Habenda autem ratio est rei familiaris quam quidem dilabi sinere flagitiosum est, sed ita ut illiberalitatis avaritiaeque absit suspicio; posse enim liberalitate uti non spoliantem se patrimonio nimirum est pecuniae fructus maximus (Cicero, *Off.* 2.18 [64]).

135. ἐπώλησεν κτῆμα καὶ ἐνοσφίσατο ἀπὸ τῆς τιμῆς, συνειδυίης καὶ τῆς γυναικός, καὶ ἐνέγκας μέρος τι παρὰ τοὺς πόδας τῶν ἀποστόλων ἔθηκεν (Acts 5:1-2).

136. BDAG, 679.

reversal of fortune brought about by that intervention, these economically virtuous characters become examples of illiberality, precisely as a result of their economic prudence. Those who, on the other hand, appeared to be foolhardy and indiscriminate—the host in the parable of the great feast, Zacchaeus, and Barnabas—become the virtuous liberals in the Christian community. Luke has evoked the ideology of the contemporary morality but has upended conventional expectations. Thus it seems clear that he was deliberately attempting to address and persuade those who might have been influenced by the views of the Greco-Roman moralists. As a result, these individuals were sensitive to criticism from their peers and superiors and, therefore, resistant to Luke's alternative subsistence strategy out of fear that it might hinder their social advancement.

Conclusion

In this chapter, I have argued that in Acts 2:42–47 and Acts 4:32–35, Luke articulates an alternative subsistence strategy to be employed by the urban Christian groups for whom he wrote. This strategy was concerned most of all with human need and, therefore, resembles the traditional economic morality of peasant societies. The fact that Luke articulates this vision in the narrative context of an urban (Jerusalem) Christian community for the benefit of his urban Christian audience suggests that he is attempting to revive old rural practices in a new, urban setting. In this sense, Luke's alternative subsistence strategy is both conservative and innovative. It is designed for a marginal subgroup that had been adversely affected by the social and economic impact of the Pax Romana. Rome's empire produced a number of new "winners," local elites who could align themselves with the imperial system and thereby acquire increased honor, power, and wealth. Rome's empire also produced, however, a number of "losers." These tended to be those who already faced regular subsistence struggles brought on by naturally occurring food shortages. Under imperial rule, these struggles became even more serious and pronounced. Thus, Luke's Christian communities were primarily constituted by people such as this, who were used to subsistence struggles, but who found their traditional mechanisms for dealing with food shortage increasingly undermined. The Christian community provided a means by which the old strategies could be employed, but in a new social setting among those who, having been displaced from their home territories to urban areas, had no natural connections with their immediate neighbors.

Even though Luke's alternative subsistence strategy conceived of the community as bearing the responsibility of providing for those who fell below the level necessary for survival, it was the relatively wealthy who assumed the brunt of this burden. This is not surprising, considering that this is consistent with the rural patronage common to peasant societies. In the case of Luke's model, the relatively wealthy are depicted as selling surplus properties and then handing over the proceeds to be administered by the apostles for the purpose of assisting the needy. But who would these wealthy Christians have been? Most scholars would agree that the Christian movement had very few, if any, participants who came from the socially elite class. It is quite plausible, however, that the Christian community could have claimed a fair number of relatively wealthy people who because of their lack of social status could not break into the elite classes. This group could have conceivably included freedmen, successful peasant farmers, affluent artisans, merchants, and perhaps even Roman soldiers and centurions. I would argue that much of what Luke writes concerning economic issues is meant to persuade this group to take a leading role in the alternative subsistence strategy he advances.

Yet as we have seen, there would have been ideological barriers to their adoption of Luke's agenda—most notably the social stigma attached to prodigality. Even though living at the margins of elite society, this group nevertheless took its social and cultural cues from that society. Thus, they would have been determined to conform to the moral expectations of the dominant class and quite sensitive to violations of those norms. On one level they may have eagerly embraced the opportunity to act as benefactors in the Christian community as a way to emulate their counterparts among the elite class. However, they undoubtedly wanted to do this on their own terms and would have resisted any sort of giving that looked indiscriminate and foolhardy. But in the Christian community, where need (and not virtue) was the paramount criterion for a worthy recipient, it is not surprising that their conventional expectations needed to be modified. To achieve this goal, Luke did not simply outline an alternative set of values; he composed a narrative in which these values fit naturally. If Luke's audience were to adopt this narrative as their own, then this would provide the needed ideological support for the alternative economic morality that he promotes in Acts 2 and 4. As we have seen, Luke narrated the restoration of Israel in the events surrounding the life, crucifixion, and resurrection of Jesus. This is a story of the reversal that takes place when Israel's God establishes his rule: the humble are lifted up and the mighty are humbled. This plotline not only supports, but demands, new economic values. Thus, in light of this story Luke could freely redefine concepts such as liberality and prodigality. This quickly became a necessary step in his effort to implement an alternative subsistence strategy in a new urban setting.

So far I have argued that one dimension of the purpose of the early Christian movement, beginning with the efforts of the historical Jesus, continuing with the missionary activity of Paul, and finding expression also in the later years of the first century in Luke-Acts, was an attempt to create an alternative subsistence strategy for a marginal group adversely affected by Roman rule. In the final chapter, I will examine the extent to which this objective remained in the second and third centuries, identifying a continuing interest in care for the poor.

CHAPTER 5

Christian Care for the Poor in the Second and Third Centuries CE

We have seen that care for the poor was a consistent practice of the early Christians. Beginning with Jesus and continuing as the movement expanded into the cities of the Roman Empire over the course of the first century CE, the Christians provided for the needy among them in a manner that resembled the traditional subsistence strategies of rural communities. In the peasant village, relatively wealthy patrons typically provided for their needy neighbors, as much to avoid negative gossip as to garner praise for their generosity. Such a system required a tight-knit community with a moral obligation to meet the basic subsistence needs of every village resident. One aspect of Jesus's work was to bolster these traditional village practices in Galilee during a time when economic growth under Herod Antipas put a strain on their customary subsistence strategies. As the Christian movement expanded beyond Galilee in the middle of the first century into the cities of the Roman Empire, these urban Christian assemblies replicated this basic model of care for the poor by nurturing a strong sense of fellowship and by recruiting relatively wealthy members to play the role of the village patron who would assist the needy.

Even though the Roman Empire in the first century experienced a prolonged period of peace, prosperity, and economic growth, poverty remained. A fundamentally agrarian economy is always vulnerable to food shortages, even in the best of times, because of the unpredictability of annual rainfall, temperature variation, pestilence, and other factors affecting growing conditions. Moreover, as I have argued, the economic prosperity of the Pax Romana may actually have placed further strain on traditional subsistence strategies. Wealthy patrons who in previous times had fulfilled the expectations of their rural communities might now turn their backs on the needy in the hope of new opportunities for upward social mobility. In other words, the general prosperity of the period created even greater challenges for the poor who could no longer count on the formerly reliable generosity of their well-off neighbors.

I have been arguing that the early Christians responded to these economic challenges by creating an alternative subsistence strategy that was both traditional and innovative—traditional in the sense that they replicated the values and practices of the rural village, innovative because they did so in the urban setting of their house churches. Under the Pax Romana a "middling class," enjoyed incomes that ranged from 2.4 to 10 times the level necessary for basic subsistence.[1] Few of these wealthy individuals enjoyed a social status consistent with their relative wealth, but they nevertheless tried to emulate the behaviors of their socially elite counterparts. One way was to be honored as patrons and benefactors. Voluntary associations provided one opportunity for patronage, and it seems likely that Christian assemblies provided another. But in the Christian context, a different set of rules governed the way benefactors distributed their generosity. In the Christian assembly, as in the rural village, need was the primary criterion for determining a recipient's worthiness, whereas in the urban context patrons chose their beneficiaries based on other factors, particularly by assessing their moral virtue. So, when Christian benefactors gave to the poor simply because of their need and not because of their virtue, this seemingly indiscriminate generosity appeared irresponsible and morally questionable to onlookers trained in the norms of virtuous patronage. Because of this, Christian writers and church leaders needed to construct an ideology in which indiscriminate giving based simply on need not only made sense but would become the new model for virtuous generosity in the urban context of the Christian house churches.

When we come to the second and third centuries CE, some interpreters claim that Christian economic behavior changes dramatically from the earlier patterns that we have observed.[2] According to this view, the pristine egalitarianism of the earliest Jesus movement gave way to an economically stratified institution in which the wealthy elite sought honor and attempted to dominate their poor fellow Christians in much

---

1. Scheidel and Friesen, "Size of the Economy."

2. Important examples of this perspective include, Countryman, *Rich Christian*; and Garrison, *Redemptive Almsgiving*.

the same way as in the urban Roman society at-large. Roman Garrison, for example, says that the early second century was a period when "the presence of wealthy members in the community and their dominant influence made it necessary to compromise the demand of renunciation and to promote the virtues of hospitality and charity, the good deeds of the rich."[3] Likewise, William Countryman has noted the tension found in the writings of the church fathers of this era, who on the one hand offer a critique of wealth and on the other promote almsgiving.[4] The existence of these contradictory sentiments, Countryman argues, is explained by "the necessity of the church's officers to keep the rich under control, and yet to keep them attached to the church."[5] The basic problem in the estimation of these scholars is how an originally egalitarian movement, consisting of uniformly poor members, could over time become increasingly stratified between rich and poor. The second and third centuries were a crucial stage in these developments and therefore represent for some scholars a step down the slippery slope toward the corrupt imperial Christianity that emerged in the fourth and fifth centuries CE.

When early Christian care for the poor is analyzed in light of what James C. Scott has observed in peasant societies of more recent times, however, these apparent problems and contradictions are alleviated. For instance, it is unnecessary to assume that either the early Jesus movement or the Pauline communities strove to be "egalitarian."[6] As Scott discovered, poorer members of a peasant community do not resent the wealthy, so long as they fulfill their customary obligation to provide for the needy in times of food shortage.[7] In light of these traditional peasant values, we should perhaps understand Jesus's call to renounce possessions not necessarily as a command to dispose of all that one owns but rather as a call to be willing to share one's surplus when needs arise. Likewise, there is no necessary conflict between Christian "communism" (sometimes ascribed to Luke's summary statements in Acts 2:42–47 and Acts 4:32–35) and "almsgiving." In a peasant society, the wealthy retain private ownership of their possessions but are morally obligated to assist the poor. Further-

---

3. Garrison, *Redemptive Almsgiving*, 111.

4. See Countryman, *Rich Christian*, 149–82 for the culmination of his argument.

5. Ibid., 173.

6. For a challenge to the view that the Jesus movement was egalitarian, see Elliott, "Jesus Was not an Egalitarian," 75–91. For the Pauline communities see Bartchy, "Undermining Ancient Patriarchy," 68–78.

7. Scott, *Moral Economy*, 40–44; 167–79.

more, incentives for almsgiving that promise honor and even spiritual benefits to the giver are similar to the strategies used to motivate rural patrons.[8]

In this chapter, I argue that Christian care for the poor in the second and third centuries exhibited continuity with earlier practices rather than a new direction in Christian economic behavior. The Christian assemblies of this period remained small groups that provided for their needy members by appealing to the relatively wealthy to fund this effort as their moral obligation. Christian care for the poor should be seen as an alternative subsistence strategy because it was an alternative to other types of subsistence strategies organized according to kinship or civic models. And, just as primitive Christian groups did, so the Christian groups of the second and third centuries also developed a sophisticated ideological framework for supporting their alternative subsistence strategy. My plan is first to assess evidence for the practice of Christian care for the poor and then evaluate the ways Christian writers in the second century articulated a legitimating ideology to support the Christians' potentially controversial practices. Before doing so, however, I summarize the political and economic situation of the Roman Empire in the second century and briefly describe the conditions facing the Christian movement in this period.

The Roman Empire and the Christian Movement in the Second Century

In the second century CE, the Roman Empire enjoyed a period of general peace and prosperity, an era advertised on the coins of the day as a "golden age."[9] The emperors of the second century, beginning with Trajan and continuing through Marcus Aurelius, created an orderly, efficient, and enlightened government for a large and diverse empire. Good government allowed for a period of cultural flowering, exemplified by a renaissance in rhetoric known as the Second Sophistic. Economically, commerce and trade flourished and overall prosperity was on the rise. The second century marked the high point of civic euergetism when wealthy men channeled their competitive ambitions into building up the

---

8. Ibid., 40–42.

9. For a helpful summary of the politics and cultural achievements of the second century see Wells, *Roman Empire*, 202–54.

infrastructure of their cities, which benefited the urban rich and poor alike. This "age of ambition," while creating a picture of second-century affluence and prosperity in the archaeological record, proved unsustainable, however, and may represent the origins of the "third-century crisis."[10] Be that as it may, "crisis" was not yet evident in the second century, a period which most experienced as a time of stability and prosperity. As I have stated previously, however, economic growth and general prosperity during the Pax Romana did not end poverty, particularly the short-term, conjunctural poverty that was common in Rome's fundamentally agrarian economy.

It was during the second century that Roman authorities also first became aware of the Christians as a distinct group within Roman society. Pliny's Letter to Trajan, dated to around 113 C.E., is informative in this regard. It is clear from this letter that Pliny had only a vague cognizance of the Christians prior to his term as governor of Bithynia-Pontus. Before his arrival in the province, he knew nothing about Christian beliefs and practices and had never before dealt with them in an official capacity. Soon after assuming his new post, however, Pliny found himself confronted with a number of problems associated with this group and sought guidance from the emperor Trajan about what procedures to follow. We might assume that other Roman magistrates and members of the elite class were also experiencing in the early second century their own first encounters with the Christians, and that they only became more familiar with them over the course of the second century as Christian numbers grew, and their presence became more visible in the cities of the empire. The Christians faced occasional persecution in the second century, though it is impossible to determine how deeply this penetrated the Christian rank and file. There were a handful of high-profile martyrs in the second century, but the question of whether ordinary Christians were vulnerable to persecution at the hands of imperial authorities is a matter of debate.[11] While Trajan's response to Pliny's inquiry[12] suggests

10. Brown, *Making of Late Antiquity*, 27–53.

11. See Moss, *Myth of Persecution*, for the view that persecution in the second century was a myth created by later Christians of the fourth and fifth centuries to justify their own dominant position in society. Moss exaggerates her case but does raise the legitimate question of how pervasive persecution actually was in this period.

12. "You have followed the right course of procedure, my dear Pliny, in your examination of the cases of persons charged with being Christians, for it is impossible to lay down a general rule to a fixed formula. These people must not be hunted out; if they are brought before you and the charge against them is proved, they must be punished,

that Roman magistrates were not interested in conducting a thorough campaign to eradicate the Christian movement by pursuing, arresting, prosecuting, and executing every individual Christian, it does seems likely that the Christians faced grassroots opposition from unbelieving family members, neighbors, slave owners, employers, and patrons. As a result, Christian communities would have been looked to that much more as an alternative subsistence strategy by individual members who now faced not only naturally occurring food shortages but also the negative economic repercussions of their faith commitment.

The Model of Christian Care for the Poor in the Second Century

I now turn to the Christian apologetic literature of the second century to show that the practice of Christian care for the poor in this era remained consistent with the practices of earlier generations of Christians. The second-century apologists provide us with detailed descriptions of the characteristic beliefs and behaviors of the Christians of this era, including their practice of care for the poor. Scholars debate the audience and purpose of the apologies. These texts were ostensibly written for a nonbelieving Roman audience, often being addressed to emperors and other Roman officials.[13] Fergus Millar has established that this is indeed possible; Roman emperors devoted a significant portion of their time and energy to hearing, studying, and offering judgments on legal matters.[14] Regarding the Justin's *First Apology*, Millar states, "It is at least as convincing, and far more economical, an explanation of its contents and its concrete reference to events, to suggest that it actually was presented—or was intended to be presented—to the emperors, as that it is an elaborate literary fiction."[15] Some scholars, however, find it implausible that emperors

---

but in the case of anyone who denies that he is a Christian, and makes it clear that he is not by offering prayers to our gods, he is to be pardoned as a result of his repentance however suspect his past conduct may be. But pamphlets circulated anonymously must play no part in any accusation. They create the worst sort of precedent and are quite out of keeping with the spirit of our age" (Pliny, *Ep.* 10:97).

13. For example, Justin's *First Apology* was addressed to the emperor Antoninus Pius. Tertullian addressed more generically the "rulers (*antistites*) of the Roman Empire."

14. Millar, *Emperor in the Roman World*, 203–72, 507–49.

15. Ibid., 563. T. D. Barnes likewise concludes that the *Embassy* of Athenagoras was indeed also addressed to the emperors, Marcus Aurelius and Commodus ("Embassy").

would actually consider such petitions from the Christians, concluding that the *Apology* to an emperor was instead a literary fiction, intended for internal consumption and designed to alleviate the Christians' own fears and doubts about committing to this new association and its peculiar beliefs and practices.[16] In either case, the apologists' descriptions of the Christians, in my opinion, can be taken as basically reliable, allowing, perhaps, for a certain degree of idealization, if not exaggeration, on some points. If written to Roman magistrates, it would be essential for the apologists to represent Christian beliefs and practices accurately; any sort of cover-up could be easily discovered and would prove dangerous to the Christian cause. If, on the other hand, the apologists wrote for a believing audience, their appeals would also need to ring true if their goal was to allay the fears, doubts, and second thoughts of their Christian brothers and sisters. Unless we are willing to assume that the Christian apologists completely fabricated their reports, we may take their descriptions as basically accurate, particularly regarding their economic practices and care for the poor, outward behaviors that could be readily verified by believers and unbelievers alike. Contemporary pagan writers do indicate, in fact, that the Christians were known to be generous and practiced a form of communal sharing. In his *Death of Peregrinus*, for example, Lucian of Samosata portrays the Christians as gullible dupes tricked by Peregrinus into believing that he was a Christian prophet and supporting him while he was in prison.[17] While obviously satirical, Lucian's caricature of Christian generosity must have represented an element of truth for Lucian's audience, who may have observed similar patterns of behavior among the Christians. In light of this, we find in the apologists' descriptions a sympathetic, insider's view of a phenomenon that Lucian had observed and criticized from a distance. In the paragraphs that follow, I examine two prominent second-century examples, the *First Apology* of Justin, composed in the middle of the second century (c. 155), and Tertullian's *Apology*, composed near the end of the second century (c. 197). In these texts we find a description of Christian care for the poor that closely resembles the practice of Christians from earlier periods.

As I mentioned above, Justin addressed his *First Apology* to the emperor Antoninus Pius and in it defends a litany of Christian beliefs, theological claims, and behaviors that have been either misunderstood,

---

16. See Edwards, Goodman, Price, and Rowland, "Introduction"; see also Barnes, *Tertullian*, 109–10.

17. Lucian, *Peregr.* 11–13.

misrepresented, or maligned by their pagan critics. For example, Justin rejects the charge of atheism (5–6), while adding his own critique of the foolishness of pagan idolatry (9). He argues that God is not served through material things, animal sacrifices, offerings of incense, and the like, but rather by virtuous behaviors such as temperance, justice, and philanthropy (10). Christians, Justin says, seek no new human kingdom besides Rome and are thus no threat for sedition or revolution (17); rather, the kingdom they hope for is eternal and divine (11). Justin claims that the Christians worship God with a rational mind, while the pagan worshipers of images implicitly do not (13). Christianity is rooted in antiquity. The prophets of the Old Testament promised the coming of Christ (31–53), the great Plato was indebted to Moses (59) and even advanced a doctrine of the cross (60). Justin explains Christian baptism (61) and defends the sacrament against pagan imitations (62). He then explains the Eucharist, the sacrament subject to so much popular misunderstanding (66). In the penultimate paragraph of the apology, Justin discusses the Christians' habit of gathering on the first day of the week, another Christian practice subject to much rumor and misrepresentation, and seeks to set the record straight by emphasizing the edifying nature of these weekly meetings.

It is in this paragraph on the Christian gatherings that Justin briefly describes their practice of care for the poor because it was the weekly assembly that provided the context and structure for the Christians' alternative subsistence strategy. The relevant text segments are brief. Justin states at the beginning of the paragraph, "And the wealthy among us help the needy; and we always keep together; and for all things wherewith we are supplied, we bless the maker of all though his Son Jesus Christ, and through the Holy Ghost."[18] Later in the paragraph he continues:

> And they who are well to do, and willing, give what each thinks fit; and what is collected is deposited with the president, who succors the orphans and the widows and those who, through sickness or any other cause, are in want, and those who are in bonds and the strangers sojourning among us, and in a word takes care of all those who are in need (67.6).[19]

---

18. Ἡμεῖς δὲ μετὰ ταῦτα λοιπὸν ἀεὶ τούτων ἀλλήλους ἀναμιμνήσκομεν· καὶ οἱ ἔχοντες τοῖς λειπομένοις πᾶσιν ἐπικουροῦμεν, καὶ σύνεσμεν ἀλλήλοις ἀεί. ἐπὶ πᾶσί τε οἷς προσφερόμεθα εὐλογοῦμεν τὸν ποιητὴν τῶν πάντων διὰ τοῦ υἱοῦ αὐτοῦ Ἰησοῦ Χριστοῦ καὶ διὰ πνεύματος τοῦ ἁγίου (1 Apol. 67.1–2).

19 οἱ εὐποροῦντες δὲ καὶ βουλόμενοι κατὰ προαίρεσιν ἕκαστος τὴν ἑαυτοῦ ὃ βούλεται

Let me make three observations about Justin's description. First, Justin emphasizes need as the basic criterion for determining worthy recipients of aid. At the beginning of the passage, he says that the Christian assembly cares for those who "are lacking" or "in need" (τοῖς λειπομένοις). This emphasis on need is consistent with what we have seen previously in Christian charitable giving, in contrast to typical Greco-Roman generosity in which the recipient's moral virtue was a vital consideration. Once again, this concern for need is characteristic of rural subsistence strategies, which I have been arguing provided the basis for the Christian practice of care for the poor. Furthermore, Justin specifies the kinds of "needy" people he has in mind. He mentions "orphans and widows" (ὀρφανοῖς τε καὶ χήραις) and those who were needy as a result of "illness" or "disease" (τοῖς διὰ νόσον). His reference to "those in bonds" (τοῖς ἐν δεσμοῖς οὖσι) may be to Christians imprisoned because of their Christian commitment,[20] or he could be referring to some form of debt bondage, in which case Christian assistance may have involved paying the debt in order to secure the bound person's freedom.[21] Finally Justin refers to resident foreigners within the Christian community (τοῖς παρεπιδήμοις οὖσι ξένοις). This group may have included Christian apostles, missionaries, or messengers from other cities, or perhaps Christian traders and merchants who traveled frequently. But it is also likely that Justin refers here to those who had migrated to Rome in search of employment because of adverse social and economic conditions back home. Justin's list of types of needy people suggests that the Christian community was as much concerned with "conjunctural" as with "structural" poverty.[22] We can assume that Christians assisted the chronically impoverished in their assemblies, but with the exception of orphans and widows, the reasons for need Justin mentions in this passage are temporary conditions requiring short-term assistance from the community.

Second, Justin specifies that it is the wealthy who take the leading role in the Christians' charitable giving. In the first part of the passage, Justin writes that "the haves" (οἱ ἔχοντες) provide for the "have-nots"

δίδωσι, καὶ τὸ συλλεγόμενον παρὰ τῷ προεστῶτι ἀποτίθεται, καὶ αὐτὸς ἐπικουρεῖ ὀρφανοῖς τε καὶ χήραις, καὶ τοῖς διὰ νόσον ἢ δι' ἄλλην αἰτίαν λειπομένοις, καὶ τοῖς ἐν δεσμοῖς οὖσι, καὶ τοῖς παρεπιδήμοις οὖσι ξένοις, καὶ ἁπλῶς πᾶσι τοῖς ἐν χρείᾳ οὖσι κηδεμὼν γίνεται (1 Apol. 67.6)

20. Osiek, "Ransom of Captives."

21. See de Ste. Croix, *Class Struggle*, 162–70, on debt bondage.

22. In chapter 1 see my discussion of the distinction.

(τοῖς λειπομένοις) and then later says that it is "those who prosper" (οἱ εὐποροῦντες) who assist the needy. As we have seen previously, while the Christians may have sometimes resorted to sacrificial sharing among the poor, the preferred means of supporting their alternative subsistence strategy was to appeal to the relatively wealthy to play the leading role in providing assistance. Moreover, we need not assume that Justin's Christian assembly included members of the social elite class. The expanding Roman economy of this period created an upwardly mobile segment of the population, which was not only personally secure against food shortage but also had a level of surplus income that could be used for discretionary spending. Consistent with this interpretation, Justin makes the point that when the wealthy give to support the poor, they do so voluntarily, and the amount they give is according to their own decision. He says that the wealthy who give are the ones who are willing to do so (οἱ εὐποροῦντες δὲ καὶ βουλόμενοι), and each determines for himself or herself the amount that he will give (κατὰ προαίρεσιν ἕκαστος τὴν ἑαυτοῦ, ὃ βούλεται δίδωσι). The point is not that the wealthy felt no compulsion to give; in the peasant village and in the early Christian assemblies, the community expected the wealthy to provide for the needy and rewarded them with honor when they complied and sanctioned them with criticism and gossip when they failed to do so. Justin's point may be instead that there were no formal obligations, such as the membership dues of *collegia* or the civic liturgies imposed upon the decurion class. In other words, the financial expectations upon the wealthy in the Christian assemblies were informal, though the community's expectations had no less persuasive force because of this. Justin's description here is, therefore, consistent with the characteristics of the peasant moral economy. Relatively wealthy Christians were persuaded to play the role of rural patrons. This was a more sustainable subsistence strategy than sacrificial sharing among the poor and was built upon a morality that did not necessarily require economic equality among all members but rather simply expected the relatively wealthy to share from their surplus resources when needs arose in the community. The wealthy in Justin's community were not expected to renounce all their possessions but rather were under informal moral pressure to assist the poor from their discretionary income.

A third observation is that Justin's description suggests that the Christians focused on caring for their own needy members rather than conducting a benevolence program for the poor in the society at large. As Justin describes it, care for the poor occurred in the context of the communal gatherings of the Christians on the first day of the week. Likewise, his statement that the Christians were "continually together with one another" (καὶ σύνεσμεν ἀλλήλοις ἀεί) indicates the strong communal bonds upon which care for the poor was predicated. This does not mean that Christians did not welcome needy individuals from the outside or that the Christians were unconcerned with plight of the poor in Greco-Roman society. Rather it is to acknowledge the very personal, face-to-face form in which generosity typically occurred in antiquity. The key to the success of the Christians was that they were able to construct an ideological system that brought together individuals for cooperation on the basis of a relationship not defined by citizenship or blood kinship. Thus, the communal model of Christian care for the poor was not an insular or exclusive practice but rather the only feasible means of providing for the needy. The Christian assembly provided the necessary context and structure by which wealthy Christians could assist their poor brothers and sisters.

Tertullian's treatment of Christian care for the poor in the thirty-ninth chapter of his *Apology* builds upon Justin's discussion. Tertullian looked to Justin's *First Apology* as a model for his own work, so it is not surprising that he makes use of many of the same arguments of his predecessor. Most interpreters agree, however, that Tertullian's *Apology* advances beyond earlier examples of the genre because of his masterful use of ancient rhetorical technique.[23] Tertullian's description of Christian care for the needy also adds more specificity to Justin's picture, perhaps because he intended to relate his discussion to the actual situation of the church in Carthage rather than simply reiterate standard themes inherited from those who had dealt with the subject previously.

Like Justin, Tertullian identifies types of needy people but includes some not mentioned by his predecessor. He says, for example, that gifts to the common fund were used to "support and bury poor people" indicating a point of similarity between the Christian assemblies and other voluntary associations in the Roman world that provided burials and funerary feasts for their members.[24] He refers also to assisting "boys and girls destitute of means and parents."[25] Tertullian may be referring to

---

23. See Sider, *Ancient Rhetoric*.

24. egenis alendis humandisque (*1 Apol.* 39.6). See Harland for a discussion of the funerary practices of voluntary associations (*Associations, Synagogues, and Congregations*, 84–86).

25. et pueris ac puellis re ac parentibus destitutis (*1 Apol.* 39.6).

orphans here, as in Justin's description, but he could also have in mind exposed children who were claimed and raised by the Christian community, a topic of particular interest for him.[26] Rather than Justin's widows, Tertullian mentions "old persons confined to the house," most likely the aged in the Christian community who, for whatever reason, could not depend upon the support of their children, which was the typical means of elder-support in antiquity.[27] Tertullian also mentions those who had suffered "shipwreck," referring perhaps to maritime traders (Carthage was a prosperous port city in the western Mediterranean) who had lost their livelihood at sea.[28] Though in some cases these merchants were relatively affluent, they might experience need as a result of unfortunate catastrophic circumstances. Tertullian also refers to those banished to mines, exiled to islands, or shut up in prison because of their Christian confession.[29] Tertullian's categorization of the needy demonstrates his concern not only for short-term, "conjunctural" poverty (shipwreck) but also for situations of long-term need: children without parents, the aged, and those imprisoned for their faith commitment. In short, Tertullian's description suggests that the Christian assembly in Carthage acted as an alternative subsistence community and responded to need that resulted from a variety of circumstances.

Tertullian also agrees with Justin that the relatively wealthy in the community are the ones who should bear the financial burden of care for the needy. Through a careful analysis of Tertullian's writings, Georg Schöllgen has argued that the Christian community of Tertullian's day did not consist solely of the lowest classes but was made up of a wide spectrum of the population, including a number who possessed wealth and relatively high levels of education and social status, though not belonging to the ruling class.[30] Schöllgen's view is supported by the findings of Scheidel and Friesen, who identify a "middling class" of relatively wealthy non-elites in Roman society, a key premise in this present study. The presence of this relatively wealthy group explains Tertullian's need to

---

26. 1 Apol. 9.17.

27. iamque domesticis senibus (1 Apol. 39.6). Sider (*Christian and Pagan*, 60) suggests another possible translation, "aged domestic servants," presumably those too old to work.

28. item naufragis (1 Apol. 39.6).

29. et si qui in metallis et si qui in insulis vel in custodiis, dumtaxat ex causa dei sectae, alumni confessionis suae fiunt (1 Apol. 39.6).

30. Schöllgen, *Ecclesia Sordida*, 13–14.

distinguish the benevolence practices of the Christian community from that of pagan associations (*collegia*) with which they would have likely been personally familiar. One important difference is that the gifts to the communal fund were not spent on "feasts, drinking parties, and disagreeable devouring," but rather were given to the poor.[31] Likewise, the Christian common meal was not a lavish affair but rather quite modest and was focused on simple sustenance, especially for the needy. Tertullian writes:

> Our feast explains itself by its name. The Greeks call it "love." Whatever it costs, our outlay in the name of piety is gain, since with the good things of the feast we benefit the needy; not as it is with you, do parasites aspire to the glory of satisfying their licentious propensities, selling themselves for a belly-feast to all disgraceful treatment—but as it is with God himself, a peculiar respect is shown to the lowly.[32]

Instead of contributing to a fund to support lavish banquets for members of the *collegia*, relatively wealthy Christian patrons hosted meals that provided for the basic needs of the poor.

Tertullian also stresses that giving in the Christian community was entirely voluntary, another difference from pagan associations, which imposed mandatory membership dues. Tertullian writes: "Though we have our treasure-chest, it is not made up of purchase-money, as of a religion that has its price. On the monthly day, if he likes, each puts in a small donation; but only if it be his pleasure, and only if he be able: for there is no compulsion; all is voluntary."[33] Several points can be highlighted

---

31. Haec quasi deposita pietatis sunt. Nam inde non epulis nec potaculis nec ingratis voratrinis dispensator (*1 Apol.* 39.6). Harland observes, however, that comments such as Tertullian's may represent the common slander of one group against its rivals (*Associations, Synagogues, and Congregations*, 74–75). It is conceivable that the feasts of the voluntary associations may also have been designed, in part at least, as a means of alleviating the need of their poor members; thus, the associations may also have been concerned with providing an "alternative subsistence strategy" for their members.

32. Cena nostra de nomine rationem sui ostendit: Id vocatur quod dilectio penes Graecos. Quantiscumque sumptibus constet, lucrum est pietatis nomine facere sumptum, siquidem inopes quosque refrigerio isto iuvamus, non qua penes vos parasiti affectant ad gloriam famulandae libertatis sub auctoramento ventris inter contumelias saginandi, sed qua penes deum maior est contemplatio mediocrium (*1 Apol.* 39.16).

33. Etiam, si quod arcae genus est, non de honoraria summa quasi redemptae religionis congregator. Modicum unusquisque stipem menstrua die, vel cum velit et si modo velit et si modo possit, apponit. Nam nemo compellitur, sed sponte confert (*1*

in this statement. First of all, contributions to the communal fund were made monthly, presumably on a Sunday when the church was gathered and on a day regularly designated for that purpose (the first Sunday of the month, for example). The regularity of this system would allow for advance planning on the part of those who chose to give. Tertullian also states that the donations are small (*modicum*) and are given only if the donor is able and if he or she desires to do so (*vel cum velit et si modo velit et si modo possit, apponit*). He emphasizes that donors are not compelled to give; they give voluntarily (*Nam nemo compellitur, sed sponte confert*). The voluntary nature of the giving is consistent with the pattern that we have seen throughout this study. Relatively wealthy members of the Christian movement were not typically required to renounce all their possessions to give to the general fund but rather retained private ownership and gave regularly from their surplus wealth.

Finally, Tertullian, like Justin, implies that Christian care for the poor was directed toward members of the community and not generally to the needy in society at large. Tertullian uses the language of kinship to describe relationships among Christians in this section of the *Apology*, arguing that Christian "brotherhood" is in fact superior to that of pagan blood kin. Whereas natural brothers dispute about family possessions, the Christians do not:

> But on this very account, perhaps, we are regarded as having less claim to be held true brothers, that no tragedy makes a noise about our brotherhood, or that the family possessions, which generally destroy brotherhood among you, create fraternal bonds among us. One in mind and soul, we do not hesitate to share our earthly goods with one another. All things are common among us but our wives.[34]

As we have seen from the beginning, Christians used sibling language to indicate their fictive kinship relationship. This assumption about the nature of the Christian fellowship enabled them to practice a generalized form of reciprocity in which a return, though expected for an act of generosity, could be delayed and different in kind.[35] The point here is that the

---

Apol. 39.5).

34. Sed eo fortasse minus legitimi existimamur, quia nulla de nostra fraternitate tragoedia exclamat, vel quia ex substantia familiari fratres sumus, quae penes vos fere dirimit fraternitatem. Itaque qui animo animcommunicatione dubitamus. Omnia indiscreta sunt apud nos praeter uxores (*1 Apol.* 39.10-11).

35. Hellerman, *Ancient Church as Family*, 180-82.

Christians created an alternative subsistence strategy modeled after the practices of the peasant village, in which the intimate relations of that setting insured that the basic subsistence needs of all community members were met. While the Christians were presumably concerned about the general problem of poverty, they addressed it in the very tangible way of providing for the needy in their own assemblies.

Let me highlight three key points about the practice of Christian care for the poor that emerge from the apologies of Justin and Tertullian. First, Justin and Tertullian agree that Christian generosity was directed toward the needy. This probably included some who were chronically poor, but when the writers discuss specific categories of needy people, they refer especially to those who were experiencing need that was temporary and brought on by specific, adverse circumstances. This supports a picture of vulnerable people coming together for mutual assistance, presumably because more traditional strategies had failed them. A second observation is that it was the relatively wealthy who provided most of the resources for the Christian subsistence strategy. This is consistent with the pattern of peasant societies in which a rural patron is praised as good and honorable if he uses his surplus to supply the needs of his neighbors during times of shortage. These sources also support the observation that Christian care for the needy was for members of the community rather than for the society's poor in general, and that this was made possible by the intimacy of the Christian's fellowship expressed in their use of kinship language.

Ideological Support for Christian Care for the Poor in the Second Century

I turn now to second-century texts that provide ideological support for the Christian practice of care for the poor. Whereas the apologies of Justin and Tertullian give us a straightforward description of the Christians' alternative subsistence strategy, these texts provide a rationale for behavior that, as we have seen, appeared irresponsible and morally questionable under the scrutiny of conventional assumptions about virtuous generosity. As Christians had in earlier generations, these writers supply their readers with extensive arguments for adopting new patterns of charitable giving. Though the texts I consider here are diverse in terms of literary genre, they share certain fundamental theological beliefs and values. My selection of sources here is not meant to be comprehensive but rather representative of the diverse ways in which second-century Christians sought to support their practice of care for the poor.

The "Two Ways" Literature

Care for the poor features prominently in the Christian "Two Ways" literature of the second century. The Two Ways model of theological and moral instruction originated in the Hebrew Bible and continued to be utilized extensively in Second Temple Jewish literature.[36] Its use in the *Didache* and in the Epistle of Barnabas suggests that various Christian groups, perhaps especially those in a Jewish milieu which had not yet clearly separated from the Jews, also found this instructional form to be particularly effective. The essence of its teaching is that there are two ways of life: the way of darkness that leads to judgment and destruction and the way of light characterized by obedience to God and is rewarded with abundant life. The appeal of this system is in its simplicity; there is no need for complex moral reasoning because the choice is clear. The way which leads to life is indeed rigorous and difficult. It requires constant watchfulness and effort, but by choosing this path, one knew quite clearly what very specific behaviors were required while also being assured of the reward that he or she would one day receive. Two examples will be used here to illustrate this genre and its treatment of care for the poor: the *Didache* 1–5 and the Epistle of Barnabas 19–20. Early second-century Alexandria is the generally accepted provenance of the *Epistle of Barnabas*,[37] while most scholars assume that the *Didache* originated in Syria or Palestine also in the late first or early second century CE.[38]

In the Two Ways system of morality, care for the poor is required of those who strive to follow the path that leads to life. The Epistle of Barnabas, for example, encourages the sharing of possessions in the Christian community: "Share everything with your neighbor, and do not say: 'It is private property'; for, if you are sharers in what is imperishable,

---

36. The Book of Deuteronomy and the Deuteronomic history assume the Two Ways model as a guide for obedience to the covenant. Deuteronomy 28, for example, clearly outlines the paths of obedience and disobedience, along with their corresponding rewards and punishments. See also Psalm 1, *Testaments of the Twelve Patriarchs*, and Qumran's *Manual of Discipline* for examples of the Two Ways model.

37. Treat, "Barnabas, Epistle of," 613.

38. Kraft, "Didache," 197.

how much more so in the things that perish"[39] Similarly, the Didache states: "Do not turn away from the needy; rather share everything with your brother and do not say: 'It is private property.' If you are sharers in what is imperishable, how much more so in the things that perish!"[40] One thing to notice here is the emphasis on helping the needy. As we have seen previously, the early Christians resembled the peasant village in prioritizing need as the basic criterion for determining the worthiness of the recipient of generosity. Another thing to note is that these citations provide a link between the perishable and the imperishable, the temporal and the eternal. A gift to the needy, therefore, is not merely a momentary, inconsequential act but an act that has eternal significance. And this provides an incentive for generosity: the temporal act of giving to the needy is implicitly linked to one's eternal reward.

On the other hand, the path that leads to destruction is filled with those who stand against the poor. The *Didache* warns that the way of death is the way of those who "love vanities, and fee hunters; of men that have no heart for the poor, are not concerned about the oppressed, do not know their Maker; of murderers of children, destroyers of God's image; of men that turn away from the needy, oppress the afflicted, act as counsels for the rich, are unjust judges of the poor."[41] Some of the evidence here suggests the influence of the values of the city. For example, "men who love vanities" suggests a fascination with urban culture that spends its resources on frivolous pleasures. "Those who act as counsels of the rich and are unjust judges of the poor" may have been wealthy non-elites who served as agents of the ruling class: managers of their business affairs, overseers of their properties, or similar types of retainer roles. All of this may suggest a scenario in which imperial rule was creating a number of social and economic opportunities for the non-elite, perhaps rural-dwelling, wealthy, who were being drawn into the ethos of the city while turning their backs on their moral obligation to the needy in the village community. Both the teaching of the historical Jesus and the Two Ways

39. κοινωνήσεις ἐν πᾶσιν τῷ πλησίον σου καὶ οὐκ ἐρεῖς ἴδια εἶναι· εἰ γὰρ ἐν τῷ ἀφθάρτῳ κοινωνοί ἐστε, πόσῳ μᾶλλον ἐν τοῖς φθαρτοῖς; (*Barn.* 19.8).

40. Οὐκ ἀποστραφήσῃ τὸν ἐνδεόμενον, συγκοινωνήσεις δὲ πάντα τῷ ἀδελφῷ σου καὶ οὐκ ἐρεῖς ἴδια εἶναι· εἰ γὰρ ἐν τῷ ἀθανάτῳ κοινωνοί ἐστε, πόσῳ μᾶλλον ἐν τοῖς θνητοῖς; (*Did.* 4.8).

41. μάταια ἀγαπῶντες, διώκοντες ἀνταπόδομα, οὐκ ἐλεοῦντες πτωχόν, οὐ πονοῦντες ἐπὶ καταπονουμένῳ, οὐ γινώσκοντες τὸν ποιήσαντα αὐτούς, φονεῖς τέκνων, φθορεῖς πλάσματος θεοῦ, ἀποστρεφόμενοι τὸν ἐνδεόμενον, καταπονοῦντες τὸν θλιβόμενον, πλουσίων παράκλητοι, πενήτων ἄνομοι κριταί (*Did.* 5.2).

instruction attempted to recall this class of people back to a traditional form of economic morality. It is important to note here that the way of darkness is populated not only by those who actively oppress the needy but also by those who show indifference toward them. In the Two Ways system of morality there is little difference between those who actively exploit the poor and those who stand by and do nothing. When it comes to care for the poor, the Epistle of Barnabas and the *Didache* offer a clear choice: providing for the needy is an essential activity for those who seek to inherit eternal life and avoid the path of destruction.

The Shepherd of Hermas

The Shepherd of Hermas also provides examples of ideas that second-century Christians used to give legitimacy to their practice of care for the poor. The Shepherd was written for the Christian community in Rome most likely in the mid-second century.[42] The work consists of three parts. It begins with a series of visions received by Hermas for the church in Rome. Though he does not use the title in reference to himself, Hermas is a Christian prophet, a class of Christian leaders in this era whose presence in the community points to the ongoing importance of revelation in the pastoral ministry of the church, particularly for addressing the problem of postbaptismal sin.[43] A series of commandments, the Mandates, come next and provide direct moral instruction to the church based on themes arising out of the Visions. The third part of the work is the Similitudes, a set of parables that depict ideal relations among members in the Christian community.

Care for the poor is a prominent theme in the Shepherd of Hermas, a fact that suggests not only that addressing economic need was a key challenge facing the church but also that a proper relationship between the rich and poor was believed to provide a remedy for postbaptismal sin. According to Helen Rhee, the Shepherd is an apocalyptic text that reflects an important ideological shift in the second and third centuries.[44] Whereas apocalyptic texts of an earlier period featured the "pious poor" and the "wicked rich" and an eschatological "great reversal," the texts of the second and third centuries offer more dominantly "the symbiosis or

42. Snyder, "Hermas' The Shepherd," 148.
43. Lane Fox, *Pagans and Christians*, 388.
44. Rhee, *Loving the Poor*, 58–62.

reciprocity theme."[45] This change in tone may reflect the church's need to integrate the increasing numbers of wealthy Christians during this era.[46] Yet, as we have seen, arguments designed to persuade the relatively affluent Christians to give generously to the poor were part of their alternative subsistence strategy from the beginning.

Evidence in the text also suggests that the practices associated with care for the poor in the church of Rome at this time continued to follow the basic patterns that we have seen so far in this study. The relatively wealthy are encouraged to give to the poor simply on the basis of their need without reference to any other set of criteria for judging their worthiness. Mandate 2, for example, states, "Practice goodness; and from the rewards of your labors, which God gives you, give to all the needy in simplicity, not hesitating as to whom you are to give or not to give."[47] The wealthy in this church are not members of the Roman elite class but more likely individuals of humble status whose economic condition has recently improved. In Carolyn Osiek's view these would include "members of the lower classes of Rome who have enough money to advance in the acquisition of possessions and in social standing . . . freedmen and women who made up the majority of the tradesmen, craftsmen, and small business people of the city, and Hermas himself belonged to this class."[48] As we will see, care for the poor played a critical role in Hermas's pastoral vision for the Christian community in Rome as reflected in his efforts to provide theological legitimacy for this practice.

To begin with, the Shepherd of Hermas as a whole rests upon a fundamental theological premise summarized in the concluding paragraph of the fifth and final vision. After writing down the commandments and similitudes revealed to him by the shepherd, Hermas says to his audience: "If then, when you have heard these, ye keep them and walk in them, and practice them with pure minds, you will receive from the Lord all that He has promised to you. But if, after you have heard them, ye do not repent, but continue to add to your sins, then ye shall receive from the Lord the opposite things."[49] The theological rationale here is very

45. Ibid., 59.
46. Ibid.
47. Ἐργάζου τὸ ἀγαθὸν καὶ ἐκ τῶν κόπων σου ὧν ὁ θεὸς δίδωσίν σοι πᾶσιν ὑστερουμένοις δίδου ἁπλῶς, μὴ διστάζων, τίνι δῷς ἢ τίνι μὴ δῷς (Herm. Mand. 2.4).
48. Osiek, *Rich and Poor*, 136. The work of Scheidel and Friesen ("Size of the Economy") supports Osiek's conjecture.
49. Ἐὰν οὖν ἀκούσαντες αὐτὰς φυλάξητε καὶ ἐν αὐταῖς πορευθῆτε καὶ ἐργάσησθε

similar to that of the Two Ways teaching discussed above. The Lord is a God who keeps promises, rewarding those who obey his commands and judging the guilty accordingly. Similarly, the first Mandate states, "First of all, believe that there is one God who created and finished all things, and made all things out of nothing . . . Have faith therefore in Him, and fear Him; and fearing Him, exercise self-control. Keep these commands, and you will cast away from you all wickedness, and put on the strength of righteousness, and live to God, if you keep this commandment."[50] Thus, the subsistence strategy of Hermas's Christian community rested on the fundamental belief that the sovereign, creator God commands care for the poor and rewards those who are obedient to his will.

The first similitude further explores this fundamental theological premise as it relates to Christian care for the poor. In this parable, the experience of the Christian is likened to that of a foreigner who lives temporarily in a city that is not his true home. He hopes to return to his native city one day, but Hermas points out that if in the meantime he adopts the laws, customs, and values of the place where he temporarily resides, then his future homecoming will be spoiled because he would come back as a foreigner and no longer a citizen. This parable of course is speaking of the inherent conflict between the empire of Rome and the kingdom of God. And in this conflict, the Christians to whom Hermas wrote faced a choice. Would they become "citizens" of Rome, adopting the customs and values of the city in which they were merely temporary residents? Or would they continue to observe the laws of their home city, the heavenly city, anticipating their eventual return? Once again, the options in this moral system are simple and clear in a manner reminiscent of the Two Ways theology.

The image of the two cities was especially poignant for Hermas's audience of Christians in Rome because many of them must have felt existential anxieties about citizenship and social status. These relatively wealthy non-elites were undoubtedly sensitive about the ambiguity of their social position, and thus, quite aware of what it would take for

---

αὐτὰς ἐν καθαρᾷ καρδίᾳ, ἀπολήμψεσθε ἀπὸ τοῦ κυρίου, ὅσα ἐπηγγείλατο ὑμῖν· ἐὰν δὲ ἀκούσαντες μὴ μετανοήσητε, ἀλλ'ἔτι προσθῆτε ταῖς ἁμαρτίαις ὑμῶν, ἀπολήμψεσθε παρὰ τοῦ κυρίου τὰ ἐναντία (Herm. Vis. 5.7).

50. Πρῶτον πάντων πίστευσον, ὅτι εἷς ἐστὶν ὁ θεός, ὁ τὰ πάντα κτίσας καὶ καταρτίσας καὶ ποιήσας ἐκ τοῦ μὴ ὄντος . . . Πίστευσον οὖν αὐτῷ καὶ φοβήθητι αὐτόν, φοβηθεὶς δὲ ἐγκράτευσαι. Ταῦτα φύλασσε, καὶ ἀποβαλεῖς πᾶσαν πονηρίαν ἀπὸ σεαυτοῦ καὶ ἐνδύσῃ πᾶσαν ἀρετὴν δικαιοσύνης καὶ ζήσῃ τῷ θεῷ ἐὰν φυλάξῃς τὴν ἐντολὴν ταύτην (Herm. Mand. 1.1-2).

them to make inroads into elite society, if even only at the margins as clients and retainers of the upper classes. The self-consciousness of this upwardly mobile, non-elite segment of the Roman population had significant implications for their economic attitudes and behaviors. In the previous chapter, I argued that Luke attempted to redefine the concept of "prodigality," and I think Hermas must have had a similar purpose as well. As he reflects on the economic consequences related to the image of the two cities, Hermas concludes that the economic morality of one city cannot be reconciled with that of the other. To the temporary sojourner who might be tempted to adopt the economic morality of the earthly city he says there is a better way, one consistent with his true citizenship:

> Instead of lands, therefore, buy afflicted souls, according as each one is able, and visit widows and orphans, and do not overlook them; and spend your wealth and all your preparations, which ye received from the Lord, upon such lands and houses. For to this end did the Master make you rich, that you might perform these services unto Him; and it is much better to purchase such lands, and possessions, and houses, as you will find in your own city when you come to reside in it.[51]

We find here a nice summary of the alternative subsistence strategy promoted by Hermas and the ideological framework he created to support it. Since wealth is a gift from God, one should not hoard it or even invest it in lands and houses for his or her own personal enrichment; rather, he should use his surplus wealth to support afflicted souls, widows, and orphans. As we have seen before, the point was not that the wealthy should renounce all their possessions or even that they should give more than they could really afford. Rather, the wealthy person gives from his surplus, "according to what he is able" (καθά τις δυνατός ἐστι), in a pattern reminiscent of the peasant moral economy in which economic equality in the village is not the goal but rather that everyone's subsistence needs are met. This alternative set of economic values and behaviors finds validation in the fact that caring for the needy is the will of the sovereign God, who rewards one's earthly generosity with heavenly riches.

---

51. ἀντὶ ἀγρῶν οὖν ἀγοράζετε ψυχὰς θλιβομένας καθά τις δυνατός ἐστι, καὶ χήρας καὶ ὀρφανοὺς ἐπισκέπτεσθε καὶ παραβλέπετε αὐτούς, καὶ τὸν πλοῦτον ὑμῶν καὶ τὰς παρατάξεις πάσας εἰς τοιούτους ἀγροὺς καὶ οἰκίας δαπανᾶτε, ἃς ἐλάβετε παρὰ τοῦ θεοῦ. εἰς τοῦτο γὰρ ἐπλούτισεν ὑμᾶς ὁ δεσπότης, ἵνα τούτας τὰς διακονίας τελέσητε αὐτῷ· πολὺ βέλτιόν ἐστι τοιούτους ἀγροὺς ἀγορίζειν καὶ κτήματα καὶ οἴκους, οὓς εὑρήσεις ἐν τῇ πόλει σου, ὅταν ἐπιδημήσῃς εἰς αὐτήν (*Herm. Sim.* 1.8–9).

In Similitude 2, Hermas begins by making the point that reciprocity between rich and poor in the Christian community is mutually beneficial, even if it might seem at first glance that the poor have little to offer in the exchange. According to Hermas, "the poor man makes intercession; a work in which he is rich, which he received from the Lord, and with which he recompenses the master who helps him. And the rich man, in like manner, unhesitatingly bestows upon the poor man the riches he received from the Lord."[52] Hermas envisions a scenario here in which there is equality in the reciprocal relationship between the rich and the poor. Each one gives from his wealth to the other who is lacking. The materially poor man is spiritually wealthy and can intercede with God on behalf of the rich man. In exchange for this service, the rich man supports the poor man from his material abundance. This is a "great work" (ἔργον μέγα), Hermas says, and "pleasing to God" (δεκτὸν παρὰ τῷ θεῷ).[53] The parable of the elm tree and the vine, which follows, conveys these ideas. The elm tree and the vine, according to Hermas, are mutually supportive. The elm produces no fruit, but in times of drought it supplies water to the vine, enabling the vine to produce a double portion of fruit, enough for both itself and the tree.[54] "So also," Hermas says, "poor men interceding with the Lord on behalf of the rich, increase their riches; and the rich, again, aiding the poor in the necessities, satisfy their souls. Both therefore are partners in this righteous work."[55] Hermas concludes by saying, "He who does these things shall not be deserted by God, but shall be enrolled in the books of the living. Blessed are they who have riches, and who understand they are from the Lord. For they who are of that mind will be able to do some good."[56] There is mutuality between the rich and the poor in the Christian community; each provides a necessary service to the other.

---

52. ὁ μὲν πένης ἐργάζεται τῇ ἐντεύξει, ἐν ᾗ πλουτεῖ ἣν ἔλαβεν παρὰ τοῦ κυρίου· ταύτην ἀποδίδωσι τῷ κυρίῳ τῷ ἐπιχορηγοῦντι αὐτῷ. Καὶ ὁ πλούσιος ὡσαύτως τὸ πλοῦτος. ὃ ἔλαβεν παρὰ τοῦ κυρίου, ἀδιστάκως παρέχεται τῷ πένητι (*Herm. Sim.* 2.7).

53. Ibid.

54. *Herm. Sim.* 2.8.

55. οὕτως καὶ οἱ πένητες ὑπὲρ τῶν πλουσίων ἐντυγχάνοντες πρὸς τὸν κύριον πληροφοροῦσι τὸ πλοῦτος αὐτῶν, καὶ πάλιν οἱ πλούσιοι χορηγοῦντες τοῖς πένησι τὰ δέοντα πληροφοροῦσι τὰς εὐχὰς αὐτῶν. γίνονται οὖν ἀμφότεροι κοινωνοὶ τοῦ ἔργου τοῦ δικαίου (*Herm. Sim.* 2.8–9).

56. ταῦτα οὖν ὁ ποιῶν οὐκ ἐγκαταλειφθήσεται ὑπὸ τοῦ θεοῦ, ἀλλ᾽ ἔσται γεγραμμένος εἰς τὰς βίβλους τῶν ζώντων. μακάριοι οἱ ἔχοντες καὶ συνιέντες, ὅτι παρὰ τοῦ κυρίου πλουτίζονται, ὁ γὰρ συνίων τοῦτο δυνήσεται καί τι ἀγαθόν (*Herm. Sim.* 2.9–10).

Let me make three observations. First, Hermas says that the rich man gives to the poor "unhesitatingly" (ἀδιστάκτως) because he knows that the Lord has blessed him with his wealth for this very purpose. Hermas here may be trying to allay the concern of wealthy Christians that they would be viewed as prodigal if they gave indiscriminately to the needy. As we saw in the last chapter, wealthy Christians of this era were closely attuned to Greco-Roman assumptions about virtuous generosity and therefore needed reassurance that giving liberally to the poor would be culturally acceptable. Hermas says not to be concerned about this; in the Christian context it is virtuous to give unhesitatingly because it is the will of God. Second, Hermas offers no negative judgment of wealth. Wealth is not sinful, and the rich Christian should feel no need to renounce it. If used correctly, wealth places no hindrances on one's spiritual growth. In fact, wealth is good. It is a blessing from God, and having it is essential if one hopes to assist the needy. Last, to an outside observer, Christian care for the poor appeared to be a form of Roman patronage. The patron-client bond was an unequal relationship, and this was largely the point. Patrons took on clients to gain honor by having subordinates beneath them. But in the Christian context, what looked like an unequal relationship was actually more like friendship between equals. This is because in Hermas's view each man is wealthy, but in a different way. The materially poor man is spiritually rich, and on that basis stands on equal terms with the materially wealthy man. Instead of inequality and subordination, Hermas envisions a mutually beneficial relationship in which the rich and the poor each has something to give to the other.

The idea that wealthy Christians could gain spiritual benefits (ultimately, salvation for their souls) by giving to the poor became an increasingly prominent theological idea in the second century. In the view of some scholars, this concept of "redemptive almsgiving" represents the corruption of the primitive church's egalitarianism in which the wealthy were expected to renounce their possessions when they joined the movement.[57] However, my argument in this study has been that from the beginning the Christians encouraged the participation of the wealthy and that Christian teachers and authors consistently articulated an ideology to support the expectation that these wealthy members would care for the poor. "Redemptive almsgiving," therefore represents simply another argument to support a practice that seemed imprudent and immoral to

---

57. Countryman, *Rich Christian*; Garrison, *Redemptive Almsgiving*.

many wealthy people. Moreover, the idea that wealthy Christians could gain spiritual benefits from giving to the poor was really nothing new. Already in the mid-50s CE, Paul stated this as a premise for his collection project when he wrote in Rom 15:27: "For if the Gentiles have come to share in their spiritual blessings, they ought also to be of service to them in material things."[58] Similarly, in Luke 14:12–14, Jesus tells the host who had invited him for a meal in his home not to invite his "friends or your brothers or your relatives or rich neighbors" with the hope that they would invite him in return and he would be "repaid."[59] Instead, Jesus says, when giving a banquet, "invite the poor, the crippled, the lame, and the blind. And you will be blessed, because they cannot repay you, for you will be repaid at the resurrection of the righteous."[60] The ideas expressed by Hermas and others in the second century simply expand on the basic premises incipient in these New Testament texts. Finally, the "moral economy of the peasant" also represents a set of ideological assumptions used by village communities to compel wealthy villagers to fulfill their responsibilities to the poor. In the village, the rural patron's motive for giving—whether it be altruism or self-interest—was beside the point. The important thing was that the needs of the poor were met. The Christians, as they developed their alternative subsistence strategy also needed a repertoire of arguments to persuade the wealthy to act, and one of these important arguments was that giving to the poor would help them accrue spiritual benefits.

Clement of Alexandria

A fourth example of a second-century text which provides ideological support for the Christians' alternative subsistence strategy is a treatise written by Clement of Alexandria, titled, *Who Is the Rich Man That Is to Be Saved?* Clement wrote this text most likely during the last decade of the second century as the head of the catechetical school in Alexandria. The works of Clement, and this text in particular, are often taken

---

58. εἰ γὰρ τοῖς πνευματικοῖς αὐτῶν ἐκοινώνησαν τὰ ἔθνη, ὀφείλουσιν καὶ ἐν τοῖς σαρκικοῖς λειτουργῆσαι αὐτοῖς.

59. τοὺς φίλους σου μηδὲ τοὺς ἀδελφούς σου μηδὲ τοὺς συγγενεῖς σου μηδὲ γείτονας πλουσίους . . . γένηται ἀνταπόδομά (Luke 14:12).

60. ἀλλ᾽ ὅταν δοχὴν ποιῇς, κάλει πτωχούς, ἀναπείρους, χωλούς, τυφλούς· καὶ μακάριος ἔσῃ, ὅτι οὐκ ἔχουσιν ἀνταποδοῦναί σοι, ἀνταποδοθήσεται γάρ σοι ἐν τῇ ἀναστάσει τῶν δικαίων (Luke 14:13–14).

as evidence that the church of the late second century was rising in social prominence and, as a result, had become more accommodating to a wealthy and culturally sophisticated membership. Clement's treatise reflects thorough engagement with Hellenistic philosophy and offers a rationale for wealthy Christians to hold onto their possessions. In light of this, some insist that Clement represents an accommodating form of Christianity that has lost touch with its more rigorous and egalitarian roots.[61] Moreover, some claim that Clement seems more concerned with the spiritual condition of the rich than with the physical needs of the poor. Helen Rhee has observed that in Clement's thought, "almsgiving seems to be encouraged more for salvation of the giver than for the alleviation of poverty."[62] But I argue here that the basic model of care for the poor which Clement depicts in this treatise, along with its supporting ideology, is remarkably consistent with that of earlier generations of Christians. Certainly, Clement's urban, culturally sophisticated audience in Alexandria was quite different in many respects from the wealthy rural farmers addressed by Jesus. Yet, when we look at Christian care for the poor as an alternative subsistence strategy, we can see similarities that would otherwise go unnoticed.

Though Clement draws heavily upon contemporary Hellenistic moral philosophy, Eric Osborn argues that his ethical system is a synthesis in which priority is given to the biblical tradition.[63] Clement's ethics are summed up in what Osborn refers to as the "two-fold hope," a concept which is both Platonic and Pauline.[64] According to Plato, the human practice of virtue participates in the eternal Good but cannot fully realize it. Paul thinks of this as the tension between the "now" and the "not yet," which is the space between one's present condition in Christ and the completed salvation that is to come. In both traditions, eventual assimilation to God is the goal of human life. Clement uses Gen 1:26 to describe this "now" and "not yet" quality of the human experience. Gen 1:26 says that humans were created in the "image" and "likeness" of God. Clement picks up on this and makes the claim that to be created in God's "image" means that humans were created with the potential to attain assimilation to God. Attaining the "likeness" of God, however, comes only

---

61. Countryman, *Rich Christian*, 47–68.
62. Rhee, *Loving the Poor*, 77.
63. Osborn, *Clement of Alexandria*, 226–53.
64. Ibid., 229.

through intentional discipline and moral progress and involves a partnership between the human and divine wills. In making this distinction between "image" and "likeness," Clement "sets out the vision of every human as capable of growing like God. The perfection of this ideal finds its fulfillment in deification and life in the eternal vision of God."[65] With its distinction between image and likeness, "Gen 1:26 sets out, according to Clement, God's saving plan for humanity, a plan which begins at creation and is not yet perfected. Only Jesus Christ, who is both God and man, has fulfilled the plan. God has given to him the human race that he might bring that race into his own divine likeness."[66] In Clement's view, all humans are born with the potential of assimilation to God, but only in Christ can this potential be realized.

For Clement, one characteristic of the "likeness" of God is ἀπάθεια, "passionlessness" or "detachment." Clement is clearly indebted to Stoicism on this point, but Osborn observes that this term is an important example of the way in which Clement subordinates Hellenistic philosophical categories to biblical ideas in his ethical synthesis.[67] For Clement, ἀπάθεια refers to one's detachment from the passions associated with pleasure, but the Christian concept of love, which takes priority, enables the Christian to avoid the Stoic pitfall of disinterest toward the needs of one's neighbor, inherent in the concept of ἀπάθεια.[68] This is similar to the Christian redefinition of "prodigality" that we examined in the previous chapter. For Clement freedom from desire, but love for others, imitates the divine character and is part of the Christian's journey to assimilation with God.

These basic concepts of Clement's moral reasoning underlie his treatise, *Who Is the Rich Man that Shall Be Saved?* Clement begins this composition with the premise that it would not be consistent with the divine nature to exclude the wealthy from salvation; Christ has shown to them also the way to assimilation to the likeness of God. God has granted this potential as a gift of his grace, but actually reaching God's likeness requires human effort, much like the pursuit of virtue in the tradition of Hellenistic moral philosophy. Clement writes, "Let not the man that has been invested with worldly wealth to proclaim himself excluded from

---

65. Ibid.
66. Ibid., 233–34.
67. Ibid., 239.
68. Ibid., 240. See also the discussion in Rhee, *Loving the Poor*, 77–83.

the Savior's lists, provided he is a believer and one who contemplates the greatness of God's philanthropy; nor let him, on the other hand, expect to grasp the crowns of immortality without struggle and effort, continuing untrained, and without contest."[69] Here we see the tension between the "now" and the "not yet." God makes possible the salvation of the rich, but they must be earnest and diligent in their effort toward this end, for as Clement states, "God conspires with willing souls."[70]

How then can the rich attain the likeness of God? Clement insists that it would not be possible merely by renouncing one's possessions as Cynics and even some Christians had proposed.[71] Clement admits that this might appear to be the thrust of Christ's command to the rich man when he says, "Sell what you own, and give the money to the poor, and you will have treasure in heaven; then come, follow me."[72] But for Clement, this is where the concept of ἀπάθεια comes into play. Clement argues that Christ's command should not be interpreted literally because even when a person renounces everything, he or she may continue to be attached to material things in his inner disposition.[73] Instead, the Christian seeking to attain the likeness of God must demonstrate ἀπάθεια, a freedom from the *desire* for wealth and the things of this world.

It is precisely at this point that we see a clear illustration of the way in which Clement integrates Stoic ἀπάθεια into his Christian ethics. Having ἀπάθεια toward worldly possessions, rich Christians are then free to put their wealth toward its divinely intended use by assisting their needy neighbors. For Clement, wealth falls into the Stoic category of ἀδιάφορα, "matters of indifference." The ἀδιάφορα are things in themselves that are morally neutral but accrue a moral value depending on how one uses them. Clement writes:

> Riches, then, which benefit also our neighbors, are not to be thrown away. For they are possessions, inasmuch as they are possessed, and goods, inasmuch as they are useful and provided

---

69. τις καὶ τὴν ἐπίγειον ταύτην περιβεβλημένος περιβολὴν μήτε τὴν ἑαυτὸν τῶν ἄθλων τοῦ σωτῆρος ἐκκηρυσσέτω, πιστός γε ὢ καὶ τὸ μεγαλεῖον συνορῶν τῆς τοῦ θεοῦ φιλανθρωπίας, μήτε μὴν αὖθις ἀνάσκητος καὶ ἀναγώνιστος μείνας ἀκονιτὶ κἀνιδρωτὶ τῶν στεφάνων τῆς ἀφθαρσίας ἐλπιζέτω μεταλαβεῖν (Clement, Quis div. 3.5).

70. βουλομέναις μὲν γὰρ ταῖς ψυχαῖς ὁ θεὸς συνεπιπνεῖ (Clement, Quis div. 21.2).

71. Clement, Quis div. 11.1–4.

72. ἕν σε ὑστερεῖ· ὕπαγε, ὅσα ἔχεις πώλησον καὶ δὸς πτωχοῖς, καὶ ἕξεις θησαυρὸν ἐν οὐρανῷ, καὶ δεῦρο ἀκολούθει μοι (Mark 10:21).

73. Clement, Quis div. 12.1–5.

> by God for the use of men; and they lie to our hand, and are put under our power, as material and instruments which are for good use to those who know the instrument. If you use it skillfully, it is skillful; if you are deficient in skill, it is affected by your want of skill, being itself destitute of blame. Such an instrument is wealth. Are you able to make a right use of it? It is subservient to righteousness. Does one make a wrong use of it? It is, on the other hand, a minister of wrong.[74]

Wealth for Clement is not in itself immoral. What matters is the attitude with which one holds wealth or the use to which he puts it. Since this is so, Clement continues: "So let no man destroy wealth, rather than the passions of the soul, which are incompatible with the better use of wealth. So that, becoming virtuous and good, he may be able to make a good use of these riches."[75] Renunciation is not, therefore, primarily about renouncing one's material possessions, but rather renouncing the passions of the soul. In Clement's view, wealth is good when it is used to care for the needy, which is impossible, in fact, without wealth. Therefore, retaining wealth with ἀπάθεια provides the only possible way to fulfill God's command to care for the poor.

The call to care for the poor simply on the basis of need appeared to Clement's audience, perhaps even more than to Luke's audience, as indiscriminate and morally questionable generosity, or "prodigality." Clement wrote his treatise to counteract the stigma of this vice by redefining virtuous generosity. One passage in particular clearly demonstrates Clement's goal. He writes:

> Do not you judge who is worthy or who is unworthy. For it is possible you may be mistaken in your opinion. As in the uncertainty of ignorance it is better to do good to the undeserving for the sake of the deserving, than by guarding against those

---

74. Οὐκ ἄρα ἀπορριπτέον τὰ καὶ τοὺς πέλας ὠφελοῦντα χρήματα: κτήματα γάρ ἐστι κτητὰ ὄντα καὶ χρήματα κρήσιμα ὄντα καὶ εἰς χρῆσιν ἀνθρώπων ὑπὸ τοῦ θεοῦ παρεσκευασμένα, ἃ δὴ παράκειται καὶ ὑποβέβληται καθάπερ ὕλη τις καὶ ὄργανα πρὸς χρῆσιν ἀγαθὴν τοῖς εἰδόσι. τὸ ὄργανον ἐὰν χρῇ τεχνικῶς, τεχνικόν ἐστιν, ἐὰν ὑστερῇς τῆς τέχνης, ἀπολαύει τῆς σῆς ἀμουσίας χρῆσθαι δικαίως αὐτῷ: πρὸς δικαιοσύνην καθυπηρετεῖ: ἀδίκως τις αὐτῷ χρῆται: πάλιν ὑπηρέτης ἀδικίας εὑρίσκεται (Clement, Quis div., 14.1–3).

75. ὥστε μὴ τὰ κτήματά τις ἀφανιζέτω μᾶλλον ἢ τὰ πάθη τῆς ψυχῆς, τὰ μὴ συγχωροῦντα τὴν ἀμείνω χρῆσιν τῶν ὑπαρχόντων, ἵνα καλὸς καὶ ἀγαθὸς γενόμενος καὶ τούτοις τοῖς κτήμασι χρῆσθαι δυνηθῇ καλῶς. τὸ οὖν ἀποτάξασθαι πᾶσι τοῖς ὑπάρχουσι καὶ πωλῆσαι πάντα τὰ ὑπάρχοντα τοῦτον τὸν τρόπον ἐκδεκτέον ὡς ἐπὶ τῶν ψυχικῶν παθῶν διειρημένον (Clement, Quis div. 14.5–6).

that are less good to fail to meet in with the good. For though sparing, and aiming at testing, who will receive meritoriously or not, it is possible for you to neglect some that are loved by God; the penalty for which is the punishment of eternal fire. But by offering to all in turn that need, you must of necessity by all means find some of those who have power with God to save.[76]

In this passage, Clement offers two arguments against judging the worthiness of one's beneficiaries. First, by employing what his culture would approve as virtuous discernment of proper recipients of generosity, the Christian benefactor risked overlooking the needy person who was approved by God. Second, the needy person has the power to save the wealthy giver, a concept which we have already encountered in the Shepherd of Hermas.

Clement makes two additional points that provide theological support for the alternative subsistence strategy he was advancing. The first is that in helping the needy, the wealthy person is actually giving to the Father and to the Son:

> Open thy compassion to all who are enrolled as the disciples of God; not looking contemptuously to personal appearance, nor carelessly treating in accordance with one's place in life. Nor if one appears penniless, or ragged, or ugly, or feeble, do thou fret in soul at this and turn away. This form is cast around us from without, the occasion of our entrance into this world, that we may be able to enter into this common school. But within dwells the hidden Father, and His Son, who died for us and rose with us.[77]

---

76. σὺ μὲν μὴ κρῖνε, τίς ἄξιος καὶ τίς ἀνάξιος· ἐνδέχεται γάρ σε διαμαρτεῖν περὶ τὴν δόξαν· ὡς ἐν ἀμφιβόλῳ δὲ τῆς ἀγνοίας ἄμεινον καὶ τοὺς ἀναξίους εὖ ποιεῖν διὰ τοὺς ἀξίους ἢ φυλασσόμενον τοὺς ἧσσον ἀγαθοὺς μηδὲ τοῖς σπουδαίοις περιπεσεῖν. ἐκ μὲν γὰρ τοῦ φείδεσθαι καὶ προσποιεῖσθαι δοκιμάζειν τοὺς εὐλόγως ἢ μὴ τευξομένους ἐνδέχεταί σε καὶ θεοφιλῶν ἀμελῆσαι τινων, οὗ τὸ ἐπιτίμιον κόλασις ἔμπυρος αἰώνιος· ἐκ δὲ τοῦ προΐεσθαι πᾶσιν ἑξῆς τοῖς χρῄζουσιν ἀνάγκη πάντως εὑρεῖν τινα καὶ τῶν σῶσαι παρὰ θεῷ δυναμένων (Clement, Quis div. 33.2–3).

77. πᾶσιν ἄνοιξον τὰ σπλάγχνα τοῖς τοῦ θεοῦ μαθηταῖς ἀπογεγραμμένοις, μὴ πρὸς σῶμα ἀπιδὼν ὑπερόπτως, μὴ πρὸς ἡλικίαν ἀμελῶς διατεθείς, μηδ᾽ εἴ τις ἀκτήμων ἢ δυσείμων ἢ δυσειδὴς ἢ ἀσθενὴς φαίνεται, πρὸς τοῦτο τῇ ψυχῇ δυσχεράνῃς καὶ ἀποστραφῇς. σχῆμα τοῦτ᾽ ἐστιν ἔξωθεν ἡμῖν περβεβλημένον τῆς εἰς κόσμον παρόδου προφάσει, ἵν᾽ εἰς τὸ κοινὸν τοῦτο παιδευτήριον εἰσελθεῖν δυνηθῶμεν· ἀλλ᾽ ἔνδον κρυπτὸς ἐνοικεῖ ὁ πατὴρ καὶ ὁ τούτου παῖς ὁ ὑπὲρ ἡμῶν ἀποθανὼν καὶ μεθ᾽ ἡμῶν ἀναστάς (Clement, Quis div., 33.5–6).

Three points are significant here. First, it is clear that care for the needy was to be directed toward members of the community, "those who are enrolled as the disciples of God." Second, Clement provides specific descriptions of the needy: they are those who appear penniless, ragged, ugly, and feeble. It is impossible to tell whether Clement could have distinguished between chronic and conjunctural poverty, but it seems clear that Clement was aware of real need around him and wrote in support of a system to alleviate it. Finally, Clement is trying to address the concern of his wealthy audience that giving to such as these was a morally irresponsible thing to do. While the poor might not appear worthy of patronage according to contemporary norms of virtuous generosity, Clement puts forth the idea that wealthy Christians were actually giving to the Father and to the Son when they gave to the poor.

Clement makes one final point in support of the Christian practice of care for the poor. He insists that when wealthy Christians give to the needy, they emulate the very nature of God and take a step toward Godlikeness, the very goal of Christian salvation. Clement writes:

> For this also He came down. For this He clothed Himself with man. For this He voluntarily subjected Himself to the experience of men, that by bringing Himself to the measure of our weakness whom He loved, He might correspondingly bring us to the measure of His own strength. And about to be offered up and giving Himself a ransom, He left for us a new Covenant-testament: "My love I give unto you." And what and how great is it? For each of us He gave His life—the equivalent for all. This He demands from us in return for one another. And if we owe our lives to the brethren, and have made such a mutual compact with the Saviour, why should we any more hoard and shut up worldly goods, which are beggarly, foreign to us and transitory.[78]

According to Clement the purpose of the incarnation was that in becoming like us, God provided the means by which we might become like God.

---

78. διὰ τοῦτο καὶ αὐτὸς κτῆλθε, διὰ τοῦτο ἄνθρωπον ἐνέδυ, διὰ τοῦτο τὰ ἀνθρώπων ἑκὼν ἔπαθεν, ἵνα πρὸς τὴν ἡμετέραν ἀσθένειαν οὓς ἠγάπησε μετρηθεὶς ἡμᾶς πρὸς τὴν ἑαυτοῦ δύναμιν ἀντιμετρήσῃ. καὶ μέλλων σπένδεσθαι καὶ λύτρον ἑαυτὸν ἐπιδιδοὺς καινὴν ἡμῖν διαθήκην καταλιμπάνει· ἀγάπην ὑμῖν δίδωμι τὴν ἐμήν. τίς δέ ἐστιν αὕτη καὶ πόση; ὑπὲρ ἡμῶν ἑκάστου κατέθηκε τὴν ψυχὴν τὴν ἀνταξίαν τῶν ὅλων. ταύτην ἡμᾶς ὑπὲρ ἀλλήλων ἀνταπαιτεῖ. εἰ δὲ τὰς ψυχὰς ὀφείλομεν τοῖς ἀδελφοῖς, καὶ τοιαύτην τὴν συνθήκην πρὸς τὸν σωτῆρα ἀνθωμολογήμεθα, ἔτι τὰ τοῦ κόσμου, τὰ πτωχὰ καὶ ἀλλότρια καὶ παραρρέοντα, καθείρξομεν ταμιευόμενοι; (Clement, *Quis div.* 37.3–5).

The incarnation, the joining together of the divine and human natures, was soteriological in intent: it was the means of reconciliation between God and humankind. Likewise, giving to the poor by the wealthy is also soteriological in the sense that the physical needs of the poor are met, and also the means for solidarity between the two groups is provided. Moreover, just as the incarnation was a great sacrifice—the giving of one life for that of the many—so also does the relationship between rich and poor involve sacrifice when the wealthy individual gives from surplus for the needs of another.

In sum, Clement of Alexandria, though thoroughly conversant with contemporary Hellenistic philosophy, presents an economic morality that is consistent with what we have seen from earlier times in the Christian movement. In Clement's system the wealthy assist the poor within the Christian community on the basis of their need rather than because of other criteria such as their moral virtue. Though Clement works with ideas derived from the moral philosophical tradition, such as the Platonic "twofold end" and Stoic ἀπάθεια, he refines and adapts these concepts in accordance with biblical ideas. Christ's incarnation is an important example of his synthesis of Hellenistic and biblical concepts. Just as God took on human nature in order to make humans divine, so also do the rich care for the poor as a means of emulating God and thereby making progress toward the ultimate goal of assimilation to the divine nature. Thus, care for the poor in the Christian churches is intelligible only in light of foundational elements of Christian theology.

The Apocryphal Acts

The *Apocryphal Acts of the Apostles* provides another example of second and third-century Christian literature that offers ideological support to the Christians' alternative subsistence strategy. The designation "Apocryphal Acts" refers to a set of five ancient compositions dated to the second and third centuries CE.[79] Scholars debate the relationship of these texts to the canonical book of Acts as well as their relative historical reliability. Traditionally, the *Apocryphal Acts* have been judged to be later compositions and inauthentic imitations of the generally reliable canonical Acts.

---

79. Klauck, *Apocryphal Acts*, 3. Klauck provides tentative dates for these *Acts* as follows: *Acts of John* (c. 150–160 CE), *Acts of Paul* (c. 170–180 CE), *Acts of Peter* (c. 190–200 CE), *Acts of Andrew* (c. 200–210 CE), *Acts of Thomas* (c. 220–240 CE).

Richard Pervo, however, challenges this explanation and argues that the *Apocryphal Acts* have as much claim to historicity as the canonical Acts—that is, not much; both the canonical and the apocryphal *Acts*, in his view, are compositions intended to "entertain as well as edify" their audiences.[80] The wide distribution of the *Apocryphal Acts* is indicated by the number of ancient translations. Manuscripts exist, for example, in Latin, Coptic, Syriac, Ethiopic, Armenian, and Georgian.[81] This is a clear indication of their enduring popularity in early Christianity.

A leading theory regarding the genre of the *Apocryphal Acts* is that they were modeled after the popular Hellenistic novel.[82] Pervo defines the ancient novel as a "relatively lengthy work of prose fiction depicting or deriding certain ideals through an entertaining presentation of the lives and experiences of a person or persons whose activity transcends the limits of ordinary living as known to its implied readers."[83] Popular during the cosmopolitan and politically unstable Hellenistic and Roman periods, these novels represent the "creation of an ideal world without the disorder, ambiguity, and limitations of the known world."[84] Novelists tended to reinforce traditional social values in their narratives, creating a world for their readers that reflected the ideals that seemed to be slipping away from them.[85] The *Apocryphal Acts*, on the other hand, offer a counterculturial imitation of the Hellenistic novel. Whereas the novel sought to reinforce traditional civic virtues in a world that was changing, the *Apocryphal Acts* promoted a new worldview that undermined the values of Greco-Roman society, particularly in their idealization of virginity, renunciation, and the ascetic life.[86]

Yet, in spite of (or rather because of) their countercultural orientation, the *Apocryphal Acts* played a significant role in the formation of Christian identity in the second and third centuries and later in defining

---

80. Pervo, *Profit with Delight*, 122.

81. Rhee, *Early Christian Literature*, 38.

82. An early and influential proponent of this view was Rosa Söder, *Die apokryphen Apostelgeschichten*. The *Apocryphal Acts* may have appealed to the same audiences. Tomas Hägg states, "the same readership which provided a market for the Hellenistic novel was now devouring stories about apostles, martyrs, and saints" (*Novel in Antiquity*, 161).

83. Pervo, *Profit with Delight*, 105.

84. Ibid., 111.

85. Ibid.

86. Cooper, *Virgin and the Bride*, 45–67.

the nature of the Christian empire of late antiquity. Averil Cameron writes:

> While second-century writers like Clement of Alexandria developed a presentation of Christian ideas in terms of Greek philosophy, and Tertullian applied to Christian themes the skills of traditional rhetoric, these works, "popular" or even heretical by orthodox standards, created a set of Christian stories for the next generations. Not just in the canonical books, or through official church teaching, but in the whole spread of Christian inventiveness in the first centuries it was thus established what kind of reality Christianity would construct for the empire when the time came.[87]

Cameron emphasizes the importance of religious storytelling for shaping Christian culture. In contrast to the more theoretical arguments of the apologists and the Christian philosophers, like Clement and Origen, whose audiences may have been very small, the stories of the *Apocryphal Acts* were popular and widely known.[88] Though actually read only by the literate and relatively well educated, the stories of the *Apocryphal Acts* would have been widely known through Christian preaching, which itself was a ubiquitous and influential phenomenon in this period.[89] The stories of the *Apocryphal Acts* assumed and contributed to a larger plotline, a master narrative that provided the ideological foundation upon which the Christians established their distinctive forms of religious practice and communal life, including their alternative subsistence strategy.

The theological premise underlying the master narrative of the *Apocryphal Acts* is that the Christian God is sovereign, superior to the pagan gods, and thus deserving of worship and obedience. The main figure in these narratives is the apostle who serves as the agent and authoritative representative of God. God works through him by displaying acts of power which typically result in Christian conversions among those who witness the miracles.[90] The idea is that the Christian God is all-powerful and thus worthy of exclusive commitment, devotion, and

---

87. Cameron, *Christianity and the Rhetoric of Empire*, 115.

88. Ibid., 118–19.

89. Ibid., 79.

90. In light of stories such as these and the lack of other compelling explanations, Ramsay MacMullen concludes that miracle reports constituted one of the chief causes of Christian numerical growth in this period (*Christianizing the Roman Empire*, 25–42).

obedience. Converts come from the provincial, urban elite class, and acts of generosity to the poor typically accompany their conversions and are portrayed as the appropriate response when one decides to follow Christ. Frequently read in the fourth and fifth centuries, the accounts in the *Apocryphal Acts* of the wealthy converts' generosity toward the poor served as a "direct form of exhortation" to almsgiving for Christians in late antiquity.[91]

Three brief examples illustrate this motif. In the *Acts of Paul*, the apostle's devoted disciple Thecla, through her courage in the face of martyrdom and the miracle of her eventual release, inspires the faith and conversion of a wealthy noblewoman named Tryphaena.[92] As Thecla prepares to leave the city to join Paul in Iconium, the text states that "Tryphaena sent her much clothing and gold, so that she could leave it with Paul for the service of the poor."[93] In the *Acts of Peter*, a Christian senator named Marcellus had formerly been a caretaker of the poor, but in the interim between Paul's departure from Rome and the arrival of Peter he had come under the influence of Simon Magus. Now as a result of Simon's influence and under pressure from the emperor Nero to fulfill his customary senatorial duties, Marcellus had turned his back on the Christian assembly and ceased caring for the poor as he had formerly done. Upon Peter's arrival, the Christians of Rome report to him the terrible change that had come upon Marcellus: "Believe us brother Peter; no one was so wise among men as this Marcellus. All the widows who hoped in Christ found refuge in him; all the orphans were fed by him. And what more, brother? All the poor called Marcellus their patron, and his house was called (the house) of pilgrims and the poor."[94] But not only had he ceased his former generosity; he now regretted that he had ever given to "these imposters" (*illis impostoribus*) in the first place.[95] Upon hearing this, Peter goes to the house of Marcellus where Simon Magus is lodging. At the door is a large guard dog. Peter unties him, and the

---

91. Finn, *Almsgiving*, 130.

92. *Acts Paul* 3.26–43.

93. ἡ μὲν οὖν Τρύφαινα πολὺν ἱματισμὸν καὶ χρυσὸν ἔπεμψεν αὐτῇ, ὥστε καταλιπεῖν τῷ Παύλῳ εἰς διακονίαν τῶν πτωχῶν (*Acts Paul* 3.41).

94. Crede nobis, frater Petre: nemo fuit tam sapientior inter homines, quam hic Marcellus. Viduae omnes sperantes in Christo ad hunc refugium habebant; omnes orfani ab eo pascebantur. Quid plura, frater? Marcellum omnes pauperi patronum vocabant; cuius domus peregrinorum et pauperorum vocabulum habebat (*Acts Pet.* 8).

95. Ibid.

dog begins to speak in a human voice. Peter gives the command, the dog enters the house, stands on two legs, and announces to Simon and the whole household that Peter has come. Simon is dumbfounded by the sight, and Marcellus comes out to greet Peter, falls at his feet, and repents of his sin.[96] Later in the Acts, we see that Marcellus, consistent with his repentance, has returned to his former ways and once again cares for the poor.[97] Last, in the *Acts of John*, a man named Antipatros offers the apostle ten thousand gold pieces to heal his demon-possessed twin sons.[98] John responds to the request by saying, "My physician takes no reward in money, but when he heals for nothing he reaps the souls of those who are healed ... What then are you willing [to give], Antipatros, in exchange for your children? Offer your soul to God, and you shall have your children healthy by the power of Christ."[99] At this point, John prays, Antipatros's sons are healed, and he bows down to give thanks to the apostle. With this, the text says that John "enjoined Antipatros to give money to those who were in need."[100] This he did, and they went away "praising and blessing God."[101]

Each of these scenes follows a similar pattern. A wealthy individual, perhaps even a member of the ruling class, has an encounter with an apostle through whom he or she experiences in some firsthand way the supernatural power of the Christian God, confirming for the individual God's authority over all the pagan deities and spirits. Because of this encounter the wealthy man or woman confesses faith and demonstrates the fruit of that faith by giving generously to the needy. While it may be historically unlikely that there were many members of the senatorial class or the ultrarich (the top 1 to 2 percent of Roman society) who had actually joined the Christian movement by this time in the second and early third centuries, these fictional accounts nevertheless inspired those of lesser means, the relatively wealthy non-elites who were a significant

---

96. Ibid., 9–10.

97. Ibid., 19.

98. *Acts John* 56.

99. Ὁ ἐμὸς ἰατρὸς μισθὸν ἀργυρίου οὐ λαμβάνει, ἀλλ' ἰώμενος δωρεὰν τὰς τῶν ἰαθέτων ψυχὰς κατάλλαγμα τῶν νόσων καρπίζεται. τί ἄρα θέλεις, Ἀντίπατρε, κατάλλαγμα τῶν παίδων; τὴν ἰδίαν ψυχὴν τῷ θεῷ παραστήσας καὶ ἕξεις τοὺς παῖδάς σου ὑγιεῖς τῇ δυνάμει τοῦ Χριστοῦ (*Acts John* 56).

100. καὶ παρήγγειλεν τῷ Ἀντιπάτρῳ ὁ Ἰωάννης χρήματα δοθῆναι τοῖς χρείαν ἔχουσιν (*Acts John* 57).

101. αἰνοῦντας καὶ εὐλογοῦντας τὸν θεόν (*Acts John* 57).

constituency in the church, to engage in their own acts of generosity. It might be that these narratives, even more so than the more theoretical texts that we have examined in this chapter, helped shape the Christian worldview for this "middling class" of upwardly mobile individuals who were seeking opportunities to act as patrons and benefactors but were concerned to avoid the stigma of giving to those considered unworthy by the rest of society. Stories like these created an alternative worldview in which generosity to the poor and needy was no longer considered immoral and "prodigal" behavior but rather virtuous, because it was concerned first and foremost with addressing human need. And once again, as we have seen throughout this study, this consistent Christian concern with assisting the needy resembles the traditional values of rural communities; in other words, Christian care for the poor reflects the "moral economy of the peasant."

Christian Care for the Poor in the Writings of Cyprian of Carthage

To conclude this chapter, I now turn to Christian care for the poor in the writings of Cyprian of Carthage. It is appropriate to conclude this study with Cyprian because his career in the middle decades of the third century CE bridges two eras in Christian history. On the one hand, as a Christian bishop in Carthage, Cyprian was the leader of a persecuted minority group that at this time was facing perhaps the most systematic opposition and danger from the Roman authorities that they had ever experienced. At the same time, however, Cyprian was also a well-educated member of the social elite class and a former teacher of rhetoric whose voluminous writings testify to the excellence of his abilities.[102] Cyprian's career therefore reflect's Christianity's changing status in the Roman world, a process that would come to fruition over the next three centuries. The fact that someone of Cyprian's social position would become a Christian and eventually enter the highest levels of Christian leadership suggests that though still a minority group within Roman society, the Christians were no longer socially and politically insignificant. The second half of the third century, in fact, was a crucial period for Christianity's development and position in Roman society. Not only did the Christians experience significant overall numerical growth, they also began to attract increas-

---

102. Rives, *Religion and Authority*, 285–94.

ing numbers of members from the elite orders of Roman and provincial society.[103] In this light, Constantine's favor toward the Christians may not have been so much the result of his own personal religious conversion as an astute political maneuver that recognized the political benefit of becoming the patron of this rising segment of the population.[104]

Similarly, Christian care for the poor in the writings of Cyprian also seems to span two eras. As we will see, the practice of care for the poor that appears in Cyprian's letters and treatises is consistent with the basic model that I have presented over the course of this study. Stated simply, Cyprian promoted an alternative subsistence strategy that benefited members of the Christian community for whom other more traditional strategies had failed for one reason or another. Similar to earlier Christian writers, Cyprian also articulated a theological rationale designed to alleviate the concerns of wealthy Christians who were reluctant to give to the poor because of negative perceptions about the morality of doing so. But Cyprian's efforts to promote a program for poor relief also anticipated developments in the fourth and fifth centuries CE when Christian bishops became increasingly vocal proponents of care for the poor and took on large-scale institutional efforts to address need as a primary duty of their pastoral ministry in a Christian empire in which all the poor were now the responsibility of the church.[105] In Cyprian's writings we discover that the church in Carthage had a well-organized system of caring for the poor, which was overseen by the bishop and implemented by the lower-ranking clergy. We also see that Cyprian assumed full authority for this system, even during his absence from Carthage during the Decian persecution. During this period of exile, he wrote letters to encourage the clergy to continue to provide for the needy even during such trying times, he continued to assess who was worthy to receive the church's benevolence, and he even contributed to the effort with his own personal resources. In doing so, Cyprian resembled the wealthy Christians of earlier times who took upon themselves the role of the patron to the poor; but at the same time, we also can detect in Cyprian's efforts the growing institutionalization of the church's care for the poor. After a brief discussion of Cyprian's context in third-century Carthage, I turn first to the practice of care for the poor as it emerges in the letters of Cyprian. Then, I will examine the

---

103. See Brown, *World of Late Antiquity*, 60–69, for an insightful discussion of Christianity's development in the third century.

104. Ibid., 86.

105. Brown, *Poverty and Leadership*, 26–73.

theological rationale that Cyprian used to support the church's practice. In both cases, I will draw attention to points of continuity with Christian care for the poor of earlier periods.

In the decades from 235 to 284 CE (from the assassination of Severus Alexander to the rise of Diocletian), the Roman imperial government faced a combination of serious political, military, demographic, and economic challenges that created a period of instability often referred to as the "Third-Century Crisis."[106] During this fifty-year period, approximately twenty-seven emperors claimed the throne, an extraordinary rate of turnover due mainly to death in battle or military coup-d'état. The Roman military faced serious challenges: barbarian incursions along the Danubian border and a new expansionist Persian state (under the Sassanian dynasty) to the east. An outbreak of plague compounded the problems, shrinking both the Roman labor necessary to fill the ranks of the army as well as the tax revenue needed to fund the military build-up.[107] The debasement of the coinage may be a sign of a bureaucracy struggling to make ends meet.[108] During these decades, professional soldiers filled the ranks of the army, and the emperors were promoted from this new class of military professionals. To many modern observers, this militarization of the imperial government is a sure sign of the collapse of the Pax Romana of the first two centuries; the days of high culture, peace, and prosperity were over. But in the words of Peter Brown, "the Roman empire was saved by a military revolution."[109] In his view, it was the energy, efficiency, and capable leadership of these military men that kept the empire intact, and it was they who "emerged as the heroes of the imperial recovery of the late third and early fourth centuries."[110]

While it is generally assumed that the Roman Empire faced a long and widespread economic depression in the third century, evidence suggests that this was not uniformly the case, and that some provinces were spared the impact of this economic contraction and even experienced

---

106. For a concise description of this period see Cameron, *Later Roman Empire*, 1–12. Giardina argues against recent "minimalistic interpretation" of the third century crisis and upholds the view that this period witnessed serious and momentous changes which help explain the transition to late antiquity ("Transition to Late Antiquity," especially 757–64).

107. Ibid., 757–58.

108. Ibid., 759–60.

109. Brown, *World of Late Antiquity*, 24.

110. Ibid., 24, 26.

relative prosperity during this period.[111] One such region was Roman North Africa. Archaeological surveys show only a small decrease in the number of rural settlements during the second half of the third century, a period when a much more dramatic drop might be expected.[112] This may indicate that North Africa was spared at least some of the disruption caused by barbarian incursions in the north, military hostilities with the Sassanian Persians in the east, labor shortages, and a crippling tax burden that other provinces may have felt more acutely. In other words, the "Third-Century Crisis" may not have been experienced as such by the people of North Africa. This evidence for "business as usual" might suggest that when Cyprian discusses care for the poor he is addressing the normal, conjunctural poverty inherent in agrarian economies rather than the extraordinary conditions faced in other provinces as a result of the political instability of the times.

A major event that shaped Cyprian's tenure as bishop of Carthage was the edict of the emperor Decius, issued upon his accession to the imperial throne in the year 249 CE. This edict required all inhabitants of the empire, who were now all Roman citizens since the time of Caracalla's decree in 212 CE, to offer sacrifices to the traditional gods of the Roman state. Upon doing so, they would be given a *libellus*, or certificate of sacrifice, by the attending priests. The traditional view of Decius's intent is that he specifically targeted the Christians with this measure.[113] One argument in support of this position is that it would have been a "bureaucratic nightmare" to issue a *libellus* to every inhabitant of the empire; perhaps the surviving *libelli* can be explained, then, as a "second stage [of the decree], aimed only at suspect Christians."[114] Paul Schubert, however, has shown persuasively that the physical format of surviving papyrus *libelli* indicates an efficient, standardized, and workable system in which Decius's decree reached the Egyptian prefect, who then passed it on to the *strategoi* of the various nomes (administrative districts), who

---

111. See for example, Corbier, "Coinage, Society, Economy," 393–439; Duncan-Jones, "Economic Change," 20–52; and Rathbone, "Roman Egypt," 698–719. Brown regards the "decline" of the third century as merely a "return to reality"; in his view the prosperity of the second century is the anomaly that requires explanation (*Through the Eye of A Needle*, 8–11).

112. Duncan-Jones, "Economic Change," 34.

113. This was the view of Eusebius and other ancient writers. Eusebius reports that Decius issued the edict out of hatred for his predecessor, Philip, who, according to Eusebius, was a Christian (*Hist. eccl.* 6.34.1; 6.39.1).

114. Lane Fox, *Pagans and Christians*, 455–56.

in turn saw to its implementation in the towns and villages by local officials and professional scribes.[115] The administrative structure was already in place in the census system, so the issuance of a certificate of sacrifice for all citizens is by no means implausible.[116] Thus, Decius's edict can be understood as directed not specifically against the Christians but to all inhabitants of the empire. Therefore, it was most likely a conservative measure designed to achieve imperial unity by restoring traditional religious practices[117] and by seeking the favor of the gods during a time of political instability.[118] As Rives argues, Decius's attempt to universalize Roman religion by imposing normative cultic behavior from the top down (when, previously, pagan religion had been a local phenomenon) actually prefigured the universalizing goals of Constantine in the next century.[119] But even though Decius's edict aimed for compliance from all Roman citizens, the Christians, of all people, would have felt this order most acutely. So it is not surprising that they experienced the trauma of this decree as an act of persecution directed solely against them.

In the remaining pages I first examine the model of care for the poor that we see reflected in Cyprian's letters both before and during the Decian persecution.[120] The goal here is to show that the system of caring for the needy remained consistent throughout Cyprian's tenure, and that it was flexible enough to accommodate those adversely affected by Decius's edict. Following this, I then examine Cyprian's theological argument in support of Christian care for the poor and note its similarity to what we have seen previously in the work of other Christian thinkers.

Because Cyprian wrote Letter 2 prior to the edict, his discussion of assisting the needy in this document can be taken as evidence for the normal model of care for the poor practiced by the church in Carthage. In this letter, Cyprian writes to a fellow bishop about the church's responsibility to support an actor, who, though apparently retired from actual

---

115. Schubert, "Form and Content."

116. Ibid., 189–91. James Rives also makes this suggestion ("Decree," 150–51).

117. Rives refers to Decius's goal of establishing a religious "orthopraxy" for all Roman citizens ("Decree," 153).

118. Allen Brent argues that after defeating Philip in battle, Decius sought to "secure upon nature as well as on society the 'peace of the gods' (*pax deorum*)" by proposing "a universal *supplicatio*" (*Cyprian*, 6).

119. Rives, "Decree," 153–54.

120. For the chronological order of Cyprian's letters, I have relied upon the judgments of Clarke, *Letters of Cyprian*.

stage performance, continued to earn his livelihood as a teacher of the craft. The early church considered the theater to be immoral and acting a profession forbidden to Christians, but this prohibition created the very practical problem of how actors who became Christians would support themselves after their conversion. Cyprian's position was that since the church made this moral demand, it was now the church's responsibility to offer the necessary financial support. Cyprian writes: "If such an instructor pleads poverty and straitened circumstances, his needs can be alleviated along with those of others who are supported by the provisions of the church—on condition, of course, that he can be satisfied with more frugal, and harmless, fare."[121] Two points are significant here: First, Cyprian states that the actor should be grouped with others who are sustained by the church's support (*ecclesiae alimentis sustinentur*). Though he does not specify here who these others are, this statement does indicate that the church had a regular system of poor relief. Second, Cyprian focuses on the actor's need (*paenuriam talis et necessitatem paupertatis*) and makes the point that the church is obligated to provide for his basic subsistence, but not the lifestyle to which he is accustomed; he should be satisfied with "more frugal fare" (*fugalioribus cibis*).

If G. W. Clarke is correct that Letter 7 should be dated immediately following Decius's edict but prior to incidents of persecution,[122] then Cyprian's discussion of care for the poor here may also be taken to reflect the typical practices of the church. In this letter, Cyprian urges the clergy in Carthage to remain diligent in caring for the poor in spite of his absence.[123] Cyprian writes: "Be scrupulous in your care for the widows, the sick, and all the poor, and further that you meet the financial needs of any strangers who are in want out of my personal funds which I have left in the care of our fellow presbyter Rogatianus."[124] Cyprian first of all notes the types of individuals eligible for the church's assistance. In the case of widows and some of the sick, poverty was a chronic condition,

---

121. Quod si paenuriam talis et necessitatem paupertatis optendit, potest inter ceteros qui ecclesiae alimentis sustinentur huius quoque necessitas adiunari, si tamen contentus sit frugalioribus et innocentibus cibis (Cyprian, *Ep.* 2.2).

122. Clarke, *Letters of Cyprian*, 1:198.

123. Cyprian fled Carthage and went into hiding at the outbreak of the persecution. His biographer, Pontius, insists that he did so not out of fear but so that he could avoid martyrdom and continue to provide pastoral care to his flock (*Vit. Cyp.* 7).

124. Viduarum et infirmorum et omnium pauperum curam peto diligenter habeatis. Sed et peregrinis si qui indigentes fuerint sumptus suggeratis de quantitate mea propria quam apud Rogatianum compresbyterum nostrum dimisi (Cyprian, *Ep.* 7.2).

and the church's support would be ongoing, but for the others we can imagine a situational type of poverty resulting from specific, temporary hardships that would require only short-term relief. It may be that Cyprian has this kind of conjunctural poverty in mind when he refers to the general category of "all the poor" (*omnium pauperum*). Cyprian also mentions needy "strangers" (*et peregrinis si qui indigentes fuerint*). These could be individuals who have migrated to Carthage hoping to improve their economic prospects but, finding themselves alone in the city, are now worse off than they were before because they no longer have the social support network of their hometown or village. It is also noteworthy here that Cyprian provides the funds for these poor-relief efforts with his own personal wealth, yet he calls upon the church's clergy to oversee the distribution. The church's system of care for the poor has become more institutionalized, but the personal resources of the wealthy are still needed to fund it.

The Decian persecution created a new category of needy Christians in Carthage and placed a heavy strain on the church's system of care for the poor. While it is impossible to know the numbers involved and how extensively the persecution affected the Christian population in the city, exile, confiscation of property, imprisonment, and in some cases martyrdom must have impoverished some relatively wealthy families who had previously been immune to subsistence concerns. In Letter 5, Cyprian encourages the clergy to assist those who are in economic need as a result of the persecution:

> I ask that there be nothing wanting in furnishing supplies for those who have confessed the Lord with words of glory and who are now to be found in prison, as equally to those who are suffering from need and want but yet continue faithful in the Lord. For all the funds collected have been distributed amongst the clergy in Carthage precisely to meet emergencies of this kind, thus putting a number in the position to ease individual cases of hardship and necessity.[125]

Cyprian seems to distinguish here between two classes of needy people: those who were in prison because of their Christian confession, and the

---

125. Quantum ad sumptus suggerendos, sive illis qui gloriosa voce Dominum confessi in carcere sunt constituti, sive his qui pauperes et indigentes laborant et tamen in Domino perseverant, peto nihil desit, cum summula omnis quae redacta est illic sit apud clericos distributa propter eiusmodi casus, ut haberent plures unde ad necessitates et pressures singulorum operari possint (Cyprian, *Ep.* 5.1).

general poor and needy whom the church had regularly assisted prior to the outbreak of the persecution. The fact that he insists that the confessors should be helped at the same level as the regular poor suggests that there may have been some initial uncertainty about how to manage this influx of new recipients of the church's assistance. Cyprian's statement that the funds had been collected and given to the clergy for distribution "precisely to meet emergencies of this kind" is also revealing for what it says about the intended purpose of the church's system of care for the poor: it was designed to address short-term, emergency situations. This is what we have seen consistently from the beginning, that the early Christians intentionally organized themselves, in part at least, for the purpose of providing an alternative subsistence strategy for their members.

Like his predecessors surveyed in previous chapters, Cyprian also provided ideological support designed to encourage relatively wealthy Christians to contribute to the church's system of care for the poor. In his treatise *On Works and Alms*, which is devoted to the topic, Cyprian presents a number of arguments for giving generously for the sake of the poor. For those who were concerned that almsgiving would deplete their patrimony upon which they depended for financial security for themselves and for their children, Cyprian reminds them that God will provide. Echoing the words of Jesus, he writes:

> God feeds the fowls, and daily food is afforded to the sparrows, and to creatures which have no sense of things divine there is no want of food or drink. Thinkest thou that to a Christian—thinkest thou that to a servant of the Lord—thinkest thou that to one given up to good works—thinkest thou that to one that is dear to the Lord, anything will be wanting?[126]

Giving to the poor requires trust in God. Cyprian adds that almsgiving removes the fear of having one's property confiscated by the state: "The state neither takes away the property entrusted to God, nor does the exchequer intrude on it, nor does any forensic calamity overthrow it. The inheritance is placed in security which is kept under the guardianship of God."[127] For those who were used to the normal patterns of Greco-

---

126. Volucres Deus pascit et passeribus alimenta diurnal praestantur et quibus nullus divinae rei sensus est eis nec potus nec cibus deest: tu christiano, tu Dei servo, tu operibus bonis dedito, tu Domino suo caro aliquid existimas defuturum? (Cyprian, *Eleem.* 11).

127. Patrimonium Deo creditum nec respublica eripit nec fiscus invadit nec calumnia aliqua forensis evertit. In tuto hereditas ponitur quae Deo custode servatur

Roman benefaction and the honor that would come from giving generous gifts, Cyprian reminds them that God is the audience when one gives to the poor. He writes:

> If, in a gift of the Gentiles, it seems a great and glorious thing to have proconsuls or emperors present, and the preparation and display is the greater among the givers, in order that they may please the higher classes, how much more illustrious and greater the glory to have God and Christ as the spectators of the gift.[128]

Honor and glory are still the goal, but instead of trying to impress one's peers and social superiors, the goal for the Christian is to impress God, and the reward for doing so, Cyprian says, is "eternal life" (*vita aeterna praestatur*).[129]

Cyprian's most important argument for giving to the poor is that it is a remedy for postbaptismal sin. We have seen this idea already in the *Shepherd of Hermas*. As I noted above, the concept of "redemptive almsgiving" became increasingly important in this period, and Cyprian was a prominent advocate for it. According to Cyprian, God provided a once-for-all redemption through his Son, but as a graceful response to human frailty, he also established almsgiving as a means by which "we may wash away whatever foulness we subsequently contract."[130] The theological challenge of postbaptismal sin took an extreme form in the case of "the lapsed" in the Decian persecution. Confronted on the one side by the Novatians, who denied readmission to the lapsed, and on the other side by the "confessors," who claimed that their suffering authorized them in the eyes of God to offer restoration, Cyprian sought middle ground that would both preserve the intergity of the church and would also demonstrate a measure of forgiveness consistent with the nature of God. Cyprian gave almsgiving an important place in his penitential system. In his treatise *On the Lapsed*, Cyprian states that in addition to prayer and lamentation, fasting, wearing sackcloth and ashes, spending days in grief, and keeping nightly vigils with weeping, penitent ones should also "be

---

(ibid.).

128. Si in gentilium munere grande et gloriosum videtur proconsules vel imperatores habere praesentes, et apparatus ac sumptus apud munerarios maior est ut possint placere maioribus, quanto inlustrior muneris et maior est gloria Deum et Christum habere spectatores (ibid., 21).

129. Ibid.

130. ut sordes postmodum quascumque contrahimus eleemosynis abluamus (ibid.).

earnest in righteous works, whereby sins may be purged; frequently apply yourself to almsgiving, whereby souls are freed from death."[131]

We have seen in this section that under the leadership of Cyprian, the church in Carthage practiced a system of care for the poor very similar to the basic model we have observed from the beginning of the Christian movement. Human need was the basic criterion in determining the worthiness of recipients of the church's benevolence. While the church in Carthage provided for the chronically poor, their system also accommodated those who experienced temporary, short-term, conjunctural poverty, including those in need as a result of the Decian persecution, and in that manner provided an alternative subsistence strategy for those who found themselves lacking other kinds of support. It is clear from Cyprian's letters and treatises on care for the poor that it was the relatively wealthy who were expected to contribute, but in a sign of things to come, this personal wealth, donated by the relatively wealthy, non-elite Christians of Carthage, was placed increasingly under the institutional oversight of the church. And like his predecessors, Cyprian also employed a number of arguments, most notably the redemptive power of almsgiving, to lend ideological support for the counterculural practice of giving to the needy to a class of Christians still caught between two worlds and competing value systems: the kingdom of this world and the kingdom of God.

Conclusion

In this chapter, I have tried to show continuity in Christian care for the poor as the Christian movement passed from its earliest days in the first century into the second and third centuries, a time when it experienced geographical expansion, numerical growth, and rising social prominence. Even though the Christians of this period developed new ideas to support their alternative subsistence strategy, the basic model remained the same. The relatively wealthy of the Christian assemblies were expected to play the role of patrons of the community, in much the same way that the rural patron of the peasant village did, by providing for the subsistence needs of the poor during times of food shortage. The urban Christian assemblies were structured, in part at least, in the interest of providing an alternative subsistence strategy for their members. The Christians

---

131. Oportet iustis operibus incumbere quibus peccata purgantur, eleemosynis frequenter insistere quibus a morte animae liberantur (Cyprian, *Laps.* 35).

were traditional in that their economic model resembled the rural village; they were innovative in that they replicated the village in the city. One of the challenges they faced in doing so was that upwardly mobile urban residents who were accustomed to the norms of urban patronage and benefaction viewed the Christian practice of giving to the needy as irresponsibly indiscriminate and morally questionable behavior. Thus, the Christians had to address these concerns by creating a conceptual world in which care for the poor, simply on the basis of their need, not only made sense but became the new norm for virtuous generosity in this alternative community. Even though "redemptive almsgiving" appears to be a new theological direction taken by the Christians of this era which some modern historians see as compromising their egalitarian roots, when it is assessed from the standpoint of the Christians' alternative subsistence strategy, redemptive almsgiving may be viewed instead as simply one more argument in their repertoire to persuade the relatively wealthy to fulfill their vital role as patrons to the poor.

Conclusion

Two central conclusions emerge from this study. The first is that the early Christian practice of care for the poor should not be regarded as an entirely new phenomenon in the ancient Roman world. As we have seen, it was modeled after the communal economic morality of the rural village, the "moral economy of the peasant," to use the terminology of James Scott. Thus, the basic patterns of the Christian practice would undoubtedly have been familiar to a large segment of the ancient population whose livelihood depended upon agricultural labor. A second conclusion is that Christian care for the poor from the earliest Jesus movement up to the time of Cyprian of Carthage exhibited a remarkable degree of continuity. This provides an alternative to the standard interpretation that sees the economic practices of the earliest Christ followers corrupted, as early as in the last decades of the first century, by the presence of wealthy Christians who practiced almsgiving rather than renunciation. This is a story of a lost innocence, in which the pristine egalitarianism of the Jesus movement and the Pauline communities begins to crumble under the influence of contemporary Greco-Roman values. A movement of the poor becomes a stratified religion dominated by the rich, who control not only the church's purse strings but also its developing orthodox theology. According to this view, Christianity in the second and third centuries becomes a religion concerned with preserving the status quo and protecting the interests and power of the privileged. To see Christian care for the poor as an alternative subsistence strategy, however, suggests a different conclusion. Certainly changes can be identified, but one contention of this study has been that these changes represent superficial responses to evolving circumstances rather than a fundamental alteration of the basic model.

The peasant farmer in the ancient Mediterranean world faced a life of economic uncertainty. This was the result of climatic variation, which caused frequent and sometimes drastic fluctuations in annual crop production. The possibility of personal misfortunes, such as disease, disability, or premature death added to the peasant family's insecurity. In good years there might be plenty, and they could hope to fill their stockpiles. In bad years, however, these families might not even have enough to survive without some form of assistance. This chronic uncertainty made subsistence strategies an absolute necessity. As we have seen, these included production strategies (crop distribution and diversification as well as storing one's surplus and selling cash crops in the marketplace). Another line of defense included social strategies, the primary focus of this study. In times of shortage, peasants often turned to kin, close neighbors, and even wealthy villagers, who, based on the norm of reciprocity and the assumption that subsistence is a fundamental right for all in the community, were obligated to provide assistance, risking personal shame and judgment from the community for not giving assistance.

Roman imperial rule created conditions that undermined these traditional strategies. In part, some of the oppressive features of Roman rule created need among lower classes. Yet, scholars debate the impact of these factors. According to one school of thought, taxes and rents could not have been overly burdensome, or the whole system would have collapsed. Moreover, it is likely that overall prosperity increased under Roman rule. In light of this, indirect social changes associated with imperialism may have been more detrimental than the actual economic impact. One such detrimental social change was that ruling class values and ideals increasingly influenced wealthy rural patrons, hindering their willingness to provide for the poor because they became concerned that they would be identified as prodigals, a category of benefactor condemned by the ancient moralists for giving indiscriminately to unworthy recipients. Thus giving to the needy peasant in one's village was no longer a morally acceptable option for those interested in joining elite society, even if only marginally. Moreover, with new opportunities in the cities for economic advancement, access to urban law courts, and new social circles, the rural wealthy no longer had to be so concerned with conforming to the consensual morality of the village community. In many cases, the village lost much of its power to impose social sanctions upon those not observing its communal ideals. In sum, imperial rule undermined a key element of the traditional peasant subsistence strategy by causing the rural patron to be less responsive to local needs. It was in this context that Christian care for the poor provided an alternative subsistence strategy to those for whom traditional strategies were no longer sufficient. At this point I can now summarize three elements that characterize Christian care for the poor as an alternative subsistence strategy, and that demonstrate its basic continuity over the first three centuries CE.

First, the Christians' alternative subsistence strategy met the needs primarily of the working poor, who experienced short-term need as a result of various types of misfortunes that could befall someone in an agrarian economy. This assumption is based on a new understanding of the Roman economy, which questions the assumption that Roman society was made up of two social groupings divided by a wide economic gulf. This influential model maintains that the social elite class, made up no more than 2 percent of the population and controlled nearly all the wealth of the empire while the other 98 percent, the oppressed lower class, faced grinding poverty with no hope for improving their lot in life. Newer research has shown more economic diversity among the non-elite population. The designations rich and poor, in fact, prove to have little explanatory power in light of this, because many who were socially or politically poor were not necessarily economically poor. Therefore, the question of a person's economic position relative to basic human subsistence proves to be the more helpful approach in identifying the poor. Some in Roman society undoubtedly fell below subsistence level as a chronic condition, but this was not the majority of the population. Most lived right at the level of subsistence or just a little bit above. Consequently, when misfortunes occurred, subsistence became a struggle, and struggling families required a variety of strategies to insure their survival. When traditional strategies failed, alternative strategies were needed. The Christians provided just such an alternative.

A second feature of the Christian alternative subsistence strategy is that it was funded by the relatively wealthy in the Christian community. Therefore, Christians attempted to replicate in an urban setting the traditional economic practices of the rural village. In other words, the relatively wealthy Christian assumed the role of the rural patron by assisting those in the Christian assembly who faced subsistence struggles. Here again the older view, which divides Roman society between rich and poor, has caused problems for interpreters. Under this model, it is difficult to see how there could be any wealthy people in the Christian community, considering that widespread participation by social elites did not happen until well into the fourth century. But if the economics of the ancient world is approached from the standpoint of wealth relative to subsistence, one can imagine in the churches members with sufficient wealth personally immune to subsistence concerns and also with some level of discretionary income in spite of their non-elite social status. Some people in this category joined Christian assemblies and were persuaded to use their surplus wealth for the needy.

As soon as it is granted that Jesus and Paul sought to persuade the relatively wealthy non-elites to fund the alternative subsistence strategy of the Christian community, then a key assumption supporting the model of decline in Christian care for the poor falls away. While Christian groups may have had to resort occasionally to a practice I have referred to as sacrificial sharing among the poor, this could not have been regarded as a sustainable strategy over the long term. More enduring would have been a strategy of recruiting the relatively wealthy in the community to assume the role of the rural patron. This is just what we see in Christian discourse from the historical Jesus to Cyprian of Carthage: an effort to persuade the wealthy that caring for the poor was not only a moral obligation but spiritually beneficial as well.

A third feature of the Christian subsistence strategy is that Christian theology legitimated the practice and remained remarkably consistent from Jesus to Cyprian. The story of the kingdom of God provided the master narrative for the earliest Christians and upheld their communal practices, including care for the poor. This was a story rooted in the traditions of Israel, in which the sovereign God enters into a covenantal relationship with his people, which for the early Christians now included both Jews and gentiles in Christ. This was also a story with powerful social and political implications, promising its adherents that one day God would bring a reversal in which the poor are exalted. Yet, this God also forgives the penitent, providing an opportunity for reconciliation to those who had formerly been unrighteous. A key element in doing the will of this God, as we have seen, is caring for the poor in the Christian assembly. Thus the Christian concept of God from the first through the third centuries established the moral framework by which the Christians legitimated their alternative subsistence strategy and cared for the poor on the basis of their need.

The early Christians responded to a specific set of social and economic circumstances, drawing upon resources that were both traditional and innovative. They created alternative communities in the Roman

Empire that provided members with needed social and economic support in a changing world. The proclamation of the early Christians certainly contained an otherworldly dimension. But these beliefs went hand in hand with the down-to-earth realities faced by those seeking another layer of social security to meet their subsistence needs, particularly when traditional strategies proved no longer sufficient. To some modern interpreters, such concerns might seem too mundane and insignificant to occupy the attention of one of the world's great religious traditions. To the majority of ancient people, however, having enough to eat was as important a religious concern as any theological doctrine or ecclesiastical dispute.

Bibliography

Ancient Sources

Greco-Roman Sources

Aristotle, *Nicomachean Ethics*:
Text: *Aristotelis, Ethica Nicomachea*. Edited by L. Bywater. *Scriptorum Classicorum Bibliotheca Oxoniensis*. Oxford: Oxford University Press, 1890.

Translation: *Aristotle, The Nicomachean Ethics*. Translated by H. Rackham. LCL. Cambridge: Harvard University Press, 1945.

Cicero, *On Duties*:
Text: *Cicéron: Lex Devoirs*, Vols. 1–2. Edited by Maurice Testard. Paris: Les Belles Lettres, 1965, 1970; Vol. 2, 2nd ed., 1984.

Translation: *Cicero, De Officiis*. Translated by Walter Miller. LCL. New York: MacMillan, 1913.

Julian, *Letter to a Pagan Priest*:
Text and Translation: *The Works of the Emperor Julian*. Vol. 2. Translated by Wilmer Cave Wright. LCL. Cambridge: Harvard University Press, 1913.

Pliny the Younger, *Letters*:
Text: *Epistulae: A Critical Edition*. Edited by Selatie Edgar Stout. Indiana University Humanity Series 49. Bloomington: Indiana University Press, 1962.

Translation: *The Letters of the Younger Pliny*. Translated with and introduction by Betty Radice. Baltimore: Penguin, 1963.

Seneca, *On Benefits*:
Text: *Sénèque, Des Bienfaits*. Edited by François Préchac. Paris: Les Belles Lettres, 1926.

Translation: *Seneca: Moral Essays*. Vol. 3. Translated by John W. Basore. LCL. Cambridge: Harvard University Press, 1935.

Seneca, *The Fortunate Life*:
Text and Translation: *Seneca: Moral Essays*. Vol. 2. Translated by John W. Basore. LCL. Cambridge: Harvard University Press, 1932.

Early Christian Sources

Acts of John:
Text: *Acta Iohannis*. Eric Junod et Jean-Daniel Kaestli. Corpus Christianorum, Series Apocryphorum 1–2. Turnhout: Brepols, 1983.

Translation: *New Testament Apocrypha*. 2 vols. Edited by Wilhelm Scheemelcher. English translation by R. McL. Wilson. Rev. ed. Louisville: Westminster John Knox, 1992.

Acts of Paul:
Text: *Les Actes de Paul et Ses Lettres Apocryphes: Introduction, textes, traduction et commentaire*. Léon Vouaux. Documents pour servir a l'étude des origines chrétiennes. Paris: Letouzey et Ané, 1913.

Translation: *New Testament Apocrypha*. 2 vols. Edited by Wilhelm Scheemelcher. English translation by R. McL. Wilson. Rev. ed. Louisville: Westminster/John Knox, 1992.

Acts of Peter:
Text: *Les Actes de Pierre: Introduction, textes, traduction et commentaire*. Léon Vouaux. Paris: Letouzey et Ané, 1922.

Translation: *New Testament Apocrypha*. 2 vols. Edited by Wilhelm Scheemelcher. English translation by R. McL. Wilson. Rev. ed. Louisville: Westminster John Knox Press, 1992.

Clement of Alexandria, *Who Is the Rich Man That Is to Be Saved?*
Text: *Clemens Alexandrinus*. Vol. 3. Edited by Otto Stählin. Berlin: Akademie, 1970.

Translation: Translated by William Wilson. *ANF*. Vol. 2. Edited by Alexander Roberts and James Donaldson. Revised and chronologically arranged with brief prefaces and occasional notes by A. Cleveland Coxe. 1908. Reprint: Grand Rapids: Eerdmans, 1971.

Cyprian of Carthage, *On the Lapsed*:
Text: *Liber de Lapsis*. Patrologia latina. Edited by J.-P. Migne. 217 vols. Paris: Migne, 1844–1864.

Translation: Translated by Ernest Wallis. *ANF*. Vol. 5. Edited by Alexander Roberts and James Donaldson. Revised and chronologically arranged with brief prefaces and occasional notes by A. Cleveland Coxe. 1908. Reprint, Grand Rapids: Eerdmans 1971.

Cyprian of Carthage, *Letters*:
Text: *Sancti Cypriani Episcopi Opera*. Pars 3/1–2. Edited by G. F. Diercks. CCSL 3. Turnhout: Brepols, 1972.

Translation: *The Letters of Cyprian*. 4 vols. G. W. Clarke. ACW 43–44, 46–47. New York: Newman, 1984–1989.

Cyprian of Carthage, *On Works and Alms*:
Text: *Cyprian de Carthage: La bienfaisance et les aumônes: introduction, texte critique, traduction, notes et index*. Michel Poirier. SC 440. Paris: Cerf, 1999.

Translation: Translated by Ernest Wallis. *ANF*. Vol. 5. Edited by Alexander Roberts and James Donaldson. Revised and chronologically arranged with brief prefaces and occasional notes by A. Cleveland Coxe. 1908. Reprint, Grand Rapids: Eerdmans, 1971.

Didache:
Text: *Didache, Zwölf-Apostel-Lehre*. Translated and introduced by Georg Schöllgen. Fontes Christiani 1. Freiburg: Herder, 1991.

Translation: *The Didache, The Epistle of Barnabas, the Epistles and the Martyrdom of St. Polycarp, the Fragments of Papias, and the Epistle to Diognetus*. Translated and annotated by James A. Kleist, SJ. ACW 6. Westminster, MD: Newman, 1961.

Epistle of Barnabas:
Translation: *The Didache, The Epistle of Barnabas, the Epistles and the Martyrdom of St. Polycarp, the Fragments of Papias, and the Epistle to Diognetus*. Translated and annotated by James A. Kleist, SJ. ACW 6. Westminster, MD: Newman, 1961.

Justin, *First Apology*:
Text: *Saint Justin, Apologies*. Introduction, critical text, translation, commentary and index by André Wartelle. Paris: Études Augustiniennes, 1987.

Translation: Translated by Alexander Roberts and James Donaldson. *ANF*. Vol. 1. Edited by Alexander Roberts and James Donaldson. Revised and chronologically arranged with brief prefaces and occasional notes by A. Cleveland Coxe. 1908. Reprint, Grand Rapids: Eerdmans 1971.

Shepherd of Hermas:
Text: *Hermas, Le Pasteur*. Introduction, critical text, translation and notes by Robert Joly. SC 53. Paris: Cerf, 1958.

Translation: Translated by F. Crombie. *ANF*. Vol. 2. Edited by Alexander Roberts and James Donaldson. Revised and chronologically arranged with brief prefaces and occasional notes by A. Cleveland Coxe. 1908. Reprint, Grand Rapids: Eerdmans 1971.

Tertullian, *Apology*:
Text: *Tertullian, Apologeticum: Verteidung des Christentums*. Translated and explained by Carl Becker. Munich: Kösel, 1952.

Translation: Translated by S. Thelwall. *ANF*. Vol. 3. Edited by Alexander Roberts and James Donaldson. Revised and chronologically arranged with brief prefaces and occasional notes by A. Cleveland Coxe. 1908. Reprint, Grand Rapids: Eerdmans 1971.

Secondary Studies

Allison, Dale C. *Jesus of Nazareth: Millenarian Prophet*. Minneapolis: Fortress, 1998.
Alexander, Loveday. *The Preface to Luke's Gospel: Literary Convention and Social Context in Luke 1.1–4 and Acts 1.1*. SNTSMS 78. Cambridge: Cambridge University Press, 1993.
Alföldy, Géza. *The Social History of Rome*. Translated by David Braund and Frank Pollock. Totowa, NJ: Barnes & Noble, 1985.
Arnal, William E. *Jesus and the Village Scribes: Galilean Conflicts and the Setting of Q*. Minneapolis: Fortress, 2001.
Ascough, Richard. "Benefaction Gone Wrong: The 'Sin' of Ananias and Sapphira in Context." In *Text and Artifact in the Religions of Mediterranean Antiquity: Essays in Honor of Peter Richardson*, edited by Stephen G. Wilson and Michael Desjardins, 91–110. Studies in Christianity and Judaism 9. Waterloo, ON: Wilfrid Laurier University Press, 2000.
Atkins, Margaret, and Robin Osborne, eds. *Poverty in the Roman World*. Cambridge: Cambridge University Press, 2006.
Aviam, Mordechai. "People, Land, Economy, and Belief in First-Century Galilee and Its Origins: A Comprehensive Archaeological Synthesis." In *The Galilean Economy in the Time of Jesus*, edited by David A. Fiensy and Ralph K. Hawkins, 5–48. SBLECL 11. Atlanta: SBL, 2013.
Bailey, Kenneth E. "Informal Controlled Oral Tradition and the Synoptic Gospels." *AJT* 5 (1991) 34–54.
———. *Jacob and the Prodigal: How Jesus Retold Israel's Story*. Downers Grove, IL: InterVarsity, 2003.
———. "Middle Eastern Oral Tradition and the Synoptic Gospels." *ExpT* 106 (1995) 563–67.
———. *Poet and Peasant, and Through Peasant Eyes*. Reprint, combined ed. Grand Rapids: Eerdmans, 1983.
Balch, David L. "Rich Pompeiian Houses, Shops for Rent, and the Huge Apartment Building in Herculaneum as Typical Spaces for Pauline House Churches." *JSNT* 27 (2004) 27–46.

Bammel, Ernst. "The Feeding of the Multitude." In *Jesus and the Politics of His Day*, edited by Ernst Bammel and C. F. D. Moule, 211–40. New York: Cambridge University Press, 1984.

Barclay, John. "Poverty in Pauline Studies: A Response to Steven Friesen." *JSNT* 26 (2004) 363–66.

Barnes, Timothy David. "The Embassy of Athenagoras." *JTS* 26 (1975) 111–14.

———. *Tertullian: A Historical and Literary Study*. 1971. Reissued with corrections and a postscript. Oxford: Clarendon, 1985.

Barrett, C. K. "The First New Testament?" *NovT* 38 (1996) 94–104.

Bartchy, S. Scott. "Community of Goods in Acts: Idealization or Social Reality?" In *The Future of Early Christianity: Essays in Honor of Helmut Koester*, edited by Birger A. Pearson in collaboration with A. Thomas Kraabel, George W. E. Nickelsburg, and Norman R. Petersen, 309–18. Minneapolis: Fortress, 1991.

———. "The Historical Jesus and the Reversal of Honor at the Table." In *The Social Setting of Jesus and the Gospels*, edited by Wolfgang Stegemann, Bruce J. Malina, and Gerd Theissen, 175–83. Minneapolis: Fortress, 2002.

———. "Undermining Ancient Patriarchy: The Apostle Paul's Vision of a Society of Siblings." *BTB* 29 (1999) 68–78.

Berger, Klaus. "Almosen für Israel: zum historischen Kontext der paulinischen Kollekte." *NTS* 23 (1976–77) 180–204.

Berger, Peter, and Thomas Luckmann. *The Social Construction of Reality*. Garden City, NY: Doubleday, 1967.

Bock, Darrell L. *Acts*. BECNT. Grand Rapids: Baker Academic, 2007.

———. *Luke*. 2 vols. BECNT. Grand Rapids: Baker Academic, 1994–1996.

Bolkestein, Hendrik. *Wohltätigkeit und Armenpflege im vorchristlichen Altertum*. 1939. Reprint, Groningen: Bouma, 1967.

Borg, Marcus J. *Conflict, Holiness, and Politics in the Teaching of Jesus*. Studies in the Bible and Early Christianity 5. Lewiston, NY: Mellen, 1984.

———. *Jesus: Uncovering the Life, Teachings, and Relevance of a Religious Revolutionary*. San Francisco: HarperSanFrancisco, 2006.

Brent, Allen J. *Cyprian and Roman Carthage*. Cambridge: Cambridge University Press, 2010.

———. "Cyprian's Reconstruction of the Martyr Tradition." *Journal of Ecclesiastical History* 53 (2002) 241–68.

Brown, Peter. *The Making of Late Antiquity*. 1978. Reprint, Cambridge: Harvard University Press, 1992.

———. *Poverty and Leadership in the Later Roman Empire*. The Menahem Stern Jerusalem Lectures. Hanover, NH: University of New England Press, 2002.

———. *Through the Eye of A Needle: Wealth, the Fall of Rome, and the Making of Christianity in the West, 350–550 AD*. Paperback ed. Princeton: Princeton University Press, 2014.

———. *The World of Late Antiquity: AD 150–750*. 1971. Paperback ed. New York: Norton, 1989.

Burns, J. Patout, Jr. *Cyprian the Bishop*. Routledge Early Church Monographs. New York: Routledge, 2002.

Cameron, Averil. *Christianity and the Rhetoric of Empire*. Sather Classical Lectuers. Berkeley: University of California Press, 1990.

———. *The Later Roman Empire: AD 284–430*. Cambridge: Harvard University Press, 1993.

Capper, Brian. "The Palestinian Cultural Context of Earliest Christian Community of Goods." In *The Book of Acts in Its Palestinian Setting*, edited by Richard Bauckham, 323–56. The Book of Acts in Its First Century Setting 4. Grand Rapids: Eerdmans, 1995.

Clarke, G. W. *The Letters of Cyprian*. 4 Vols. ACW 43–44, 46–47. New York: Newman, 1984–89.

Conzelmann, Hans. *Acts of the Apostles*. Translated by James Limburg, A. Thomas Kraabel, and Donald H. Juel. Hermeneia. Philadelphia: Fortress, 1987.

———. *The Theology of St. Luke*. Translated by Geoffrey Buswell. 1961. Reprint, Philadelphia: Fortress, 1982.

Cooper, Kate. *The Virgin and the Bride: Idealized Womanhood in Late Antiquity*. Cambridge: Harvard University Press, 1996.

Corbier, Mireille. "Coinage, Society, and Economy." In CAH, Vol. 12: *The Crisis of Empire, A.D. 193–337*, edited by Alan K. Bowman, Peter Garnsey, and Averil Cameron, 393–439. 2nd ed. Cambridge: Cambridge University Press, 2005.

Countryman, L. William. *The Rich Christian in the Early Church: Contradictions and Accommodations*. Texts and Studies in Religion 7. New York: Mellen, 1980.

Crossan, John Dominic. *The Historical Jesus: The Life of a Mediterranean Jewish Peasant*. San Francisco: HarperSanFrancisco, 1991.

Crossan, John Dominic, and Jonathan L. Reed. *Excavating Jesus: Beneath the Stones, Behind the Texts*. San Francisco: HarperSanFrancisco, 2001.

Cullmann, Oscar. "The Early Church and the Ecumenical Problem." *Anglican Theological Review* 40 (1958) 181–89, 294–301.

Dahl, Nils A. "The Story of Abraham in Luke–Acts." In *Studies in Luke–Acts*, edited by Leander E. Keck and J. Louis Martyn, 139–58. Nashville: Abingdon, 1966. Reprinted in Dahl, *Jesus in the Memory of the Church: Essays*, 66–86. Minneapolis: Augsburg, 1976.

Danker, Frederick W. *Jesus and the New Age: A Commentary on St. Luke's Gospel*. Rev. ed. Philadelphia: Fortress, 1988.

D'Arms, John H. *Commerce and Social Standing in Ancient Rome*. Cambridge: Harvard University Press, 1981.

De Ligt, L. *Fairs and Markets in the Roman Empire: Economic and Social Aspects of Periodic Trade in a Pre-Industrial Society*. Amsterdam: Gieben, 1993.

de Ste. Croix, G. E. M. *The Class Struggle in the Ancient World*. 1981. Reissued and corrected paperback ed. Ithaca: Cornell University Press, 1998.

Dodds, E. R. *Pagan and Christian in an Age of Anxiety*. 1965. Reprint, New York: Cambridge University Press, 2000.

Downing, Gerald F. "Theophilus's First Reading of Luke–Acts." In *Luke's Literary Achievement: Collected Essays*, edited by C. M. Tuckett, 91–109. JSNTSup 116. Sheffield: Sheffield Academic, 1995.

Downs, David J. *The Offering of the Gentiles: Paul's Collection for Jerusalem in Its Chronological, Cultural, and Cultic Contexts*. With a foreword by Beverly Roberts Gaventa. Grand Rapids: Eerdmans, 2016.

Duncan-Jones, Richard. "Economic Change and the Transition to Late Antiquity." In *Approaching Late Antiquity: The Transformation from Early to Late Empire*, edited by Simon Swain and Mark Edwards, 20–52. New York: Oxford University Press, 2004.

Dunn, James D. G. *Jesus Remembered*. Christianity in the Making 1. Grand Rapids: Eerdmans, 2003.

———. *Romans 9–16*. WBC 38B. Dallas: Word, 1988.
Edwards, Mark, Martin Goodman, Simon Price, and Christopher Rowland. "Introduction: Apologetics in the Roman World." In *Apologetics in the Roman Empire: Pagans, Jews, and Christians*, edited by Mark Edwards, Martin Goodman, Simon Price, in association with Christopher Rowland, 1–14. New York: Oxford University Press, 1999.
Elliott, John H. "Jesus Was not an Egalitarian: A Critique of an Anachronistic and Idealist Theory." *BTB* 32 (2002) 75–91.
———. *What Is Social-Scientific Criticism?* Guides to Biblical Scholarship: New Testament Series. Minneapolis: Fortress, 1993.
Esler, Philip Francis. *Community and Gospel in Luke–Acts: The Social and Political Motivations of Lukan Theology*. SNTSMS 57. Cambridge: Cambridge University Press, 1987.
Evans, C. F. *Saint Luke*. TPINTC. Philadelphia: Trinity, 1990.
Fee, Gordon D. *The First Epistle to the Corinthians*. NICNT. Grand Rapids: Eerdmans, 1987.
Fiensy, David A. "Assessing the Economy of Galilee in the Late Second Temple Period: Five Considerations." In *The Galilean Economy in the Time of Jesus*, edited by David A. Fiensy and Ralph K. Hawkins, 165–86. SBLECL 11. Atlanta: SBL, 2013.
Finley, M. I. *The Ancient Economy*. 1973. Berkeley: University of California Press, 1974.
Finn, Richard, OP. *Almsgiving in the Later Roman Empire: Christian Promotion and Practice (315–450)*. New York: Oxford University Press, 2006.
Fitzmyer, Joseph A. *The Acts of the Apostles: A New Translation with Introduction and Commentary*. AB 31. New York: Doubleday, 1998.
———. *The Gospel according to Luke (I–IX): Introduction, Translation, and Notes*. AB 28. New York: Doubleday, 1981.
———. *Romans: A New Translation with Introduction and Commentary*. AB 33. New York: Doubleday, 1993.
Flanagan, James G. "Hierarchy in Simple 'Egalitarian' Societies." *Annual Review of Anthropology* 18 (1989) 245–66.
Freyne, Sean. *Jesus, A Jewish Galilean: A New Reading of the Jesus Story*. New York: T. & T. Clark, 2004.
Friesen, Steven J. "Poverty in Pauline Studies: Beyond the So-called New Consensus." *JSNT* 26 (2004) 323–61.
———. "Prospects for a Demography of the Pauline Mission: Corinth among the Churches." In *Urban Religion in Roman Corinth: Interdisciplinary Approaches*, edited by Daniel N. Schowalter and Steven J. Friesen, 351–70. HTS 53. Cambridge: Harvard University Press, 2005.
Garland, David E. *1 Corinthians*. BECNT. Grand Rapids: Baker Academic, 2003.
Garnsey, Peter. *Famine and Food Supply in the Graeco-Roman World: Responses to Risk and Crisis*. Cambridge: Cambridge University Press, 1988.
———. *Food and Society in Classical Antiquity*. Key Themes in Ancient History. Cambridge: Cambridge University Press, 1999.
Garnsey, Peter, and Richard Saller. *The Roman Empire: Economy, Society and Culture*. 2nd ed. Berkeley: University of California Press, 2015.
Garrison, Roman. *Redemptive Almsgiving in Early Christianity*. JSNTSup 77. Sheffield: Sheffield Academic, 1993.
Georgi, Dieter. *Remembering the Poor: The History of Paul's Collection for Jerusalem*. Nashville: Abingdon, 1992.

Giardina, Andrea. "The Transition to Late Antiquity." In *The Cambridge Economic History of the Greco-Roman World*, edited by Walter Scheidel, Ian Morris, and Richard P. Saller, 743–768. 2007. Paperback ed. Cambridge: Cambridge University Press, 2014.

Goodman, Martin. "The First Jewish Revolt: Social Conflict and the Problem of Debt." *JJS* 33 (1982) 417–27.

González, Justo L. *Luke*. Belief: A Theological Commentary on the Bible. Louisville: Westminster John Knox, 2010.

Gouldner, Alvin W. "The Norm of Reciprocity: A Preliminary Statement." *American Sociological Review* 25 (1960) 161–78.

Green, Joel B. *The Gospel of Luke*. NICNT. Grand Rapids: Eerdmans, 1997.

———. *The Theology of the Gospel of Luke*. New Testament Theology. Cambridge: Cambridge University Press, 1995.

Hägg, Tomas. *The Novel in Antiquity*. Berkeley: University of California Press, 1983.

Hamel, Gildas H. *Poverty and Charity in Roman Palestine, First Three Centuries C.E.* University of California Publication: Near Eastern Studies 23. Berkeley: University of California Press, 1990.

Hands, A. R. *Charities and Social Aid in Greece and Rome*. Aspects of Greek and Roman Life. London: Thames & Hudson, 1968.

Hanson, K. C., and Douglas E. Oakman. *Palestine in the Time of Jesus: Social Structures and Social Conflicts*. 2nd ed. Minneapolis: Fortress, 2008.

Harland, Philip A. *Associations, Synagogues, and Congregations: Claiming a Place in Ancient Society*. Minneapolis: Fortress, 2003.

Harnack, Adolf von. *The Mission and Expansion of Christianity in the First Three Centuries*. Translated and edited by James Moffat. 1908. Reprint, Gloucester, MA: Peter Smith, 1972.

Hellerman, Joseph H. *The Ancient Church as Family*. Minneapolis: Fortress, 2001.

Henderson, Suzanne Watts. "'If Anyone Hungers . . .': An Integrated Reading of 1 Cor 11.17–34." *NTS* 48 (2002) 195–208.

Herzog, William R., III. *Jesus, Justice, and the Reign of God: A Ministry of Liberation*. Louisville: Westminster John Knox, 2000.

Holgate, David A. *Prodigality, Liberality and Meanness in the Parable of the Prodigal Son: A Greco-Roman Perspective on Luke 15:11–32*. JSNTSup 187. Sheffield: Sheffield Academic, 1999.

Holl, Karl. "Der Kirchenbegriff des Paulus in seinem Verhältnis zu dem der Urgemeinde." *Sitzungsbericht der Berliner Akademie* (1921) 920–47. Reprinted in Holl, *Gesammelte Aufsätze zur Kirchengeschichte*, vol. 2: *Den Osten*, 44–67. Tübingen: Mohr/Siebeck, 1928.

Horden, Peregrine, and Nicholas Purcell. *The Corrupting Sea: A Study of Mediterranean History*. Oxford: Blackwell, 2000.

Horrell, David. "Paul's Collection: Resources for a Materialist Theology." *Epworth Review* 22 (1995) 74–83.

Horsley, Richard A. *Galilee: History, Politics, and People*. Valley Forge, PA: Trinity, 1995.

———. *Hearing the Whole Story*. Louisville: Westminster John Knox, 2001.

———. *Jesus and Empire: The Kingdom of God and the New World Disorder*. Minneapolis: Fortress, 2003.

———. "Jesus and Galilee: The Contingencies of a Renewal Movement." In *Galilee through the Centuries: Confluence of Cultures*, edited by Eric M. Meyers, 57–74. Winona Lake, IN: Eisenbrauns, 1999.

———. *Jesus and the Spiral of Violence: Popular Jewish Resistance in Roman Palestine*. Minneapolis: Fortress, 1987.

———. *The Liberation of Christmas: The Infancy Narratives in Social Context*. New York: Crossroad, 1989.

———. "What Has Galilee to Do with Jerusalem? Political Aspects of the Jesus Movement." *HvTSt* 52 (1996) 88–104.

Horsley, Richard A., with Jonathan A. Draper. *Whoever Hears You Hears Me: Prophets, Performance, and Tradition in Q*. Harrisburg, PA: Trinity, 1999.

Horsley, Richard A., and Patrick Tiller. "Ben Sira and the Sociology of the Second Temple." In *Second Temple Studies III: Studies in Politics, Class and Material Culture*, edited by Philip R. Davies and John M. Halligan, 74–107. JSOTSup 340. New York: Sheffield Academic, 2002.

Jensen, Morten Hørning. *Herod Antipas in Galilee*. 2nd ed. WUNT 2/215. Tübingen: Mohr/Siebeck, 2010.

———. "Herod Antipas in Galilee: Friend or Foe of the Historical Jesus?" *JSHJ* 5 (2007) 7–32.

Johnson, Luke Timothy. *The Acts of the Apostles*. SP 5. Collegeville, MN: Liturgical, 1992.

———. *The Gospel of Luke*. SP 3. Collegeville, MN: Liturgical, 1991.

———. "Literary Criticism of Luke–Acts: Is Reception History Pertinent?" *JSNT* 28 (2005) 159–62.

———. *The Literary Function of Possessions in Luke-Acts*. SBLDS 39. Missoula, MT: Scholars, 1977.

Jongman, Willem M. "The Early Roman Empire: Consumption." In *The Cambridge Economic History of the Greco-Roman World*, edited by Walter Scheidel, Ian Morris, and Richard P. Saller, 592–618. 2007. Paperback ed. Cambridge: Cambridge University Press, 2014.

Kehoe, Dennis P. "The Early Roman Empire: Production." In *The Cambridge Economic History of the Greco-Roman World*, edited by Walter Scheidel, Ian Morris, and Richard P. Saller, 543–69. 2007. Paperback ed. Cambridge: Cambridge University Press, 2014.

Kloppenborg, John S. *The Formation of Q: Trajectories in Ancient Wisdom Collections*. Reprint, Harrisburg, PA: Trinity, 1999.

Kloppenborg-Verbin, John S. *Excavating Q: The History and Setting of the Sayings Gospel*. Minneapolis: Fortress, 2000.

Komter, Aafke E. *The Gift: An Interdisciplinary Perspective*. Amsterdam: Amsterdam University Press, 1996.

Kraft, Robert A. "Didache." In *ABD* 2:197–98.

Kuhn, Karl Allen. *The Kingdom according to Luke and Acts: A Social, Literary, and Theological Introduction*. Grand Rapids: Baker Academic, 2015.

Lane Fox, Robin. *Pagans and Christians*. New York: Knopf, 1987.

Lenski, Gerhard. *Power and Privilege: A Theory of Social Stratification*. 2nd ed. New York: McGraw-Hill, 1984.

Lindemann, Andreas. "The Beginnings of Christian Life in Jerusalem according to the Summaries in the Acts of the Apostles." In *Common Life in the Early Church: Essays Honoring Graydon F. Snyder*, edited by Julian V. Hills et al., 202–18. Harrisburg, PA: Trinity, 1998.

Lintott, Andrew. *Imperium Romanum: Politics and Administration*. New York: Routledge, 1993.
Lo Cascio, Elio. "The Early Roman Empire: The State and the Economy." In *The Cambridge Economic History of the Greco-Roman World*, edited by Walter Scheidel, Ian Morris, and Richard P. Saller, 619–47. 2007. Paperback ed. Cambridge: Cambridge University Press, 2014.
Lohfink, Gerhard. *Jesus and Community: The Social Dimension of Christian Faith*. Translated by John P. Galvin. Philadelphia: Fortress, 1984.
Longenecker, Bruce W. *Remember the Poor: Paul, Poverty, and the Greco-Roman World*. Grand Rapids: Eerdmans, 2010.
Lüdemann, Gerd. *Early Christianity according to the Traditions in Acts: A Commentary*. Translated by John Bowden. Minneapolis: Fortress, 1989.
Mack, Burton L. *A Myth of Innocence: Mark and Christian Origins*. Philadelphia: Fortress, 1988.
McCollough, C. Thomas. "City and Village in Lower Galilee: The Import of the Archeological Excavations at Sepphoris and Khirbet Qana (Cana) for Framing the Economic Context of Jesus." In *The Galilean Economy in the Time of Jesus*, edited by David A. Fiensy and Ralph K. Hawkins, 49–74. SBLECL 11. Atlanta: SBL, 2013.
MacMullen, Ramsey. *Christianizing the Roman Empire, AD 100–400*. New Haven: Yale University Press, 1984.
———. *Roman Social Relations*. New Haven: Yale University Press, 1974.
———. *Romanization in the Time of Augustus*. New Haven: Yale University Press, 2000.
Malherbe, Abraham J. *Social Aspects of Early Christianity*. 2nd ed. Philadelphia: Fortress, 1983.
Marshall, I. Howard. *Luke: Historian & Theologian*. 3rd ed. New Testament Profiles. Downers Grove, IL: InterVarsity, 1988.
Martin, Dale. "Review Essay: Justin J. Meggitt, *Paul, Poverty and Survival*." *JSNT* 23 (2001) 51–64.
Matilla, Sharon Lea. "Revisiting Jesus' Capernaum: A Village of Only Subsistence-Level Fishers and Farmers?" In *The Galilean Economy in the Time of Jesus*, edited by David A. Fiensy and Ralph K. Hawkins, 75–138. SBLECL 11. Atlanta: SBL, 2013.
Mauss, Marcel. *The Gift: The Form and Reason for Exchange in Archaic Societies*. Translated by W. D. Halls, with a foreword by Mary Douglas. 1990. Reissued, New York: Routledge, 2000.
Mealand, David L. "Community of Goods and Utopian Allusions in Acts II–IV." *JTS* 28 (1977) 96–99.
Meeks, Wayne A. *The First Urban Christians: The Social World of the Apostle Paul*. New Haven: Yale University Press, 1983.
Meggitt, Justin J. *Paul, Poverty, and Survival*. Studies of the New Testament and Its World. Edinburgh: T. & T. Clark, 1998.
———. "Response to Martin and Theissen." *JSNT* 23 (2001) 85–94.
Meyers, Ched. *Binding the Strong Man: A Political Reading of Mark's Story of Jesus*. Maryknoll, NY: Orbis, 1988.
Millar, Fergus. *The Emperor in the Roman World*. 1977. With a new afterword by the author. Ithaca, NY: Cornell University Press, 1992.
Mitchell, Alan C., SJ. "The Social Function of Friendship in Acts 2:42–47 and 4:32–37." *JBL* 111 (1992) 255–72.

Moessner, David P., and David L. Tiede. "Introduction: *Two* Books but *One* Story?" In *Jesus and the Heritage of Israel: Luke's Narrative Claim upon Israel's Legacy*, edited by David P. Moessner, 1–8. Harrisburg, PA: Trinity, 1999.
Moo, Douglas J. *The Epistle to the Romans*. NICNT. Grand Rapids: Eerdmans, 1996.
Moreland, Milton. "The Galilean Response to Earliest Christianity: A Cross-Cultural Study of the Subsistence Ethic." In *Religion and Society in Roman Palestine: Old Questions, New Approaches*, edited by Douglas R. Edwards, 37–48. New York: Routledge, 2004.
Morley, Neville. "The Early Roman Empire: Distribution." In *The Cambridge Economic History of the Greco-Roman World*, edited by Walter Scheidel, Ian Morris, and Richard P. Saller, 570–91. 2007. Paperback ed. Cambridge: Cambridge University Press, 2014.
———. "The Poor in the City of Rome." *Poverty in the Roman World*, edited by Margaret Atkins and Robin Osborne, 21–39. Cambridge: Cambridge University Press, 2006.
Moss, Candida R. *The Myth of Persecution: How Early Christians Invented a Story of Martyrdom*. New York: HarperOne, 2013.
Moxnes, Halvor. *The Economy of the Kingdom: Social Conflict and Economic Relations in Luke's Gospel*. Overtures to Biblical Theology. 1988. Reprint, Eugene, OR: Wipf & Stock, 2004.
———. "Patron-Client Relations and the New Covenant in Luke–Acts." In *The Social World of Luke–Acts: Models for Interpretation*, edited by Jerome H. Neyrey, 241–68. Peabody, MA: Hendrickson, 1991.
———. *Putting Jesus in His Place: A Radical Vision of Household and Kingdom*. Louisville: Westminster John Knox, 2003.
Murphy-O'Connor, Jerome. *St. Paul's Corinth: Texts and Archaeology*. Good News Studies 6. Wilmington, DE: Glazier, 1983.
Munck, Johannes. *Paul and the Salvation of Mankind*. Atlanta: John Knox, 1959.
Nickle, Keith F. *The Collection: A Study in Paul's Strategy*. SBT 1/48. Naperville, IL: Allenson, 1966.
Nolland, John. *Luke 9:21—18:34*. WBC 35B. Dallas: Word, 1993.
Oakes, Peter. *Philippians: From People to Letter*. SNTSMS 110. Cambridge: Cambridge University Press, 2001.
Oakman, Douglas E. "The Countryside in Luke–Acts." In *The Social World of Luke–Acts: Models for Interpretation*, edited by Jerome H. Neyrey, 151–79. Peabody, MA: Hendrickson, 1991.
———. "Debate: Was the Galilean Economy Oppressive or Prosperous? Late Second Temple Galilee: Socio-Archaeology and Dimensions of Exploitation." In *Galilee in the Late Second Temple and Mishnaic Periods: Life, Culture, and Society*, Vol. 1, edited by David A. Fiensy and James Riley Strange, 346–56. Minneapolis: Fortress, 2014.
———. "Execrating? Or Execrable Peasants!" In *The Galilean Economy in the Time of Jesus*, edited by David A. Fiensy and Ralph K. Hawkins, 139–64. SBLECL 11. Atlanta: SBL, 2013.
———. *Jesus and the Economic Questions of His Day*. Studies in the Bible and Early Christianity 8. Lewiston, NY: Mellen, 1986.
———. *Jesus and the Peasants*. Matrix: The Bible in Mediterranean Context 4. Eugene, OR: Cascade Books, 2008.

———. *Jesus, Debt, and the Lord's Prayer: First-Century Debt and Jesus' Intentions.* Eugene, OR: Cascade Books, 2014.

———. *The Political Aims of Jesus.* Minneapolis: Fortress, 2012.

Osborn, Eric. *Clement of Alexandria.* Cambridge: Cambridge University Press, 2005.

Osborne, Robin. "Introduction: Roman Poverty in Context." In *Poverty in the Roman World,* edited by Margaret Atkins and Robin Osborne, 1–20. Cambridge: Cambridge University Press, 2006.

Osiek, Carolyn. "The Ransom of Captives: Evolution of a Tradition." *HTR* 74 (1981) 365–86.

———. *Rich and Poor in the Shepherd of Hermas: An Exegetical-Social Investigation.* Catholic Biblical Quarterly Monograph Series 15. Washington, DC: Catholic Biblical Association of America, 1983.

Overman, J. Andrew. "Late Second Temple Galilee: A Picture of Relative Economic Health." In *Galilee in the Late Second Temple and Mishnaic Periods: Life, Culture, and Society,* Vol. 1, edited by David A. Fiensy and James Riley Strange, 357–65. 2 vols. Minneapolis: Fortress, 2014.

Palmer, Darryl W. "Acts and the Ancient Historical Monograph." In *The Book of Acts in Its Ancient Literary Setting,* edited by Bruce W. Winter and Andrew D. Clarke, 1–29. The Book of Acts in Its First Century Setting 1. Grand Rapids: Eerdmans, 1993.

Parkin, Anneliese. "'You Do Him No Service': An Exploration of Pagan Almsgiving." In *Poverty in the Roman World,* edited by Margaret Atkins and Robin Osborne, 60–82. Cambridge: Cambridge University Press, 2006.

Parsons, Mikeal C., and Richard I. Pervo. *Rethinking the Unity of Luke and Acts.* Minneapolis: Fortress, 1993.

Pervo, Richard I. *Acts.* Hermeneia. Minneapolis: Fortress, 2009.

———. *Profit with Delight: The Literary Genre of the Acts of the Apostles.* Philadelphia: Fortress, 1987.

Rathbone, Dominic W. "Poverty and Population in Roman Egypt." In *Poverty in the Roman World,* edited by Margaret Atkins and Robin Osborne, 100–114. Cambridge: Cambridge University Press, 2006.

———. "Roman Egypt." In *The Cambridge Economic History of the Greco-Roman World,* edited by Walter Scheidel, Ian Morris, and Richard P. Saller, 698–719. 2007. Paperback ed. Cambridge: Cambridge University Press, 2014.

Redfield, Robert. *The Little Community: Viewpoints for the Study of a Human Whole.* Comparative Studies of Cultures and Civilization. Chicago: University of Chicago Press, 1955.

———. *Peasant Society and Culture: An Anthropological Approach to Civilization.* Chicago: University of Chicago Press, 1956.

Reed, Jonathan L. *Archaeology and the Galilean Jesus.* Harrisburg, PA: Trinity, 2002.

Rhee, Helen. *Early Christian Literature: Christ and Culture in the Second and Third Centuries.* New York: Routledge, 2005.

———. *Loving the Poor, Saving the Rich: Wealth, Poverty, and Early Christian Formation.* Grand Rapids: Baker Academic, 2012.

Richardson, Peter. *Herod: King of the Jews and Friend of the Romans.* Studies on Personalities of the New Testament. 1996. Reprint, Minneapolis: Fortress, 1999.

Rives, J. B. "The Decree of Decius and the Religion of Empire." *JRS* 89 (1999) 135–54.

———. *Religion and Authority in Roman Carthage from Augustus to Constantine.* Oxford: Clarendon, 1995.

Winter, Bruce W. *After Paul Left Corinth: The Influence of Secular Ethics and Social Change*. Grand Rapids: Eerdmans, 2001.

———. "The Lord's Supper at Corinth: An Alternative Reconstruction." *RTR* 37/3 (1978) 73–82.

Wilson, Carol Bakker. *For I Was Hungry and You Gave Me Food: Pragmatics of Food Access in the Gospel of Matthew*. Eugene, OR: Pickwick Publications, 2014.

Wright, Benjamin G., III. "The Discourse of Riches and Poverty in the Book of Ben Sira." In SBLSP 37/2, 559–78. Atlanta: Scholars, 1998.

Wright, N. T. *Jesus and the Victory of God*. Christian Origins and the Question of God 2. Minneapolis: Fortress, 1996.

Zanker, Paul. *The Power of Images in the Age of Augustus*. Translated by Alan Shapiro. Jerome Lectures 16. Ann Arbor: University of Michigan Press, 1990.

Index of Ancient Sources

HEBREW BIBLE

Exodus
15:21	115
21:1—23:19	41
22:25	45n97

Leviticus
23:36–37	45n97
25:8–55	116

Deuteronomy
15:4–5	110
15:11	24n1
23:19–20	45n97
28	155n36

Judges
5:2–31	115

1 Samuel
2:1–10	115

2 Kings
4:42–44	50

Psalms
1	155n36

Isaiah
2:2–4	76
58:6	115n74
60:5	76
61:1–2	115n74

Ezekiel
17:23	50
31:6	50

Micah
4:1–2	76

NEW TESTAMENT

Matthew
5:3–12	116n78
5:9–13	28
5:25–26	46n101
6:19–20	42n82
7:7–11	49
9:9–13	56n135
11:18–19	56n135
18:23–35	28
21:31–32	56n135
22:1–10	43n85
25:14–30	58n145

Mark

2:13–17	56n135
3:31–35	51
3:35	54
6:30–44	50
8:1–10	50
10:17–22	40–42
10:21	166n72
10:22	133
10:28–30	52
14:7	24n1

Luke

1:1	107n33
1:3	102n3, 106n22
1:4	106n26
1:46–55	115n71
4:16–30	115–16
4:18	107n32
4:18–19	116n75
5:27–32	56n135
6:20–21	50n113
6:20–26	116
6:24–26	130
7:1–10	104n15
7:33–34	56n135
9:22	106n28
9:57–62	53n126
10:9	116n79
10:25–37	54
11:2–4	28
11:4	45n96
12:16–21	42
12:22–31	48
12:30	49
12:33	42n82
12:41–48	57–58
12:46	58n143
12:49–53	53
12:57–59	46n101
12:58–59	46n102
14:12	163n59
14:12–14	163
14:16–24	43n85, 131–33
14:21	44n91
14:23	44
14:26	53
15:1–2	56n135
15:3	59
15:11–32	125–29
16:1	59
16:1–9	28, 58–60
16:19–31	130–31
18:9–14	56n135
18:18	40n77
18:18–30	133–34
19:1–10	56n135, 133–35
19:11–27	58n145
21:20–24	103n8
23:1–25	103n14
23:25	104n13
23:47	104n15

John

6:1–15	50

Acts

1:1	106n22
1:8	103n12
2:42–47	97, 108–13, 119, 137, 142
4:1–22	110
4:32–35	97, 108–13, 119, 137, 142
4:36—5:11	111–13, 135–37
10:1–48	104n15
16:10–17	102n4
17:3	117n80
17:6	116–17
18:12–17	104n14
20:5–15	102n4
20:35	63
21:1–18	102n4
22:25–26	104n15
23:23—24:27	104n14
24:23	104n15
25:1—26:32	104n14
25:25	104n13
27:1–3	104n15
27:1—28:16	102n4
27:43	104n15
28:30–31	107n32

Romans

12:1–2	93–94
12:1—15:13	93
12:3–8	94–96
12:3—13:14	94
12:9–13	96–98
14:1—15:13	92, 94
15:22–33	68n15, 77, 79, 81–82
15:24	92
15:25	95
15:26	76n41
15:27	75n39, 84, 163
16:23	71, 72

1 Corinthians

1:26	71–72
11:2	86
11:2–16	86
11:17–34	86–91
11:23–26	99
12—14	86
16:1–4	68n15, 77, 79–80
16:2	83

2 Corinthians

8—9	68n15, 77, 79, 80n58, 83, 84, 95
8:1–5	83
8:2	81
8:3	81n62
8:4	81n63
8:7	83
8:9	85, 99
8:13	81n61
8:13–14	84
8:13–15	80
9:1–5	83
9:6–15	80–81
9:7	95
9:10	85
9:12	82n65

Galatians

2:1–10	68–70
2:10	76, 91

Ephesians

5:18	126n107

Philippians

2:1–5	98–99
2:6–11	99

1 Thessalonians

1:6	81

Titus

1:6	126n107

1 Peter

4:4	126n107

∽

EARLY CHRISTIAN LITERATURE

Acts of John

56–57	174

Acts of Paul

3.26–43	173n92
3.41	173n93

Acts of Peter

8	173n94
9–10	174n96
19	174n97

Clement of Alexandria, *Who Is the Rich Man That Shall Be Saved?*

3.5	166n69
11.1–4	166n71
12.1–5	166n73

212 INDEX OF ANCIENT SOURCES

Clement of Alexandria (*cont.*)
14.1–3	167n74
14.5–6	167n75
21.2	166n70
33.2–3	168n76
33.5–6	168n77
37.3–5	169n78

Cyprian, *On the Lapsed*
35	184n131

Cyprian, *Letters*
2	179–80
5	181–82
7	180–81

Cyprian, *On Works and Alms*
11	182n126
21	183n128

Didache
4.8	156n40
5.2	156n41

Epistle of Barnabas
19.8	156n39

Eusebius, *Church History*
3.17	105n19
6.34.1	178n113
6.39.1	178n113

Gospel of Thomas
64	43n85

Justin, *First Apology*
67	147

Pontius, *Life of Cyprian*
7	180n123

Shepherd of Hermas
Mandates
1.1–2	159n50
2.4	158n47

Similitudes
1.8–9	160n51
2.7	161n52
2.8–9	161n55
2.8	161n54
2.9–10	161n56

Visions
5.7	158n49

Tertullian, *Apology*
39	150–54
9.17	151n26

∾

GRECO-ROMAN AUTHORS

Aristotle, *Nicomachean Ethics*
4.1.5	121n97
4.1.12	120n94
4.1.14	121n95
4.1.34–35	121n96

Cicero, *On Duties*
1.14 [45]	122n100
2.16 [55–56]	122n99
2.16 [63]	121n98

Julian, *Letter to a Pagan Priest*
305C	xv

Lucian of Samosata, *The Passing of Peregrinus*
11–13	xv, 146n17

Plato, *Republic*
449C   109n47

Pliny the Younger, *Epistles*
10.97   144n12

Seneca, *On Benefits*
1.2.1   123n101

Seneca, *On the Fortunate Life*
23.5—24.1   123n102

Index of Modern Authors

Alexander, Loveday, 103
Alföldy, Géza, 2, 21
Arnal, William E., 54
Ascough, Richard, 113
Atkins, Margaret, 4
Aviam, Mordechai, 32, 33

Bailey, Kenneth E., 39, 58, 59, 60, 87, 125, 127
Balch, David L., 73
Bammel, Ernst, 50
Barnes, Timothy David, 145, 146
Barrett, C. K., 114
Bartchy, S. Scott, ix, 41, 43, 90, 108, 109, 113, 131, 142
Berger, Klaus, 76
Berger, Peter, 108
Bock, Darrell L., 103, 106, 116
Bolkestein, Hendrik, 2
Borg, Marcus J., 26, 57
Brent, Allan J., 179
Brown, Peter, xvii, 2, 22, 144, 176, 177, 178
Cameron, Averil, 172, 177
Capper, Brian, 111
Clarke, G. W., 179, 180
Conzelmann, Hans, 104, 108
Cooper, Kate, 171
Corbier, Mireille, 178
Countryman, L. William, xvii, 141, 142, 162, 164
Crossan, John Dominic, 26, 34, 38

Dahl, Nils A., 114, 131

Danker, Frederick W., 106, 116
D'Arms, John H., 118
De Ligt, L., 6
De Ste. Croix, G. E. M., 148
Dodds, E. R., xvii
Downing, Gerald F., 103
Downs, David J., 76, 77, 78, 93
Dunn, James D. G., 38, 39, 49, 54, 93, 95, 96, 97

Edwards, Mark, 146
Elliott, John H., 142
Esler, Philip Francis, 108, 114
Evans, C. F., 133

Finley, M. I., 2, 6
Finn, Richard, 173
Fitzmyer, Joseph A., 95, 97, 103, 106, 111, 116
Freyne, Sean, 49
Friesen, Steven J., 3, 4, 5, 10, 11, 22, 36, 73, 74, 75, 79, 117, 141, 151, 158,

Garnsey, Peter, 5, 6, 7, 8, 21, 22, 42, 47, 65, 66, 118
Garrison, Roman, xvii, 141, 142, 162
Georgi, Dieter, 76
Giardina, Andrea, 177
Goodman, Martin, 46, 146
González, Justo L., 114
Gouldner, Alvin W., 12, 77
Green, Joel B., 103, 107

INDEX OF MODERN AUTHORS 215

Hägg, Tomas, 171
Hamel, Gildas H., 26, 36
Hands, A. R., 2, 8, 9, 119
Hanson, K. C., 26
Harland, Philip A., 118, 150, 152
Harnack, Adolf von, xvii
Hellerman, Joseph H., 51, 96, 153
Henderson, Suzanne Watts, 91
Herzog, William R., 26, 57
Holgate, David A., 126
Horden, Peregrine, 5, 6, 7, 21
Horsley, Richard A., 26, 27, 29, 31,
    41, 43, 45, 50, 51, 54, 56, 115

Jensen, Morten Hørning, 29, 30, 31
Johnson, Luke Timothy, 102, 107,
    108, 109, 114, 116, 130, 133
Jongman, Willem M., 10

Kautsky, John H., 26
Kehoe, Dennis P., 10, 21, 66
Kloppenborg (-Verbin), John S., 38
Komter, Aafke E., 12
Kraft, Robert A., 155
Kuhn, Karl Allen, 104

Lane Fox, Robin, xvii, 157, 178
Lenski, Gerhard, 56
Lindemann, Andreas, 111, 112
Lintott, Andrew, 8
Lo Cascio, Elio, 10
Lohfink, Gerhard, 51, 52
Longenecker, Bruce W., 65, 68, 69,
    74, 76
Luckmann, Thomas, 108
Lüdemann, Gerd, 111

Mack, Burton L., 39
McCollough, C. Thomas, 33, 34
MacMullen, Ramsey, 2, 21, 22, 65,
    172
Malherbe, Abraham J., 70
Martin, Dale, 72
Mattila, Sharon Lea, 34, 35
Mauss, Marcel, 12, 43
Mealand, David L., 109
Meeks, Wayne A., 70, 71, 118
Merz, Annette, 39

Meyers, Ched, 39
Millar, Fergus, 145
Mitchell, Alan C., 109
Moessner, David P., 114
Moo, Douglas J., 93, 94, 95, 96, 97
Moreland, Milton, 55
Morley, Neville, 4, 5, 10, 21, 66, 67
Morris, Ian, 10
Moss, Candida R., 144
Moxnes, Halvor, 49, 51, 52, 53, 54,
    109, 117, 119, 130, 131
Munck, Johannes, 76

Nickle, Keith F., 76
Nolland, John, 116, 125

Oakes, Peter, 98, 99
Oakman, Douglas E., xvii, 26, 27,
    28, 29, 35, 36, 50, 57, 101
Osborn, Eric, 164, 165
Osborne, Robin, 4

Palmer, Darryl W., 103
Parkin, Anneliese, 4
Parsons, Mikeal C., 103
Pervo, Richard I., 103, 108, 171
Price, Simon, 146
Purcell, Nicholas, 5, 6, 7, 21

Rathbone, Dominic W., 4, 5, 178
Redfield, Robert, 19
Reed, Jonathan L., 26, 34
Rhee, Helen, 157, 164, 165, 171
Richardson, Peter, 31
Rives, J. B., 175, 179
Rohrbaugh, Richard L., 125, 126,
    127
Rowe, C. Kavin, 102
Rowland, Christopher, 146

Sahlins, Marshall, 12, 84
Saller, Richard P., 8, 10, 21, 22, 65,
    118
Scheidel, Walter, 3, 4, 5, 10, 22, 36,
    65, 73, 74, 75, 79, 117, 141,
    158
Schnabel, Eckhard J., 108
Schöllgen, Georg, 151

Schottroff, Luise, 101
Schreiner, Thomas R., 92, 93, 95, 96, 97
Schubert, Paul, 178, 179
Schwartz, Seth, 60
Scott, Bernard Brandon, 50
Scott, James C., xix, 1, 11–19, 27, 38, 40, 41, 45, 47, 60
Shaw, Brent D., 105
Sider, Robert Dick, 150, 151
Snyder, Graydon F., 157
Söder, Rosa, 171
Stark, Rodney, xvii
Strathmann, Hermann, 82
Stegemann, Wolfgang, 101

Talbert, Charles H., 103
Tannehill, Robert C., 102, 107, 108, 109

Theissen, Gerd, xvii, 39, 53, 70, 71, 72, 88, 90
Tiede, David L., 114
Tiller, Patrick, 56
Treat, Jay Curry, 155

Udoh, Fabian, 31, 32
Uhlhorn, G., xvi, xvii

Veyne, Paul, 8, 82, 118, 120

Wallace-Hadrill, Andrew, 8
Wedderburn, A. J. M., 77
Wells, Colin, 104, 143
Wilson, Carol Bakker, 6, 102
Wright, Benjamin G., 56
Wright, N. T., 46, 51, 56, 125

Zanker, Paul, 21

www.ingramcontent.com/pod-product-compliance
Lightning Source LLC
Chambersburg PA
CBHW020408230426
43664CB00009B/1229